JESUS WINS THE SERIES

Bill Medley

JESUS WINS THE SERIES

THE BOOK OF REVELATION EXPLAINED AND EXPLORED

VOLUME 3

Bill Medley

WHINE PRESS

Unless otherwise indicated, Scripture taken from the Holy Bible, NEW INTERNATIONAL VERSION®, NIV® Copyright © 1973, 1978, 1984, 2011 by Biblica, Inc.® Used by permission. All rights reserved worldwide.

© 2020 Bill Medley

ISBN 978-0-6484159-0-9

All rights reserved. No part of this publication may be reproduced, stored in a retrieval system, or transmitted, in any form, by any means, electronic, mechanical, photocopying, recording or otherwise without the prior permission of the publisher.

Cover Design by Andrew Clarke Studios

Published by Whine Press, Melbourne, Australia

Printed by Ingram Spark, Melbourne, Australia

Reprinted 2023

ACKNOWLEDGEMENTS

Thanks to those who took part in proof reading. Special thanks to Jayni Manners for countless hours of proof reading, corrections and transposing the sermons into text, but also for providing the inspiration to tackle this work in the first place.

To my beloved Diana
my best friend always

Contents

1.	The Great Prostitute	(Revelation 17:1-4a)	11
2.	The Mother	(Revelation 17:4b-5)	21
3.	The Beast Comes	(Revelation 17:6-8)	31
4.	Astonished by the Beast!	(Revelation 17:8)	41
5.	The Ten Kings United	(Revelation 17:9-14)	49
6.	Beast Attacks the Prostitute	(Revelation 17:15-18)	59
7.	The Fall of Babylon	(Revelation 18:1-4a)	67
8.	Come Out of Her	(Revelation 18:4b-8)	77
9.	The Great Crash	(Revelation 18:9-19)	87
10.	The Tribulation Timeline	(Revelation 18:20)	97
11.	And Crashing with Her…	(Revelation 18:21-24)	109
12.	The Hallelujah Chorus	(Revelation 19:1-5)	119
13.	The Wedding	(Revelation 19:6-9)	127
14.	The Wedding Preparation	(Revelation 19:7-8)	137
15.	Marriage	(Revelation 19:7-9)	147
16.	Jesus' Hidden Name	(Revelation 19:10-16)	157
17.	The War	(Revelation 19:17-21)	167
18.	The 1000 Years	(Revelation 20:1-2)	177
19.	Satan Bound	(Revelation 20:1-3)	189
20.	Jews in the 1000-Years?	(Revelation 20:4-6 Part 1)	199
21.	The Two Resurrections	(Revelation 20:4-6 Part 2)	213
22.	Tormented Forever	(Revelation 20:7-10)	223
23.	The Great White Throne	(Revelation 20:11-15)	233
24.	The New Heaven and Earth	(Revelation 21:1)	243
25.	The New Jerusalem	(Revelation 21:2-4)	253
26.	The Fiery Lake	(Revelation 21:5-8)	263
27.	The Heavenly City	(Revelation 21:9-21)	273
28.	Nothing Impure Can Enter	(Revelation 21:22-27)	285
29.	Paradise	(Revelation 22:1-6)	295
30.	I Am Coming Soon	(Revelation 22:7-11)	305
31.	Testimony for the Churches	(Revelation 22:12-17)	315
32.	Overview of Revelation 1-22	(Revelation 22:18-21)	323

1
The Great Prostitute
(Revelation 17:1-4a)

One of the great things about watching sport either on TV or live at the game is the action replay. We love the replay of the great goal, the big hit, the spectacular sequence of play, or the hard-hitting tackle. As soon as we see a great move, we immediately want to see it again from all the angles, and in slow motion. Do you notice how if someone gets crunched in a heavy tackle, the broadcaster loves to replay it over and over? We have the side-cam, close-cam, drone-cam and cameras attached to goal posts and leg posts.

Well, long before modern sport, the book of Revelation was crafted by the Master film director, Jesus. And the action replay was put into effect long ago in this book. It's been one of the main features of Revelation as we have studied this book. The seals, trumpets and bowls are all leading to the final judgment and are different camera angles of the same period. We have just finished looking at the seven bowls of God's wrath that were the 'completion of God's wrath' (15:1). Well, what more can there be if Judgment Day has come and God's wrath is completed?

Answer: The action replay! Rev. 17 starts with a close-up camera angle replay of details we couldn't have seen from the wide-angle lens of the action in the sixth and seventh bowls. One of the reasons why we know this is an action replay in Rev. 17-18 is by looking at who is giving the message. It's none other than one of the very angels who delivered one of the seven bowls of judgment! So this is one of those postgame interviews. The replay footage is being played while one of the players from the actual game is being interviewed to give commentary. This angel played in the Super Bowl. He kicked the final bowl …

> One of the seven angels who <u>had</u> the seven bowls [we have seen him

> before with the bowls in the actual game!] came and said to me, 'Come, I will show you the punishment of the great prostitute, who sits by many waters' (17:1).

Here is the angel saying, 'I'll show you the detail of what you just saw, that is, what my teammates and I did (the other angels with the seven bowls) when we handed out judgment, when we delivered those seven bowls. Here is the action replay. Here is a close-up. You might have missed some detail before, but here is another camera angle.' Now we see the camera zoom in on a particular part of this judgment. It's to do with the **great prostitute, who sits on many waters**. By the time we get to 17:5, we discover this great prostitute is the great city Babylon. We have already been introduced to her previously (14:8, 16:19), but here we get the close-up.

John the apostle, the first viewer of the action, recognized the description of Babylon *the great prostitute who sits by many waters*, because he knew the OT book of Jeremiah (51:12). Jeremiah speaks of Babylon who lives by many waters ('by the rivers of Babylon') being cut off. And typical of Revelation, the OT history is being used as metaphor to describe current events and figures. The OT historical Babylon was literally by many waters, whereas our text says she *sits by many waters*. We are told later that the *many waters* are a symbol. What do they symbolize?

> Then the angel said to me, 'The waters you saw, where the prostitute sits, are <u>peoples, multitudes, nations and languages</u>' (17:15).

It's symbolic! It's not a literal Babylon with literal waters. She sits by many waters that are *peoples and nations!* In fact, in the original language it literally says she sits *on* many waters. This alone suggests we are dealing with something which has a worldwide influence, and is not a single city. So who is this woman, Babylon the great city? Who is the great prostitute? Who or what does she represent?

There are a few suggestions. The Historicist says Babylon is the RC church. The Preterist has Babylon the great city as Jerusalem or the city of Rome. The Futurist says she could be a revived Rome or a revived Babylon. There are good arguments for some of these interpretations. In fact, it seems within the views themselves there are several options, but which one is right?

We have deduced before that for the first readers, the description of the great prostitute fits perfectly in their day with that great city of adultery, Rome. Rome was the epitome of worldly lust, idolatry and anti-Christian spirituality. And the city of Rome just happens to sit on seven hills, which fits with 17:9, where we read that 'Babylon' sits on seven hills! Rome was the ancient city from which the Empire (the Beast) ruled. It persecuted God's people, and later we learn that one of the great charges against the prostitute is her bloodshed against the saints. So is Babylon also the Beast?

By the time we get to 17:3, it says the great city Babylon *rides* the Beast, so she (Babylon) can't *be* the Beast. She is supported by the Beast, but is not the Beast herself. Yet many of the things we have learned about the Beast are part of what the great prostitute does. So if she is not the Beast, who is she? Back in Rev. 14 and 16 we said she is the great 'city where you live', but that doesn't explain everything.

We need this close-up angle to find out what part she plays. For example, why is she described as the 'great city Babylon', and yet in 17:5 she is described as a 'great prostitute'? That's certainly a good metaphor for seduction. Throughout history the attack on God's people has not always been blatant persecution, but weapons of allurement. Seduced away from Jesus by the seducer, the great *prostitute!* But how does she fit into the equation? She has power. She sits *on* the nations. *Sitting* generally points to sovereign power, like a monarch 'sits' on a throne.

> One of the seven angels who had the seven bowls came and said to me, 'Come, I will show you the punishment of the great prostitute, who sits by many waters. With her the kings of the earth committed adultery and the inhabitants of the earth were intoxicated with the wine of her adulteries' (17:1-2).

But aren't the **kings of the earth** manifestations of the Beast (government worldly powers persecuting God's people)? Here the kings (worldly powers) are committing adultery *with* this great prostitute. And the **inhabitants of the earth were intoxicated with the wine of her adulteries.**

Adultery is a familiar metaphor for unfaithfulness in Israel's history. But here it is not only the kings of the earth, but all

inhabitants of the earth, who are taken in by her! So who is she?

We noted the Historicists have said this woman is the RC church, and there are features which fit with that idea. The Seventh Day Adventists are big on the RC church as the great prostitute. The RC church held power through the Middle Ages, when 'kings' were subservient to the Pope. Also, the RC church is famous for shedding blood of the saints. But even if you could say that the RC church fits the description, isn't the second Beast (the False Prophet) the proponent of false religion? Is Babylon the second Beast? And wait a minute. Who was Revelation first written to? First century Christians. It has to have meaning to them and be a blessing to them (1:3). So how can Babylon be the RC church to them? The RC church didn't exist in the first century! It did not become the RC church as we know it until the Middle Ages.

As we go further into Rev. 17-18, we find that her seduction is not only spiritual, but also has to do with the economy. She is the great city that entices with material prosperity. And by the time we get to Rev. 18, we see her seduction and adultery are tied to material comforts and wealth …

> 'For all the nations have drunk the maddening wine of her adulteries. The kings of the earth committed adultery with her, and the merchants of the earth <u>grew rich</u> from her <u>excessive luxuries</u>' (18:3).

It doesn't fit with the RC church that the merchants of the earth grow rich from her, and kings committing adultery with her. She promised luxury and economic security, but now her judgment comes because of her seduction of the nations and kings (more explicit in 18:2). Who gave in to the great prostitute? Well it seems almost everyone—kings and nations. They are drunk on her wine. They love what she has to offer. *'With her the <u>kings of the earth</u> committed adultery and the <u>inhabitants of the earth</u> were intoxicated with the wine of her adulteries.'*

If we combine the thoughts of what we are told in Rev. 18 about the economic prosperity and idolatry of Babylon (the prostitute), her enticements are *both* economic *and* spiritual, and are allied with the political or state powers.

But how does that work when those are the things we have already seen in the Beast! We are told explicitly that Babylon is not the Beast because she is sitting *on* the Beast. What else are we told?

> Then the angel carried me away in the Spirit into a wilderness. There I saw a woman <u>sitting on</u> a scarlet <u>beast</u> that was covered with <u>blasphemous names and had seven heads and ten horns</u> (17:3).

As careful readers of Revelation, we don't have to look too closely to know which Beast she is sitting on. *Blasphemous names, seven heads and ten horns* ...

> And the dragon stood on the shore of the sea. And I saw a beast coming out of the sea. He <u>had ten horns and seven heads</u>, with ten crowns on his horns, and on each head a <u>blasphemous name</u> (13:1).

It's that same ugly Beast that came up out of the sea! And the great prostitute is riding him like a bronco! She is supported by this first Beast and is even at the reins.

The scarlet color (17:3) reminds us of the red Dragon. The blood of the saints is on his hands. In fact, it's all over him. So who is Babylon, the great city, the great prostitute? She is so closely aligned with the Beast we might have thought she *was* the Beast. But she can't be. She works *with* the Beast to persecute the saints (both have that red color for the blood of the saints, 17:6). She seduces and deceives the people of the earth. But she is also spiritually deceptive. But false religion is the second Beast, the False Prophet. So again, she must have some connection with the False Prophet Beast, but she is not that Beast either. She is the prostitute. She is the great city where you live, she is Babylon. But where does she fit into the scheme of things?

Who is the enemy of God in Revelation? Ultimately, it's Satan. He opposes the true God. The true God is three persons, the Father, the Son and the Holy Spirit. Remember the counterfeit—the unholy Trinity? The Dragon, The Beast and the False Prophet. They form the complete counter, opposition, imitation and enemy of God. So where does 'Babylon the great prostitute' fit in if she is none of them? Well let's reflect on the book of Revelation. The book has introduced us to a woman before. We already met the woman of beauty ...

> A great sign appeared in heaven: a woman clothed with the sun, with the moon under her feet and a crown of twelve stars on her head (12:1).

She is beautifully adorned with the sun and moon. Now in Rev. 17 we meet another woman. The counterfeit. The seductive prostitute. She is the OTHER woman. She is unholy. She is a great city (Babylon). And she influences the world. She sits on many waters, which are the nations. The first woman of Revelation is pure and holy. She also is *a great city*! She also influences people of every nation, but for good. Revelation climaxes with this holy woman—who is what? The Holy City! She is the *holy* city who is the pure bride!

> I saw the Holy City, the new Jerusalem, coming down out of heaven from God, prepared as a bride beautifully dressed for her husband (21:2).

How is she dressed? *Beautifully dressed* for her husband, in contrast to the great prostitute who is adorned *seductively*. What we have here in the 'great prostitute Babylon' is the completion of Satan's work to oppose, imitate and counterfeit God and his work. The woman mocks and seeks to offer an *alternative* to the pure woman, the church, as the counterfeit! She is truly the *other* woman.

So just as Father, Son and Holy Spirit are counterfeited by the unholy Trinity, the Dragon, the Beast and the False Prophet, this woman is also the opposite number of the pure woman, the church! That's how we can make sense of all these other components. She is supported by the Beast (government powers), but is not the Beast. As a counterfeit to the church, she also includes counterfeit religion, though she is not exclusively false religion, because she is more far reaching than that. She offers another *salvation!* She is the direct antithesis of the church, she is the *other* woman in that she competes directly for our affections and entices, even seduces us to compromise and draw us into her *counterfeit salvation*—her idols. Her allurements go beyond just false formal religions (like the False Prophet).

So she might appear as a false church, such as a works salvation in the RC church, the cults, or liberal theology. But not all the *inhabitants of the earth* are seduced by formal false religion, so she gives them other seductive alternatives to promise fulfillment (salvation). Other idols. We see from Rev. 17-18 that she offers more than just alternative spirituality. She offers materialism! She is the *great city!* She offers the lusts and desires of this world. She uses the weapon of seduction, trying to get the church, the saints, to compromise in her purity. As the *other* woman, she doesn't attack so obviously as the Beast with persecution, but she still has blood on her hands (17:6). She is drunk on the blood of the saints, but she uses slow silent daggers rather than the Beast's open attacks. She uses economic enticements. Materialism and compromise. She uses those *kings* of this world (the Beast) to enact the laws to give her the opportunity to do her thing to *all the inhabitants of the earth*. She uses all the idols. She is where you find satisfaction, pleasure and worship. She offers another salvation! How attractive she is …

> The woman was dressed in <u>purple and scarlet</u>, and was <u>glittering with gold, precious stones and pearls</u>. She held a golden cup in her hand, filled with abominable things and the filth of her adulteries (17:4).

This is virtually the same description she is given in 18:16, where she is clothed in fine linen, purple and scarlet, and glittering with gold, precious stones and pearls. There she is referred to as *the great city* and we are given her list of trade products (18:12). She is the epitome of provision of prosperity. She is the great seductive alternative to the church! Whether she comes in the form of a prostitute religion, a prosperity gospel, or a literal great city with all it promises in its luxuries and pleasures, she provides the great alternative. Throughout the church age she has always been around. So she was the city of Rome in the first century. She is the RC church and the cults. She is every literal city today that offers those seductions and alternative 'salvation'. Young people know her well. When children brought up in the church under their parents teaching get out into the 'great city' all on their own, how many will be seduced by her? She is very attractive.

For our first readers of Revelation in the first century, the great city was clearly Rome. Jews even used *Babylon* as a nickname for Rome. All that Rome had to offer was mentioned in those letters to the seven churches. The challenges to Christians of compromise which lead them away from being part of the true church, such as sexual immorality and idols. She is the alternative salvation.

She has the seductive clothing of a prostitute and she seeks to attract through her material prosperity. **A golden cup in her hand, filled with abominable things and the filth of her adulteries.** We will see the development of a great contrast as it unfolds. Jeweled attire that is a mockery of the Lamb's bride, the *Holy City*, the one *adorned with precious stones, pearls* and *gold* (21:2, 9-23). All those temptations look so amazing. That's why we need this action replay. Look at the close-up. Do you see what is actually in that cup? *She held a golden cup in her hand, <u>filled with abominable things and the filth</u> of her adulteries.*

Wasn't there a TV program called *Sex in the City?* Wonder what that was about? I never did find out. Surely it was meant to sound seductive. Well, this woman is *the* city of seduction. This is the promise and all the stuff looks so good. Her cup is filled with *abominable things and the filth of her adulteries.* She seduces and says these things are good. She lies to you. This is the action replay on how the people of the earth got duped in the lead up to the Judgment. You actually get to see how she looked so good. We are in the game that is being replayed. Can you see yourself? Which woman did you go with? Did you go with this woman, who looked so ravishing and attractive? Did you love her? Well, the action replay close-up reveals she turned out to be nothing more than a prostitute using you. This is looking back now on the replay. Then we see all who were choked by the city and all she has to offer. Not just the obvious things like gambling, drunkenness, drugs, sexy clothes, easy money, pornography, and other sexual immorality, but the subtler seductions. The upgrades, the expensive toys and more and more, the expensive clothes, cars, houses. Idols. She offers them all. And her great seduction and deception is to convince the nations that what she offers is good. And how deceptive? Who has your affection?

Jesus went to the cross to take away your sin and give you new life to join you to his bride—the *faithful* woman. Jesus actually took the cup of God's fury at sin so that you could be free and no longer live in sin. But which cup means more to you? The cup of the woman or God's cup of wrath poured out on his Son? Has Jesus captured your heart? Or do you still have an eye for the *other* woman. Are you still secretly drinking her maddening wine? Look at her picture. She is riding high on the Beast. And that is the surprise. You would expect the action replay to go straight to the bit about how the adulterous woman is fallen. Isn't that what action replays highlight? The big tackle and crunch! But so much of this replay is the close-up of how seductive she looks *before* she falls. She looked so good! She is the alternative salvation which looks so promising ... right up to her fall. And that's what she does. She gets you distracted away from what is really happening. Her promises are all a lie. They not only will never fulfill you in this life, but Judgment is *just around the corner!* The crash is coming!

How many people have you met who *appeared* to become Christians? They appeared to be part of the true bride of Christ, but the *other* woman deceived them. Remember the parable of the sower? Some received it with joy, but fell away because of trouble with the word. It was just all too hard. Or the deceitfulness of wealth and the worries of this world? *It's the other woman!* She enticed them. It never fails to amaze me how people can fall away. I take them at their word when they say they are Christians and they seem to start out living the Christian life. But after a while, there is no fruit. Choked. By what? The *other* woman. She is the alternative to the church. Those who fall away have their reasons, good reasons, such as how they have been hurt by someone in the church, or it's too hard to live the Christian life and be part of the church. I have to work. I have needs. I have to go with the other woman. It all seems so reasonable. They can't even see they have been seduced.

In that parable of the sower only one of the four types of seeds produced a crop. Some fell away quickly. If they fall away from attending church worship, that is an obvious outward sign. They have left the faithful pure woman. But being enticed by the prostitute woman doesn't necessarily mean people stop attending church. Look back on the action replay of your life. Look at the woman there riding high. If you didn't know what was about to happen, you would never imagine her crash is coming. You are cruising along in this life distracted by all the glitter. And where is this crash? She is such fun! Pleasure? Look at her. Which woman are you walking with? The parable of the sower said the good seed would produce a crop 100, 60, 30 times. Is there a crop in your life? How are you producing compared to a few years ago? Have you become lukewarm? Which woman are you drawn to? The true church, or the *other woman*?

Study Questions

1. If the seven bowls have already been poured out, what is going on in Rev. 17, and how does that fit with the rest of Revelation?

2. How can we tell this Babylon is symbolic?

3. Give examples and the difficulties of some of the ways Babylon has been interpreted.

4. Give reasons why ancient Rome seems like a good candidate for 'Babylon' to the first readers.

5. What features does Babylon share with the Beast?

6. How does the pure woman of Revelation help us understand this woman?

7. What are the ways in which this woman, Babylon, seduces?

8. Are there ways in which we can see how the first readers had already been warned about this woman in those seven letters?

9. What ways do you need to be on your guard against the *other* woman?

2
The Mother
(Revelation 17:4b-5)

We have discovered the identity of the *other* woman. The alternative salvation she offers may come in the form of false religion, or it could be in the form of materialistic idols. She is the *great city* and manifests in those alluring cities of the world where you live. Well, now her mystery is revealed. The seven bowls of God's wrath completed his judgment. It all came crashing down. We read, at the end of Rev.16, that this woman, Babylon the Great, was devastated …

> God remembered Babylon the Great and gave her the cup filled with the wine of the fury of his wrath. Every island fled away and the mountains could not be found (16:19b-20).

It was all over. But now in Rev. 17-18 here she is again. What could be left of her? Well, 17:1 told us John is now given the action replay of her judgment. *Come, I will show you the <u>punishment</u> of the great prostitute.* The word translated *punishment* in the original Greek language can also be translated literally as *judgment*. So the angel says 'I will show you her judgment.' John is about to see the replay of what happened in her judgment at the end of the seven bowls—her punishment. But instead, at first, John sees this mesmerizing seductive woman dressed in finery with every kind of allurement. Instead of seeing her ruined and judged, she looks so enticing. Is this her judgment? Yes. But the message here is that *right up to the crash* she looked so appealing. And that is the point.

Throughout history she appeared so beautiful and seductive. You would have never realized her downfall, and yours, if you drank the wine of her adulteries, because now it is revealed she was just a prostitute. She is a sensual harlot who sells herself and you down the river. John has this amazing view of it all.

> Then the angel carried me away in the Spirit into <u>a desert</u>. There I saw a woman sitting on a scarlet beast that was covered with blasphemous names and had seven heads and ten horns (17:3).

The wilderness (desert in some translations), if nothing else, is a place of isolation from the great prostitute of Babylon, where John can see her from an uncluttered perspective. He is able to view this action replay with clarity, and see this woman for who she really is.

When it says **the angel carried me away in the Spirit into a desert** ... to John this would have felt like the prophets of old, like Ezekiel who was taken up by the Spirit when he was being prepared through seeing visions to bring a message to Israel. Here is John receiving that same commissioning to pronounce judgment. How must that have felt to John? John was just a fisherman who became a ministry worker, and finally an exiled prisoner. He was languishing in a cave on the island of Patmos, and now here he is, *carried away in the Spirit into a desert.*

Picture John being swept across land to a desert. It's like something out of one of those children's movies like *UP*, where the house is swept up and flies through the sky, sweeping across the globe. Or the *Bee Movie*, with bees suddenly flying through the sky with great panoramic views. And here is John saying, *then the angel carried me away in the Spirit*. He is taken up! Up! What a movie John is seeing! It's like you're sitting in the cinema and suddenly instead of the scene in the movie going up, you get swept up yourself! But it's not a movie you are seeing. You are soaring through the cosmos of time. You are seeing a sweep of history. That is what John is seeing. He is seeing Babylon through history. He is waiting to see the demise, the judgment, the punishment of this woman, but instead there she is riding! She is the seductive temptress, adorned in all finery. Look how she allured them. They were going along to church, but she offered her sexual immorality, she offered her financial security, her idols, and you left the true woman, the church, for this *other woman*.

And the message John gets is this: Everything is not what it seems. Look who she is and why there was such an allurement away from the true church. This action replay exposes the beautiful woman ... and underneath she is all wrinkles. Remember the saying, 'Beauty is only skin deep, but ugly is rotten to the core'. All is not what it seems. Outwardly sexy, alluring, but underneath she is diseased and filled with filth and ugliness. Even her cup appears to be beautiful and golden, but the end of 17:4 says inside it's filled with filth and abominations. Have you ever been deceived by outward appearances? But how can she be so deceptive? Is it just the way she looks?

There is one factor behind her seduction that we didn't look at in our previous chapter. Remember she rides the Beast (17: 3) who came up out of the sea at the beckon of the Dragon (13:1). So even her association with the Beast shows her connection with the works of the Dragon, Satan himself. But we see her demonic connection hinted at here as well ...

> The woman was dressed in purple and scarlet, and was glittering with gold, precious stones and pearls. <u>She held a golden cup in her hand, filled with abominable things and the filth of her adulteries</u> (17:4).

The word in the original Greek language translated *filth* can also be translated *unclean*. It's the same word used in Revelation and the gospels to describe *unclean* or demonic spirits. We read later in Rev. 18 that this woman, Babylon, is home for demons ...

> With a mighty voice he shouted: 'Fallen! Fallen is Babylon the Great! She has become a home for <u>demons</u> and a haunt for <u>every impure spirit</u>, a haunt for every <u>unclean</u> bird, a haunt for every unclean and detestable animal' (18:2).

Now we get it. She is an actual dwelling for *unclean* spirits, demons! So in our text her cup is filled with *abominable things*. Isn't that the term God used in the OT for idols? Abominable things? And what is the great prostitute trying to sell you with her economic luxuries and other unfaithfulness? Idols. Didn't Paul the apostle say that behind idols are demons (1 Cor. 10:20)? Yes! Behind all those idols that grieved the Lord so much stands spirituality. But not good spirituality. This is worth thinking about. Where might you be tempted by an idol from this woman? Desires and passions, 'success', even good things like our material possessions and security, but we turn them into idols. No wonder they are so enticing! No wonder her maddening wine is so intoxicating along with her idols. Now we learn they have demonic force and deception behind them!

Have you ever heard this before? *Our struggle is not against flesh and blood but against principalities and powers of darkness, spiritual forces of evil.* Every fiber of her demonic power is used to try and seduce you to her alternative salvation. She is the *other* woman. She is the 'better' church! She represents all the seductions of the world that appear so enticing, but now we see in God's sight they are clearly *abominations* and 'unclean' … *filthy*. Demonic! And they are the cause of her horrific judgment.

> The name written on her forehead was a mystery: BABYLON THE GREAT THE MOTHER OF PROSTITUTES AND OF THE ABOMINATIONS OF THE EARTH (17:5).

Wow, what a big forehead she must have! Gotta fit all those words on her forehead! But as we have read through Revelation, the idea of identification on the forehead goes much deeper than just an outward signwriting job. We have seen the significance of both the people of God and unbelievers having seals or marks on their foreheads identifying who they are and who they belong to, but it's not a literal mark. The mark is borne out in their thinking of the mind and actions of their hands.

We are also told she is the *mother* of prostitutes. She sits on the waters (nations). She has power over nations. She is, 'Babylon the Great'. That's the term big King Nebuchadnezzar used to boast in regard to his own glory (Dan. 4:30). She too is the pride of all that was of the great city of old. But what we learn now is that her allurement is demonically powered. She offers a false salvation. How?

Try and imagine you are sitting in a pew in of one of those seven churches in Asia Minor in the first century. Who is the great city, the woman? The great city filled with abominations and uncleanness that enticed with her adulteries was *Rome* and could be no other! The first readers would note that she is the *great ruling city over the kings of the earth* (17:18). That has to describe Rome. And oh, how she seduced the churches. The seventh church, Laodicea was rich *like Rome!* What's wrong with some of the good things in life? Well, Jesus said they were wretched, pitiful, poor, blind and naked. When Jezebel was teaching the fourth church (Thyatira) that sexual immorality was compatible with a Christian walk, *in Rome* you had it as part of legitimate spirituality. The wife asks her husband, 'Have you been with another woman?' Husband says, 'No, I've just been down to the temple to worship and went through my ritual with the temple prostitute.' Wife says, 'Oh, that's okay then, for a moment there I thought you were cheating on me.' In other words, abominations were *legitimate* with Babylon, the great city! And spiritual life dominated Rome. You had to burn incense to the emperor and take part in pagan rituals as part of festivals. Idolatry! Demon driven. Even in your work, depending on what sort of trade you worked in, you had to enter idolatrous rituals. And your ability to buy and sell depended on whether you were willing to compromise or not. Rome was the center of wealth, idols, luxury and prosperity, and entertainment was always lewd and crude. Rome was obsessed with pleasure. Pleasure is the end of all things. And most certainly people relied on Rome to provide their financial security, material comfort and safety. Pax Romana. It was a gay social life the 'great city' would provide. That is, if you went along with her demands.

That was then. But where would we find such a city today? Take a look around. You're living in it! There have been many other great cities throughout the last 2000 years, and this woman is the *mother* of them all! The great city is before us ... in many forms today. She is a seducer. Do you feel it? Now you know why! It's demonically driven! She wants the blood of the saints. She wants to destroy you. She offers an alternative salvation; she is an alternative to the church. She wants you to leave the true church. Not just the fellowship ... it's more than that. You can stay in the church building, but it's your soul she wants. She wants to make shipwreck of your faith through compromise, subtly and seductively. It's not a case of 'have you ever felt her seduction tugging at you?' You need to ask, *how* is she trying to seduce you now and are you standing firm? As Christians it's not just a matter of us all having different sins and failures. This is teaching us that there is a centralized, organized, demonic plot to have you. It comes from the one mother. She is **THE MOTHER OF PROSTITUTES AND OF THE ABOMINATIONS OF THE EARTH.**

She is the mother of them all! She offers greed, lust, materialism, her wine of sexual immorality, and false teaching. Pride was the great hallmark of historic Babylon. Pride in all its forms. Have you ever been caught up in envy, jealous of what someone else has, or can do, their looks, or their life? Do you know where that is coming from? The mother wants to entice you. She is the Madam! She has lots of prostitutes working for her. She is the *mother* of prostitutes. She's the mother of all abominations of the earth. And these days we want to depend on her, the great city, for economic security and prosperity, rather than living by faith and not worrying about tomorrow. We are bombarded by cultural expectations and attitudes towards the stuff we *need* to buy, the self-serving, the sexual immorality promoted in music, advertising, movies and TV, the expectations on young people, the seduction and false religion. It's all coming from the *mother!* It's not just random chance that you find yourself tempted in your particular sin. It's all organized from the mother of *all* prostitutes (*all* unfaithfulness) and *all* abominations. But each temptation is tailor made to your satisfaction to offer you an alternative salvation. Are pornography and other sexual sins in there? Of course! She is the mother of *prostitutes!* But she is also the mother of all other abominations. Get what you want now. You shouldn't have to wait on God. There is no temptation that has seized you except what is common to man. Why? They all come from the same mother!

But there is more. The pressure here is that this *mother* of prostitutes works her way into the church. Prosperity gospels. Cheap grace. Gospels with no repentance. Church that is not about Jesus and serving him, but about serving me and meet my needs. Worship is not about Jesus but about making me feel good and entertaining me. And so the people of the church end up living like her alternative salvation. 'Christians' act, dress and speak like the world, and the statistics tell us there is little difference among churchgoers and the world in sexual immorality, pornography, divorce, abortion, the language we use, the addictions we don't give up, cheating, stealing illegal downloads, the way we drive, our giving to the poor, our lack of forgiveness against those who sin against us, and the way we speak to and treat our spouse. The other woman has you! Have you been seduced by the other woman? She is spiritual, this woman. She's the *mother.* Her teaching is always peace, peace, when there is no peace. 'It's okay, we are all sinners.' She gets her adulterous teachers in the church and sometimes you *can't* pick them out immediately because often it's not what they say, but what they leave out. But you can identify them because the Mother's teachers don't spend too much time on sin, repentance, holiness or judgment. That's why they don't have to spend as much time on the good news of the cross! That is the woman, the demonically driven mother of all abominations. But you just keep going and say, 'My, how Revelation is interesting. I wonder when all that is going to happen?'

It's speaking to you now! If you don't feel pain to resist her temptations, then you are probably already committing adultery with her right now.

Jesus said, ...*what is exalted among men is an <u>abomination</u> in the sight of God* (Luke 16:15). She has her cup filled with abominations! This action replay is here to give you the close-up, so you are warned what is driving this false salvation she offers.

She sells the hopes, dreams, glory and satisfaction of the things of this world. And she turns good things, given by God, into idols. When work becomes a priority over the pure woman (the church), or serving, or being there for your family; or when relationships become a goal to 'make me complete', or when providing for yourself becomes storing up ... and addictions! Or when affection for things start out innocently, but she entices with her demonic temptation. She offers satisfaction. She offers an alternative salvation ... and the message here is: It's all a big lie!

The only ultimate satisfaction will be found in what you were created for. Have you seen the rest of Revelation where it tells of being able to gaze upon true beauty, not the counterfeit? To know and be in the presence of the slain Lamb who died for me, even me. Is that your hope? Do you flee from sin because you have believed in what Jesus went through to take it away? Or do your eyes divert to the *other* woman. What she offers is satisfaction, now! You don't have to wait!

What Jesus offers, his salvation, his church, has to be taken hold of by faith. You can't always see immediately how much better it is, but you will. Sometimes you get snippets of 'sight' of the Lord's hand in your life. You pray and pray and pray and if you really seek God each day just for who he is, along the way you will see snippets of the beauty of the Lord. It's guaranteed. Ask and you shall receive! Pray and never give up. Ask him to show you his beauty. Ask him to change your self-centered heart to have a heart for his glory, to exchange your 'success' for pleasing him in his kingdom! And he will give it to you! You will see a snippet here and there. But then it's back to the battle against the seduction of the other woman and the trials. Then you pray and pray, and then another snippet. But one day it will be unbroken ecstasy. But now, in between those snippets, you have to live by faith.

The prostitute has many in *her* church when she comes to a crash, and she takes them all to hell. How? She offers the short-term pleasure that ends up being empty and painful. In this life, she lets you down! But then she promises 'one more time'. Just try me again. You will be filled. Her wine is so addictive. It gives you a headache, but as soon as you sober up, you go back for more.

How can we reach our non-Christian friends with this? They are going to think you are wacko if you start showing them prostitutes riding red beasts with seven heads. But if you bring it back to the big picture of what is being taught here, it's not so remote from what they can understand. Ask your friends this: Which worldview really fits? How have your idols served you? What idols? All the things that you place of higher importance than God. Even most unbelievers have found that their idols turn out to be a lie. Is the symbol of this woman so farfetched from what most unbelievers have experienced at some point? The hopes and promises of this world entice, entice, entice, give pleasure, but then rip your heart out and leave you empty. Talk it through with friends. Ask them if they really believe that living for the self, now, is all there is to life. Even many of your unbelieving friends will tell something is wrong.

So, if there is a God, do you think he is just going to say, 'I don't care about the evils of the city.'? And if he does care, what if you have taken part in the city? In any way, shape or form? If you have ever drunk the wine of this woman, you will drink the wine of God's fury. So, are we *all* gonners?

Well, this is the ugly world that God sent his Son into, to take judgment in the place of all who believe in him, that he might give them new life, eternal life. It's for those who were drinking the wine of this woman, but then humbled themselves before him and followed him by turning from this woman and joining the pure woman, the church. Repent and believe the good news!

But you can't share the truth that true satisfaction is found in Jesus if you don't know it yourself. Do you long for Jesus more than the wine of the other woman? Which city is winning in your life? Which woman are you living with? The seductive woman with her abominations, or the bride who is the Church?

The woman was dressed in purple and scarlet, and was glittering with gold, precious stones and pearls. She held a golden cup in her hand, filled with abominable things and the filth of her adulteries. This name written on her forehead was a mystery: BABYLON THE GREAT THE MOTHER OF PROSTITUTES AND OF THE ABOMINATIONS OF THE EARTH (17:4-5).

Study Questions

1. If John is invited to see the punishment of the woman (17:1), why is this text describing all her seductive beauty?

2. What is the significance of John being taken away in the Spirit to a desert?

3. What is behind the deceptive power of this woman, and how do we deduce this from Scripture?

4. What does this woman have in common with Babylon of old?

5. Who is Babylon to the first readers in the seven churches, and what hints do we get from this text that would help them identify her?

6. As the alternative to the church, what are some of the ways she works her way into the true church?

7. What are ways the Christian can counter the attacks of the woman both defensively and pro-actively?

8. How can we use this text to speak into the lives of non-Christians?

3
The Beast Comes
(Revelation 17:6-8)

If you were one of those first readers of Revelation in one of those seven churches in the first century, you knew who the Beast was. There was only one supreme government power, the Roman Empire. This is where the Preterist says they have the right interpretation of Revelation, by pointing out that Nero, the great persecutor of Christians, was referred to as the Beast in the first century. And remember the famous hoax in the first century that Nero had risen from the dead? The Preterist says that through the Nero myth, Nero is the one who was, and is not, and is to come.

Does that fully explain our text? We have looked at the Beast and the great prostitute who rides the Beast. She is in cahoots with Satan, she is the great city, the *other woman* who offers an alternative salvation. But this time we learn that just like the Beast, she is a great persecutor of Christians. She has blood on her hands. Even in her mouth. It's a gruesome sight ...

> I saw that the woman was <u>drunk</u> with the <u>blood</u> of God's holy people, the blood of those who bore testimony to Jesus ... (17:6).

Of course, we know **blood** is the metaphor for death. She has been riding the Beast who has been persecuting Christians for the past 2000 years. The Futurist view says this persecution happens in a future seven-year tribulation, when people will be killed for the faith in greater number. And that is possible. One of the reasons I disagree with this is that I find it hard to ignore what has been fulfilled in the last 2000 years of history. Many millions of Christians' blood has been spilt for their faith. It's unfolded in history from the first century when John wrote this book. Earlier in the first century that infamous Beast, Nero, made a spectacle murdering Christians.[1] The great city of Rome, the woman, was drunk on their blood. John wrote Revelation during the reign of Emperor Domitian, who also persecuted Christians. The very letters to the churches in Rev. 2-3 speak about those who had already given their lives for their testimony. Rome, the woman, was drunk on their blood. Remember the Coliseum and the gruesome killing of Christians for entertainment? And down through the ages it continued. Roman Emperor Diocletian committed some of the most bloodthirsty persecutions up to AD 303. It was the woman, the city. She drank their blood. Then down through the Middle Ages there was the brutal murder of multitudes of Waldensians and others at the hands of the church of Rome, which in some measure also fits the profile of this 'other woman'. Has there ever been a time when she has not drunk her fill?

Many say we need to wait until some future time to see people killed in greater numbers. But what about the multitudes, even in recent decades, of those who have died for Christ? To repeat the point again, there have been more martyrs for the faith in the last century than all the rest of the previous 2000 years put together. What do we do with their blood? When it says she is drunk on their blood, do we say, 'Well, they might have died for the faith, but they don't really count, you gotta wait until the future when those who die for the faith are *really* gonna get killed.'? Is there any more dead than dead? The Futurist might say, 'Yes, but it will be greater numbers.' Of course anything is possible in the future. But it's interesting reading the popular Futurist writers and their interpretation of conditions for a future seven-year tribulation. Indeed, they speak of many dying for the faith, but also of many more who survive. We previously referred to John MacArthur on the future seven-year tribulation. He says it will also be a time when people are saved in greater numbers than ever before.[2] So in that view, there are more people being saved *than ever*. In other words, amidst all the bad things, there will be more salvation than ever. That is perhaps in some ways a whole lot *better* than things are now! John

---

[1] Tacitus, Annals of Imperial Rome, 15:44
[2] John MacArthur, *The MacArthur Study Bible,* Word Publishing, Nashville, 1997, p. 2002

MacArthur could just as easily be describing the persecution level that has come in waves in different countries at the hands of the Beast throughout the last 2000 years, and even more in the last few years. Even as we speak, the woman is drunk on the blood of God's holy people.

Perhaps it's so popular in the West to imagine a future time when people 'really get killed', that we treat it as if the blood of people dying now doesn't count. And because we are so removed from the reality of the rest of the world, we think *our* life is normal. It would shock most Westerners to hear of the brutality in those 139 nations around the world where Christians are persecuted, and that four out of five acts of religious discrimination worldwide are directed against them. We often pray, 'Thank you for our freedom', but do we really know what we are praying? The West is not 'normal' for what Christians experience worldwide. For Western Christians it might be sarcastic ridicule, or estrangement from family or friends. People might falsely accuse you of being judgmental or intolerant. But unlike our ease in the West, many Christians have lived throughout the last 2000 years in persecution that literally could cost their lives. The churches that this book of Revelation was written to knew all about it. We have seen how it affected their livelihoods or left them like John, living in a cave on a prison island. Some in the church in Smyrna were put in prison (2:10), and others in the church in Pergamum may have lost their lives (2:13)! She gets drunk on the blood of God's people, those who bear testimony. And in the centuries that followed, millions have followed at the hands of the great city, the great prostitute of Rev. 17.

> I saw that the woman was drunk with the blood of God's holy people, the blood of those who bore testimony to Jesus. When I saw her, <u>I was greatly astonished</u>. Then the angel said to me: 'Why are you astonished? I will explain to you the mystery of the woman and of the beast she rides, which has the seven heads and ten horns. The beast, which you saw, once was, now is not, and yet will come up out of the Abyss and go to its destruction. The inhabitants of the earth whose names have not been written in the book of life from the creation of the world will be astonished when they see the beast, because it once was, now is not, and yet will come (17:6-8).

Here is Nero! He was, is not, and is to come. As always, I have to say the Preterist is not going far enough. Yes, Nero fits the profile (sort of?), but what about the rest of the church in the past 2000 years? What does it mean to the church throughout the ages when it says the Beast once was, now is not and yet will come? We have seen that sort of description before. John saw it when he thinks back to the Lord God described as the one *who is, and who was, and who is to come* (1:8, 4:8). But now the mockery is reversed with this Beast … **he once was, now is not, and yet will come.** In a way, the Beast is still mocking Jesus in his life, death and resurrection. Jesus *was* (in the beginning), *was not* (his death) but is *yet to come* (second coming). Now the Beast was, now is not and is yet to come. The Beast mocks Jesus! That's one of the reasons I don't go with this Beast being confined to the past (before AD 70), or only a future seven-year period. The Beast is active in a parallel mockery of Jesus through the *same time* as Jesus' ministry. He mimics Jesus' life, death and resurrection and reign. This is during the same time as the church! The Beast also mimics Jesus' ministry to the ends of the earth, enticing **the inhabitants of the whole earth.** Jesus is given 'authority' by his Father for his ministry to all nations, and the *Beast* is given 'authority' by *his* father, the Dragon (13:2), who is the god of this age over what? The *whole earth* for the same period of time! The mimicry is parallel to Jesus' ministry. But it couldn't be mimicry if the Beast was confined to either the first century or a future seven years.

The Beast was, now is not. But wait. *When* can we say the Beast was defeated and said to be, *now is not?* The exact same time and place Jesus was *supposedly* defeated and *was not*. But God turned it into a great reversal. See Jesus' words …

> 'Now is the time for judgment on this world; now the prince of this world will be driven out. And I, when I am lifted up from the earth, will draw all people to myself'. He said this to show the kind of death he was going to die (John 12:31-33).

In other words, the cross! We know when the devil was defeated. The Dragon in whose image the Beast is made is crushed, defeated, and *is not*. When? At the cross! Just as Jesus *apparently* was not, the devil *really* was not. It's not that the devil *will* be defeated. The cross of Christ says he already *is now* a defeated foe. He *now* is not! … *and yet…he will come.*

Unlike the genuine Christ who was, and went to death, and comes to victory over death, and is coming (3:11), the Beast comes up only to go to his destruction, not victory. *The beast, which you saw, once was, now is not, and yet will come up out of the Abyss and go to his destruction.* [But before that happens, the people are astonished, and no wonder they ...] *will be astonished when they see the beast, because he once was, now is not, and yet will come.*

This also highlights the Beast's counterfeit sovereignty over time. God in Jesus is the true Alpha and Omega, who was, and is, and is to come. But the Beast also claims that. He is the Beast who *was*. But has he been around forever? Well, not quite. He would like it that way. The faker.

But he has 'sovereign' control as the god of this age (2 Cor. 4:4), and the whole world is under his control (1 John 5:19) Well again, not quite. He is not the true God over all.

And he is the *one to come*. Again, not as he would have it. He mocks the eternal God as one who was and is to come, but this is the great reversal of mockery.

Yes, we saw the Beast manifest even in the most ancient times. Didn't we gain our understanding of the Beast from a composite of the four Beasts of Daniel 7:3-7, the worldly government powers? The Beast is in the image of Satan, and Satan certainly has been around since the beginning of the creation. Who controls those worldly kingdoms? What was the specific temptation Satan tried to throw up against Jesus? 'Bow down and I will give you the kingdoms of the world' (Matt. 4:8-9). How could Satan entice Jesus with the kingdoms of the world? Because he had the Beast in his service! All the views of Revelation, the Historicist, Preterist, Futurist, and Idealist all agree that the Beast is government power, although some say the Beast is finally revealed in one personal anti-Christ figure. But kingdoms which oppress God's people have been around at least as far back as when the father of the Beast, the Dragon, was offering them to Jesus in his temptation in the first century. The Beast has been around! He 'was'. He was there in the first century. When has there not been a manifestation of the Beast in the world who spilt the blood of God's holy people?

But praise God, when Jesus went to the cross, he defeated the Beast and the Dragon, who now has *no* power to stop Jesus saving souls. Now he, the prince of this world is driven out, said Jesus. *He is not.* And *yet will come!* And there is a sense in which he has. The unbelievers are in awe. His fatal wound is healed. Remember the same Beast in 13:3. *One of the heads of the beast seemed to have had a fatal wound, but the fatal wound had been healed* ... That was his mock resurrection. Indeed, even though the Beast is a defeated foe, there have been many times the Beast has risen in those worldly powers which persecute God's people. Also the woman is drunk on their blood.

So the Beast rises only to fall again. He was there in communism, fascism, materialism, and there are seasons where he is brought down. And yet he comes again to persecute God's people. It is the great deception that impresses those on earth who follow the Beast. They are astonished! <u>*The inhabitants of the earth*</u> ... <u>*will be astonished*</u> ... The *'inhabitants of the earth'* is a typical Revelation term for unbelievers. They see the Beast not as a defeated foe. He even has an attractive salvation in the woman who rides him, and he causes the deceived of the earth to follow him. It seemed as though the Beast was defeated—the fatal wound—yet he has risen again. The powers of the world keep Christianity down, and unbelievers put their hopes in the powers to provide. The Beast lives! They will be astonished later, but they are in awe now ... he lives!

It's one of the great arguments of unbelievers. If the Beast 'is not' how do you explain your Jesus? They don't quite say it that way, it's more like, 'And if Jesus has defeated sin at the cross, then where is the victory over sin?' The Beast has come back and is winning, isn't he? Look at the evil in the world! There are anti-Christian governments such as communist regimes, or persecuting Islamic states, or passive Western governments which squeeze out Christ. Their inhabitants say, 'Governments provide for us! Where is your Christ? We don't need him. And if he came to defeat sin and evil, he hasn't done much of a job! Evil is winning! Where is your God?'

After 9/11 occurred, AFL footballer, Shaun Hart, captain of Brisbane Lions, won the Norm Smith medal for best on ground in the Grand Final. But when he dared to thank God and openly spoke about his faith, he offended many.[3] After all, it was just shortly after

---

[3] Michael Gleeson The Age newspaper, Fairfax Media, Melbourne, Australia, May 23rd 2014

9/11 and angry people wrote into the newspapers condemning him for bad taste. How dare he talk about faith in God after 9/11 had occurred? If your God cared about evil, how come the Beast who is 'not' is still around? If Jesus defeated sin and Satan at the cross, then where is your God?

Rather, people are in awe of the Beast and proclaim that the Beast is still coming. Jesus is gone and did nothing, but the Beast is still here providing for us. The Beast is reality today. Jesus is history. (They may not use those exact words, but the implication is there.) They say Jesus has not defeated anything because evil still abounds. They hear the words, 'Jesus died on the cross for sinners,' but the pride of the human heart is so powerful that the meaning of those words never registers. Sin is only 'out there'. Evil is 9/11 or ISIS and occasionally elsewhere. The problem of the world is 'out there'. The *inhabitants of the world* would never stop to consider sin might be within themselves. G.K Chesterton reportedly wrote to a newspaper which had invited answers to the question, 'What is wrong with the world?' Chesterton apparently wrote in, 'I am.' The problem is not out there, but in here, in my heart. It's in all human hearts. But people don't see sin in themselves as that bad.

The offence of the cross has raged among unbelievers for 2000 years. It offended the Pharisees in the first century. 'The Messiah is one who kills our enemies. His victory is over Rome. Not over my sin. I am a good religious person.' And that same retort still comes from Jewish people today, who say, 'Well if the Messiah has come then he hasn't done much of a job in bringing us peace and defeating evil.' They never think for a moment that the greatest need for peace is not from wars in Palestine, or from conflicts among people, but a much more serious and deeper one.

The cross has been the same offence through the ages. Mohammed founded Islam about 600 years after Jesus and tried to give an alternative explanation for Jesus' death on the cross. Jesus never died on the cross (Surah 4:157). It must have been a case of mistaken identity. God substituted Judas or someone, anyone, but Jesus! Now why would Mohammed say that about 600 years after the fact, and in the face of all the first century historical evidence? It's one of the central events of the Bible that is more attested historically than almost any other, because you have Christian eyewitnesses in the first century saying Jesus died on a cross under Pontius Pilate. And you have a Roman first century historian, Tacitus, saying Jesus died on the cross under Pontius Pilate.[4] You also have a first century Jewish historian, Josephus, saying Jesus died on the cross under Pontius Pilate.[5] Why would Mohammed want to rewrite history 600 years later? The answer is the offence of the cross. Mohammed thought of Jesus as a great prophet and couldn't conceive of a good prophet dying the indignity of the cross. And the people were *astonished* at Mohammed and his power. Now, some of the greatest persecution still comes from some of Mohammed's followers.

So the Beast lives throughout the last 2000 years and the opponents still marvel at the Beast who comes. The Beast stamps out this foolishness of the cross.

To the world the Beast comes and continues … he was, and is not, and yet he comes. The Beast is still winning. And life goes on, doesn't it? After all, you Christians are all hung up on something that happened 2000 years ago, but here we are in the world today, and the kingdom we follow, the government, supplies all we need now! Prosperity. At least they had better supply our needs, or we will vote them out at the next election. Plus, the laws of the land let me do what I want. I can use my body however I want. It's mine. I can take other's lives before they are even born. The Beast has made it law. I can speak however I want. Blaspheme the name of Jesus. Is lightning going to strike me? No. The Beast makes it legal. The Beast was and now comes and keeps coming, and what is your God gonna do about it?

Well it turns out he is going to do plenty. But we will have to move on to find out what.

---

[4] Tacitus, Annals of Imperial Rome, 15:44
[5] Josephus, Antiquities of the Jews 18:63-64

Study Questions

1. Why might Westerners think the intense persecution to death is something yet to happen?

2. Do you think the persecution of Christians throughout history is sufficient to warrant the church age being called the tribulation?

3. What would Babylon being drunk on the blood of God's holy people mean practically to those in the seven churches?

4. What are the points for and against Nero being the Beast described here?

5. Why is the Beast described as one who was, is now, and is yet to come?

6. Does this description give any hint as to the timeframe of the operation of the Beast?

7. How do people still look to the Beast today?

8. What is the offense of the cross?

4
Astonished by the Beast!
(Revelation 17:8)

What is the most astonishing thing you have ever seen? Have you seen the Wonders of the World? I saw some astonishing sights when I visited India. A palace with enough gold in one king's chair to feed half the country! Even more astonishing were things I saw on the roads. The action at intersections was so astonishing that I missed it every time because I had my hands over my eyes. It is said of India's roads, 'Only God could run this country.' Astonishing!

Well this scene in Revelation is described as *astonishing*. It's almost like John is having a bad dream as he sees the reality behind the scenes of history. It's so astonishing that John said ... *When I saw her, I was <u>greatly astonished</u>* (17:6).

Then the inhabitants of the earth (that's Revelation speak for 'unbelievers'), are also *astonished* when they see the Beast. It's all so *astonishing*. We looked at this verse last time, and it would have been easy to skip on to the next exciting section of Rev. 17 and say, well that's nice imagery, but let's not exaggerate too much John. What is so *astonishing* about this? But John is not exaggerating. He is looking into the tunnel of history and even to the end of history, and he finds it *astonishing*!

It is important for John to see this vision because it explains a much bigger picture than what the inhabitants of the earth see. They will see the full picture in the end. But for now, they are in awe of the Beast. They put their trust in the Beast. But John gets to see the big picture of what lies behind the Beast and where he is heading ...

> The beast, which you saw, once was, now is not, and yet will come up out of the Abyss and go to its <u>destruction</u>. The inhabitants of the earth whose names have not been written in the book of life from the creation of the world will be astonished when they see the beast,

> because it once was, now is not, and yet will come (17:8).

John sees the Beast that will come. John knows that the time the Beast **is not** is from when Jesus defeated him at the cross. But after that, the Beast certainly did come up from John's time, he comes up and up. To the inhabitants of the earth, it just looks like the way it was described back in Rev. 11. The unbelievers attack the church witnesses and gloat over defeating them. And here we see they are **astonished when they see the beast, because he once was, now is not, and yet will come.** They are astonished in a positive way at first. Impressed. The Beast comes back and wins. They were astonished in the same way earlier …

> One of the heads of the beast seemed to have had a fatal wound, but the fatal wound had been healed. The whole world was <u>filled with wonder</u> and <u>followed</u> the beast (13:3).

They are *filled with wonder,* in awe of the Beast who 'comes' and stamps out that Christian witness, and they *followed* the Beast. 'We were in the right.'

Now what does this mean practically? Do people consciously worship and become astonished by the Beast? Well, in a way. When multitudes were killed in the former USSR, it was not a bunch of criminals from the street who carried it out. It was the government that wanted to suppress the church. The Northern Sudanese did not sink into *anarchy* to try and commit genocide against their Southern brothers. It was the law of the land! The Beast drove it! The government! Not vigilantes. It was not a lynch mob who attacked a 27-year-old pregnant girl for converting to Christianity. It was a judge who told her to recant and believe in Islam. The law of the land! The girl refused and was sentenced to death by hanging. It was not renegades who all but stamped out the church in any number of closed Muslim countries, in Communist China or many others. It was the government. The Beast! In Nazi Germany, it was the government that rallied a whole nation to an anti-God ideology of ethnic cleansing, as well as seeking to eradicate the church by bringing in a 'new Christianity'. The 'inhabitants' of those countries follow their lead in awe.

Or more recently, when the media and government-elected

officials push same-sex marriage, or abortion, or the removal of Christian teaching from their schools, it's Christ they are seeking to remove. Do they see it that way? No! But anti-Christian sentiment reigns and the 'inhabitants' think they are doing good by removing Christ and his teaching.

Then the inhabitants gloat! Where is this victory of Jesus? We are winning. We can now do what we want! The Beast sanctions it. They are in awe of the Beast and they gloat. Even in the Western so-called Christian countries. What do the *inhabitants* say? 'It's Christians who are bigoted. It's Christians who are intolerant. It's Christians who are trying to encroach on our freedom and rights to use sex how we want and with whom we want. Our rights. We have freedom of choice. That is why we are pro-choice. It's a woman's *right*. It is our *right* to end life—at the beginning of life, or at the end, to end our own life peacefully when we want. And it's legal! The Beast makes it law. The Beast has *come again* and given us the right. You dare to say a word against our right to choose my gender or marriage partner and you will be crushed! It is the Beast who made it law! You'd better keep that Christianity out of our faces. Out of our schools! Teaching children religion is child abuse! Yes, we can say that now, child abuse. The government (Beast) *was and is coming* alive today. He sanctions our freedom. We were right to follow the Beast and support whatever measures he uses to stamp out those intolerant, judgmental Christians. How dare they impose draconian ideals on our enlightened society? We were on the side of love and tolerance for all. Free love. Love whomever we want. We are on the side of good. They are bad. The Beast is for good and he is alive! He is *astonishing!*'

But then this day comes—they see the Beast appearing. The one who was, and is not, but here he is coming up. 'Here is our champion. We stood with him against Christ who would seek to take away our rights and freedom. And here he is, our hero coming up. Up. Up. Up, like on one of those floating podiums rising to be lauded. Up he comes. We shall cheer our hero for his victorious return! But wait. Look. Look at where is he coming up from …'

The beast, which you saw, once was, now is not, and yet will come up <u>out of the Abyss</u>. 'Wait! We thought the Beast was good!' *That* is the shock that will last forever. And they are *astonished!* The one they were following belongs to the pit of hell. He is from where?

The Abyss. Satan's domain. The realm of the demonic. Metaphorically—from the pit of hell! The Abyss is not literally the same as hell, because whether you are the Beast or anyone else, there is no crossing over or getting out of hell. The Abyss is the abode of the demonic and evil and pit of the hell-bound. The inhabitants of the earth don't realize this Beast is coming out of the Abyss, only to go to its destruction. They only find out when that happens. But John (and we), received this *Revelation* in advance.

They only find out on that day when it is too late ... it was all a big lie. It was all a deception. That's why the people act the way they do. They thought he was good, but they were deceived. The Beast is made in the image of the Dragon. And who is that Dragon? How could we forget? Jesus called him the *father of all lies*! The whole thing was driven by demonic power through the father of all lies! The Beast is the one we thought was leading us to prosperity, stamping out intolerance, and standing for the good of society, but he was actually the image of the Dragon. What *astonishment!* John is astonished because he sees the whole picture, but the inhabitants of the earth will be even more astonished when it is exposed on that final day.

The beast, which you saw, once was, now is not, and yet will come up <u>out of the Abyss and go to its destruction. The inhabitants of the earth</u> whose names have not been written in the book of life from the creation of the world <u>will be astonished</u> ...

All is revealed on that day when the Beast has risen indeed, but he rises only to his **destruction**. It's not until that day that the inhabitants of the earth will discover the secret that *will* reverberate throughout eternity. The shock for them is this ...

We were following the devil! The Beast was the devil's Beast who came up out of the Abyss. The Dragon was behind the whole thing. Deceived! And all the things of this world, all our efforts, all our self-pleasures, all our idols, everything that was in conflict with the Lordship of Christ meets ... *destruction!* Destruction in the Scriptures is not being squashed out of existence, but a ruin that crashes into eternal pain—*everlasting* ruin and despair.

This is the great deception. The followers of the Beast and his father, the devil, don't even realize whom they are following. It was there in the Scriptures. Some of them even read this and missed it ...

> As for you, you were dead in your transgressions and sins, in which you used to live when you followed the ways of this world and of <u>the ruler</u> of the kingdom of the air, <u>the spirit</u> who is now at work in those who are disobedient (Eph. 2:1-2).

What *spirit* did they follow? Who follows the *ways of this world?* Those who are disobedient! That means every unbeliever follows the spirit that is now at work in him or her. What spirit is that? The Dragon and the Beast who is made in his image. Did they know for a second that they were devil worshipers? How great is this deception! Revelation says the *inhabitants of the earth* are following the Beast who is from *the Abyss*, the realm of Satan and the demonic. Try convincing your unbelieving family and friends they are satanic Beast followers. They will say you've gone troppo! That is the measure of the deception. *All* who have not submitted to Christ are following Satan. But the deception is so great that even Christians get caught up in it. 'Aren't Satan worshipers those heavy metal guys who sacrifice chickens?' Or you might hear Christians say things like 'there is something satanic about that guy'. Well, according to the Bible, anyone, even people who come to church who have not submitted to Christ, are *all* followers of Satan and the Beast. All deceived! The spirit is now at work in *all* who are disobedient.

> The god of this age has <u>blinded the minds of unbelievers</u>, so that they cannot see the light of the <u>gospel that displays the glory of Christ</u>, who is the image of God (2 Cor. 4:4).

The god of this age (Satan) has blinded the minds of which unbelievers? *All* of them! And they actually think they are good. Ask them! 'Yes, I should get to heaven, I've been a pretty good person compared to most.' But what about the times you haven't been good? Who will take the judgment for that? 'Oh, I've done more good than bad.' So effectively it becomes, 'I don't need any Savior who provides a gospel ... the Beast has provided, I don't need it.'

They can't see the deception. But on that final day the curtain is pulled back, and look who was behind the curtain pulling the strings on the puppets! *Astonished!* Then they will say, 'We were just puppets! He not only deceived us, but he was not a hero at all. He was lying to us. He was not coming up to an ovation but to destruction.' *It was all a big lie!*

So all is not what it seems. This is what Revelation reveals like no other book in the Bible. The great division and warfare is not between the countries of the world, the religions of the world, the many ideologies, races, or political philosophies. Are we getting caught up missing the forest for the trees? There is only *one* division. Jesus put it this way: *Whoever is not with me, is against me.* You are not on neutral ground. Right now, you are either for the Beast or for Jesus. And if you are for the Beast, then you are deceived.

Some say, 'I'm not either, I'm for myself.' But that is 'Beast' rule. That is his *first* rule. Do what thou wilt. That's actually a line from Alistair Crowley, who inspired Anton Levey, the writer of the satanic Bible. 'Do what thou wilt.' Do what you want! You are your own god. Satan used it in in the Garden. Eat of the fruit. Do what you want! Don't let God tell you what to do! You be like God.

Those on the side of the Beast don't think of themselves as Beast worshipers. It is deceit. There is a secret 'Star Wars' raging in the cosmos that is unseen, because we are just little earthlings with limited vision.

> For our struggle is not against flesh and blood, but against the rulers, against the authorities, against the powers of this dark world and against the spiritual forces of evil in the <u>heavenly realms</u> (Eph. 6:12).

This is a spiritual world of deceit in the heavenly realms raging throughout this world. So if you are comfortable ruling your own life, and there are no bolts of lightning striking you down when you 'do what you want', and no one sees your secret life, then what's the big deal? 'I don't hurt people. I am free to do what I want. I would follow Jesus as long as he doesn't interfere with what I want. What difference does it make?' And the answer is in this same verse as to what difference it makes. Did you notice it's just thrown in as an aside—*your name*.

... <u>*The inhabitants of the earth*</u> *whose names have* <u>*not been written in the book of life*</u> *from the creation of the world* <u>*will be astonished*</u> *when they see the beast.* You will be astonished indeed if your name is not written in the book of life. You thought you were 'all good'. But you were deceived by the one from the Abyss. And now it's all out. Destruction. There was no neutral ground. If you think you can say, 'Hey, I am not fully for Jesus, but I am definitely not with the Beast. I am sitting on the fence.' Remember the old saying? The Beast owns the fence!

There are names written in the book of life from the creation of the world. It was all planned. Right now, either you are living to serve Christ with the time, money and gifts he gave you, or living to serve the Beast. It's all written from before the creation of the world.

But here is good news. Revelation is written as the wake-up call. Even if you have been <u>*deceived*</u> and living as one whose name is *not* written in the book of life, if God gives you the grace to take this Revelation to heart, then you are blessed. This is written for you! To wake up!

And if you do wake up and repent and believe, then it turns out your name *was* written in that book from before the creation of the world. So does that mean it will be all triumphant and easy in this life? It might even *look* like the opposite. The powerful Beast looks like *he* is winning. That's the message of Revelation. When he looks like he is winning, you need to remember—Jesus wins.

That is why there is this recurring phrase in Revelation: *names written in the book of life from the creation of the world*. It is the word of encouragement to the readers, the believers in tribulation are being told that their salvation and assurance is much bigger than how well they are going, or how much attack they are under. You have an eternal security that is mind-boggling. A book written before the creation of the world which goes way beyond merely looking at 'how am I going?' It speaks of a plan of God. Jesus said, 'I will lose none of all that you have given me' (John 6:39). Names were given from the Father to the Son. Those names are written in the book of life. Those whose names are *not* written in the book will just continue with the Beast. Just like that scary scene at the end of Revelation which says the books were opened and if anyone's name was not found in the book of life they were thrown into the lake of fire. We thought we were winning with the Beast. That's the shock and *astonishment*.

What is going to happen for you on that day when that book is opened? They scan through looking for your name. Is it there? Did the Beast and his values deceive you? The 'search' feature on that book finishes. 'I'm sorry but your name doesn't seem to be here.' 'It must be there! Maybe it's under my maiden name? But I don't have a maiden name! Scan it again. It has to be there.'

Is it? Everything hinges around your name being in that book, but it is all as simple as this: Have you truly trusted in Christ or the things of this world that the Beast provides? Examine yourself. Do you still hold to do what thou wilt? Double-check and see if you are deceived. Don't just listen to preachers. Check the Bible. Are you walking with him?

The beast, which you saw, once was, now is not, and yet will come up out of the Abyss and go to its destruction. The inhabitants of the earth whose names have not been written in the book of life from the creation of the world will be astonished when they see the beast, because he once was, now is not, and yet will come (17:8).

Study Questions

1. What are the inhabitants of the earth astonished at concerning the Beast in this life?

2. What astonishes John about the Beast?

3. Give several ways the inhabitants of the earth worship the Beast.

4. Why are the inhabitants of the earth astonished when the Beast comes up at the end?

5. Some equate the Abyss with hell. Is that correct?

6. What constitutes a follower of the devil?

7. Give examples of the deception of the Beast.

8. What is the main message of this text?

9. How could you examine yourself to see if your name is written in the book of life?

5
The Ten Kings United
(Revelation 17:9-14)

How much wisdom have you got? You are going to need it. If you have a mind with wisdom you should be able to understand the seven heads of the Beast ...

> 'This calls for a mind with wisdom. The seven heads are seven hills on which the woman sits. They are also seven kings. Five have fallen, one is, the other has not yet come; but when he does come, he must remain for a little while' (17:9-10).

So did John and his first readers have wisdom? Could they figure this out? The Beast (a worldly power) with seven heads that are seven hills? How is this for the getting of wisdom? The city of Rome is literally on seven hills! The Preterist says 'this shows *we* have the wisdom!' After all, the Preterist says Revelation is speaking *only* to the context of the first century Christians. **The seven heads are seven hills on which the woman sits**. Rome was literally known as the city *on* seven hills! How much more wisdom do you need?

Although the original Greek word translated *hill* is more usually translated *mountain*, and in Revelation (just as in the OT), *mountain* is often used as a metaphor for kingdoms (Isa. 2:2, Jer. 51:25). And sure enough, 17:10 says these *mountains* or *hills* are kings. Wisdom is required here. The Preterist still says they have wisdom because Rome is on seven hills that are seven kings, and that you can count the Roman Emperors before AD 70 from the man referred to as the Beast in his day, Caesar Nero. But which *hill* or *king* is he? ...

> They are also seven kings. Five have fallen, one is, the other has not yet come; but when he does come, he must remain for a little while (17:10).

Using wisdom and knowledge of Roman history of the time, the

Preterist sees Nero as the sixth king. Five emperors before Nero and then Nero is the one who **is**, but who is the one to come? The emperors that follow Nero don't fit quite so well. There were three kings in a row all within a year after Nero; Galba, Otho and Vitellius, which makes a non-entity like Otho the eighth king who lasted only a couple of months. Unless you skip those non-entity three and go to the next major king, Vespasian, who makes a better case for an eighth king as he ruled at the time of the fall of Jerusalem. But who decides you can skip kings? Someone with more wisdom than me. The seventh and eighth kings are supposed to be more severe than Nero (the sixth king), but that doesn't fit. In fact, trying to make Roman emperors fit sounds impressive at first, but where do you start counting from? Who has that much wisdom?

Historicists and Futurists often make the seven kings *kingdoms* instead of individual kings. This seems to have more **wisdom** than the Roman Emperors concept. For instance John MacArthur says you begin with Egypt, then Assyria, Babylon, Medo-Persia and Greece, (five fallen), then Rome is the sixth one that 'is', and then look forwards over the next 2000 years to a future power led by the Anti-Christ.[6] But even with this you have to leave out ancient worldly powers that oppressed God's people (such as the Seleucid's Antiochus Epiphanes). Then by the time we get to 18:9 it throws a whole spanner in the works because these same kings are said to mourn over the prostitute's demise.

> 'When the kings of the earth who committed adultery with her and shared her luxury see the smoke of her burning, they will weep and mourn over her' (18:9).

How does that work? No one believes the ancient Greeks, Medes and Persians will be there mourning over the great prostitute. More 'wisdom' is required. Who has enough wisdom?

Did those first readers living in the first century have enough wisdom? They are the ones who were directly called on to have wisdom. And have you got enough wisdom? Did you know Rome is built on seven hills? Do you have that historical wisdom? Did you know about ancient Assyria, Medo/Persia and Babylon? If you didn't

---

[6] John MacArthur, *Because the Time is Near*, Moody Publishers, Chicago, 2007, p. 268

already know them, look them up on Google! This calls for wisdom! At least that is one type of wisdom.

There are different kinds of wisdom. Is this calling for who is the best at history lessons? Or math, or science? We've mentioned some good arguments from the Preterist, Historicist and Futurist that require a wisdom and knowledge of *history*. But that's the kind of wisdom unbelievers can have. Is that who this is addressed to, so unbelievers could apply their wisdom to calculate?

The way the Bible uses the word *wisdom* is that of godly wisdom with the worldview of Christ. How would we apply godly wisdom here? Revelation is filled with warnings. True believers reading this over the past 2000 years will respond to those warnings. That is godly wisdom. Be wise. Be ready. Be alert. The *wise* virgins, as opposed to the foolish, showed godly wisdom! Believers might get sidetracked at times, but when they get warned, they wake up. They will act with wisdom and prepare! That is biblical wisdom. Knowledge of the Scriptures yes, but also *listening* to the word! It's like the wisdom required in figuring out the '666' (13:18). It was not a matter of who is the mathematical genius who can calculate the number of an individual. That's unbeliever's wisdom. The Bible gives wisdom. Man, the mere creature, created on the 6th day, *falls short* of God and his perfection of 7. God's perfection in trinity 777, man falls short of that. His number then is 666. Back then we were told this called for wisdom, but not by checking your math book. So here we have the same call ... *This calls for a mind with <u>wisdom</u>. The <u>seven heads</u> are <u>seven hills</u> on which the woman sits. They are also <u>seven kings</u>.*

What has the book of Revelation already taught us about the number seven? What might the significance of the number of kings be? Seven heads are seven hills are seven kings. Revelation has been showing us *sevens* all the way through as God's number of completion. This book is written to *seven* churches, so by extension to all of God's church. The seven spirits of God equals the complete Spirit of God. We could go over it all again: the seven seals, seven trumpets, and seven bowls meaning the completion of God's judgments and so on. So what should we be thinking when we see *seven* mountains in 17:9, then 17:10 *tells us* they are seven kings or kingdoms? Seven kingdoms simply mean *complete* earthly power, kings or kingdoms throughout time. All of them!

Isn't that what we have said about the Beast all along? He has these seven heads which are kingdoms spanning the ages, just like the Beast's father, the Dragon (the devil), works across the age. He has been around from before he offered Jesus the kingdoms of the world. The Beast *was and is not and yet is coming*. He is not confined either to the first century or some future time.

The NT tells us we should expect an antichrist figure, a Beast figure, perhaps only revealed just as Jesus returns, and yet the antichrist spirit has been around since John was writing this Revelation. Here is how long the Beast's influence has been around!

> Dear children, this is the last hour; and as you have heard that the antichrist is coming, <u>even now</u> many antichrists have come. This is how we know it is the last hour (1 John 2:18).

The antichrist Beast has been around! He is not only coming in some personal manifestation at the end, his work was around in John's day. This is one reason why I haven't gone with the Preterist idea that the Revelation Beast is only manifest in the first century, or the Futurist concept that the Beast is only manifest in some future seven-year period. John said it was the *last hour* from his day when the antichrist influence was around. What did he mean? We will see in 17:12 the same Beast receives authority for a period of *one hour*. The time is short. But how long is this hour? We are in it! John said we are already in this *last hour!*

Can Revelation speak to John and his first readers, but also speak to anyone who has wisdom throughout the last 2000 years? Seven kings represent the sweep of worldly power against Jesus over the last 2000 years. The seven hills that are the heads of the Beast are also said to be kings, but what about these five who have fallen? **They are also seven kings. Five have fallen, one is, the other has not yet come; but when he does come, he must remain for a little while.** Five fallen, one is, and one still to come? And he *must remain for a little while*. Instead of using wisdom of the world, math and history, if we take seven as a number indicating the sweep of all earthly kingdoms, it's not just seven individuals but also the whole! If seven is completion and five are down already, we are up to the sixth measure of completion and there is one to go. What is that saying? The same thing Revelation has been saying all along. The time is near! It's the same warning we had from Jesus in 16:15. He is coming like a thief. The time could be anytime! It's unexpected. It's nearer now than it has been before. You are up to six out of seven! It's the call of Revelation. In God's sight the time of the church is a short 'hour', and for us the end is only getting closer! We are six-sevenths there! That's what this language conveys. It's five down. One here and one to go. The devil's time is short. As is the Beast's.

> 'The beast who once was, and now is not, is an eighth king. He belongs to the seven and is going to his destruction' (17:11).

But where does an eighth king fit? How does it work if seven is completion? Well, we are told he is not distinct from the seven. **He belongs to the seven.** That's important. A final manifestation of evil, but similar to what has gone on before. It makes sense if we have the principle of worldly power across time rather than specific kings or kingdoms. Seven is complete worldly power across the ages, and the eighth and final one is distinctive by virtue of intensity, but is essentially *more of the same Beast* you experienced in the seven ... *he belongs to the seven.*

Most Christians, including myself, believe in the appearance of an antichrist figure at the end of time, although I would reiterate that he could easily be made apparent immediately upon the return of Jesus, when the people who followed the Beast will be 'astonished' (17:8). Jesus returns and the antichrist is exposed. That way it would not conflict with Jesus' words that he will come unexpectedly, *like a thief.* If the antichrist were exposed any significant time in advance, then believers would all know when Jesus is coming!

So although he is the eighth, he belongs to the seven. He is not separate from what has been going on all along. Isn't that what John said when he said many antichrist's have come into the world already? So the full manifestation of the Beast, the antichrist which we should expect near the end of time, is *not* out of line with what is right before our eyes now. The eighth is part of and belongs to the other seven.

In fact, even though historical facts show chronological problems with trying to count seven individual kings and kingdoms (as do Preterists, Historicists or Futurists), it doesn't mean those views have nothing to offer with this text. If the number seven is completion, then the seven kings (kingdoms) must include those individual kingdoms mentioned by those interpreters. So it's not a great leap to borrow from all the views and say there is relevance in the historical kingdoms they mention. But I would add 'don't stop there', and use the number seven to indicate completion, that is, *all* the kingdoms of history. So Nero and the Roman Empire are part of it—a part of the sevenfold powers that attack the cause of Christ throughout history, until one comes with a more intense manifestation. An eighth.

But then what are these ten kings?

> 'The ten horns you saw are ten kings who have not yet received a kingdom, but who for <u>one hour</u> will receive authority as kings along with the beast' (17:12).

One hour indicates a short time of intensity in later times, but the kings had **not yet received a kingdom,** at least from John's day. Ten is not God's number of completion in the same way as seven, but it stands for a decimal fullness. Ten also has been used in Revelation as a number associated with Satan's work. The saints are persecuted in Smyrna for *ten* days (2:10), as Satan's choice of time. The Dragon, Satan himself, has *ten* horns (12:3). The Beast also has *ten* horns and *ten* crowns (13:1). And these *ten* kings are united.

> '<u>They have one purpose</u> and will give their power and authority to the beast' (17:13).

And what is this *one purpose?* William Hendriksen says the purpose is explained in the following verse and it is the theme of the book of Revelation.[7] It's a crucial verse. It not only sums up the whole of Revelation, it explains life for us in the world, what is happening in your life, and what will happen in the end … Jesus wins! All that we have learned about the Beast, the woman who rides him, the opposition and the call for us to be faithful, the hope you have and need. It's all summed up in this …

> 'They will wage war against the Lamb, but the Lamb will triumph over them because he is Lord of lords and King of kings—and with him will

---

[7] William Hendriksen, *More Then Conquerors,* Baker Book House, Grand Rapids Michigan, 1967, p. 205

be his called, chosen and faithful followers' (17:14).

Previously we read that the *ten kings* were aligned with the Beast. They *formerly* had no authority (17:12). However, towards the end they have this new power with the Beast to wage war against the Lamb. Before they might have been sympathetic or indifferent to the cause of the Lamb, certainly not waging war against him. And we have no trouble finding ten powers of this world which fit this description that now make war against the Lamb and his faithful. Have you seen a shift in intensity of powers in our day? Even those powers we could have relied on previously to give Christianity a fair go, powers that are now intensifying their purpose against the Lamb and his faithful? Let me give you an example of ten kings or 'powers'. (You might think of others as it doesn't have to be an exact number. Remember ten is symbolic, representing decimal fullness.) There are political powers, the media empire (attacking the church), education (free education invented by Christianity is now turning against Christ), business empires (increasingly ethics of greed), art, literature, our legal system (formerly based on the Ten Commandments now working against the Christian worldview), medical ethics (hospitals invented by Christianity now given 'authority' by the Beast, that is, worldly powers, to legislate abortion, euthanasia etc.), sports and entertainment (not bad things in themselves, now turned into idols to take people away from worshiping God). All ten were at one time powers (kings) that could help the Christian cause, but now they are sanctioned and aligned with the Beast, now they have *authority*.

But what happened to the *One World Government?* Well, contrary to popular opinion, the book of Revelation never actually mentions the One World Government (nor is it anywhere else in the Bible). What we *are* told is that these kings or powers of the world unite, but in a particular way… **They have one purpose and will give their power and authority to the beast.** They all have *one purpose* (17:13). What is that purpose? *They all make war against the Lamb* (17:14)! Now we are getting somewhere. When you think about that *one purpose* instead of having to think about a formal One World Government, they don't even have to be joined politically or ideologically. It doesn't matter if it is a closed Muslim government persecuting Christians, or the Western media barrage against the church. All these ten powers are joined: political, media, education, business, art, literature, legal system, medical ethics, sports and entertainment. They all have *one purpose* ... to make war against the Lamb. One purpose ... anti-Christ!

If you think about the great cosmic spiritual war over the territory of this earth, then with these ten powers you can ask, 'Has there ever been a time when the world has been more at *one purpose* against Christ?' These kings are still *separate* powers or *kings*, but all of one purpose. They form a united front in the world against the Lamb, against Christ's ways and his gospel going forth.

So we would need to picture a short time when every element of power and influence in this world has one purpose, one goal—to oppose the Christ. They are all under the one authority ...

> Why do the nations <u>conspire</u> and the peoples plot in vain? <u>The kings of the earth</u> rise up and the rulers <u>band together against the LORD</u> and against his anointed, saying, 'Let us break their chains and throw off their shackles' (Ps. 2:1-3).

They are spiritual powers of evil using physical earthly powers. All these powers and influences attack God's word, ethics, his salvation, his cause and his people. So 17:14 explains life now!

But what is fascinating is how even Christians are surprised, even shocked, when they see corruption in every sphere of life, and that every ideology has some bent against the kingdom of Christ. And Christians are taken aback! 'I can't believe there is so much corruption at work, in politics, in media, in entertainment, in education! ...' You can't believe it because you haven't read this...
They <u>will make war</u> against the Lamb...

One day reading my Bible I saw afresh Jesus' words to the sinful woman, 'Your sins are forgiven'. The beauty of the Savior struck me anew. He forgives! Why? Because of 17:14. He is the Lamb! Slain, stretched, tortured for our sin! But together every religion, power and king of the world hates that. It's offensive to them so they ask, 'Why is Jesus the only way? What do you need the cross for? I am not a bad person.' In principle they are saying that God should forgive without having to deal with sin. 'Our sin is not that bad.' They are all opposed to the Lamb!

This text is the assurance that in the end, though they make war against the saints and appear to have victory, it's actually Jesus who will triumph over them because he is revealed as the true King of kings, '… **but the Lamb will overcome them because he is Lord of lords and King of kings—and with him will be his called, chosen and faithful followers.**'

Perhaps this is what the apostle Paul meant when he said we would judge the world (1 Cor. 6:2). All the way to the end they wage war, but the Lamb will defeat them *and with him will be his chosen and faithful followers*. We are involved in this invisible battle—we who are on the side of the King of kings. Yes, it looks like Satan is winning, but every little battle you fight for is one *with* Jesus on your side. Don't let that temptation drag you down. You are fighting for the King of kings and the good news is, Jesus wins!

So now do you see the heart of that battle you had against temptation last week? Who were you fighting for? And what does this tell us? It tells us that there is no neutral ground. Either you are fighting *with* the King of kings, or you are against him, in which case you will be crushed and so will all the kings you followed. The lie will not go on forever. The true King will be revealed. Everything we do and say is for *his* glory … or for the world. But the two will *not remain*. One will be decimated and exposed and judged. The other will be victorious. *Blessed are all who take refuge in him.*

Up until then, there is a unifying of the kings of the world against Christ and his people. But they didn't count on whom they were really up against. You kings, you rulers, be wise (Ps. 2)! You have no idea. *Kiss the Son, lest he be angry and you be destroyed in your way, for his wrath can flare up in a moment.* They said, 'We are kings.' And Jesus is forgotten as a 'would be' king from the ancient world. But the shock is that he is revealed as the *King* of kings—*and with him will be his called, chosen and faithful followers.*

With him! Are you one of the *chosen and faithful followers?* This is the call of Revelation. This calls for patient endurance and faithfulness on the part of God's people. It looks like the Beast is winning. Hold fast and be faithful! You will be with him. It might be sooner than you think. But not all will be faithful followers. Many will get caught up in the worries of this life, the deceitfulness of wealth, the kind of things the Beast provides! The only question on that day will be, were you faithful? Whose side are you on? Are you *with him?*

Study Questions

1. To whom is the call for wisdom made?

2. Why does the Preterist have a good argument for the seven hills and what are the shortcomings of that view?

3. What are the strengths and weaknesses of the Roman Emperors as the seven kings?

4. What are the strengths and weakness of the view that six of the seven are specific ancient world superpowers?

5. What is the kind of wisdom being called for?

6. How can Revelation's use of sevens help us understand this text?

7. Based on the previous answer how can we understand the five fallen and one to come?

8. Where can an eighth king fit when seven is completion?

9. Where do another ten kings fit when seven is completion?

10. Where might people get the idea of the One World Government and how might they have misunderstood this text?

11. How does 17:14 sum up Revelation and world history?

12. How does 17:14 speak into your life now?

6
The Beast Attacks the Prostitute
(Revelation 17:15-18)

With all these great characters of Revelation—the Beast, the Dragon and the great prostitute—it's sometimes hard to understand all that is going on. Some say we are to regard these images literally. Some don't. But every now and then, we get these reminders of what John recorded from the first verse (1:1), that this Revelation is given to *make known* by *signs and symbols*. It's good to remind ourselves of this throughout the book. The single Greek word in the original language translated *made it known* specifically refers to *make known by signs or symbols*. There is another more widely used Greek word that means *make known* which doesn't carry the meaning of signs and symbols, but John chooses to *not* use that word because he wants us to know the genre of literature we are reading. And sure enough through Revelation, we get these reminders that the images given are symbolic when occasionally the meaning of symbols are *explained*. Most of the time we have to go digging through the OT to understand the symbols. It's almost as though the Lord really wanted us to read and know his word to understand Revelation! But some symbols are explained directly and the following is one of them: From 17:1 we were told the great prostitute was sitting by many waters. How does *anyone* sit by many waters? (Other more literal translations have 'sits *on* many waters.') Well, the waters are symbolic. But symbolic of what?

> Then the angel said to me, 'The waters you saw, where the prostitute sits, are peoples, multitudes, nations and languages' (17:15).

This includes every kind of person from every possible background! Do you realize what this means? Every person in the whole world from all kinds of **peoples, multitudes, nations and languages**, all who don't know Jesus, are under the sway of the prostitute! She sits by them! Controls them. Revelation is reminding us of what we so easily forget. The corruption of humanity permeates all peoples everywhere!

But now we read about prostitute's downfall, and the metaphors used describe her as naked, eaten up like the prey of the Beast, and burned like a city ...

> 'The beast and the ten horns you saw will hate the prostitute. They will bring her to ruin and leave her naked; they will eat her flesh and burn her with fire' (17:16).

Remember some say the prostitute is the RC church. The prostitute *is* the counterfeit to the church offering an alternative salvation, so that must include any false teaching and another salvation. The RC church teaches that instead of needing Jesus to get us into heaven, we need Jesus *plus* our good works. Instead of Ephesians 2:8-9, *by grace you have been saved ... so that no one can boast*, it's Jesus plus my works so you *can* boast. 'Just be a good Catholic and you can get to heaven.' So some say the RC church fits her profile, but what did this text mean to those first century readers? We have already noted there was no RC church as we know it until the Middle Ages, so that would be of no use to the first readers of Revelation. False religion can come in other ways from within the church, such as liberal theology with its social gospel and the health-and-wealth prosperity gospels. And this prostitute has connection with all kinds of idolatry and idolatrous economic false salvation, not only religious. She is Babylon the great, the great city whose forerunner is pagan Babylon of old, marked by pride and self-sufficiency. The woman is the alternative salvation. She is the *other* woman. She is the false salvation of all kinds!

> The woman you saw is the great city that rules over the kings of the earth (17:18).

This fits with her descriptions in Rev. 18, that she is directly involved with economic systems of the world *(rules over the kings of the earth)*. So this prostitute goes way beyond just false religions, because she is steeped in other economic and political corruptions *as well as* false religions. And of course—idols, idols, idols. She is the complete counterfeit salvation. Many ways! But she is coming to ruin. Those other evil powers **will eat her flesh and burn her with fire.** There are a lot of reminders for John of OT Ezekiel, but this also sounds like Jezebel of old when the dogs came and ate her flesh. This wouldn't have been lost on our first readers of Revelation, especially the church in Thyatira (2:20) whom Jesus warned about Jezebel (as a metaphor for a false teacher), who got her way into the church and filled it with sexual immorality and no doubt other false gospel teaching.

We see the great prostitute has all these things in common with Jezebel of old, who prettied herself up before her death just as this prostitute does (17:4). Both persecute and even kill the saints (17:6), and like Jezebel of old, there were a faithful few who didn't give in to her.

So when is all this happening to the prostitute? The Preterist says the great prostitute is Jerusalem as an apostate religion. But that doesn't work because that means Judaism leading up to AD 70 was at some great height and connected with Rome's idolatry before her fall in AD 70, but that didn't happen. The Futurist position is on safe ground here as always, because it's all happening in the future, and anything can happen in the future! It will only unfold at some future time when Christians are no longer around (the non-rapture Futurist includes Christians in this tribulation, but only in a short seven-year period sometime in the future). The Historicist looks to the Roman Empire as the woman and then later Papal Rome and her demise.

My own view (Idealist) is that Revelation is speaking to all Christians over the past 2000 years, and all things are unfolding progressively and speaking into our lives, though intensifying towards the end. But *when* do the Beast and the kings turn on the prostitute? This could be the most difficult text to explain, or it could be the simplest, depending on which way you look at it.

How could the Beast hate the prostitute when they were formally in cahoots together? We have seen through Revelation the Beast attacking God's people, but 17:16 is saying the Beast's attacks are now *against* the prostitute herself. So what is going on here?

When you think about the kind of things already explained in this text, understanding this is not as difficult as it first appears. For example, we have already seen 17:15 tell us *directly* that the waters the woman sits by symbolize *people*. All kinds of people! The whole world of people! Every nation, people and tongue! And we have already learned that the Beast is based on Daniel's four beasts, which were worldly political or governmental powers that oppress God's people. So the Beast is government power that oppresses the saints. But what are governments made up of? People!

And what about this woman, the *other woman*, the alternative to the church? She is the prostitute. The fake salvation. She offers all kinds of idols, greed, materialism and other ideologies *as well as* false religions. But even those things are mostly made up of and/or carried out by—*people!* What is our text really saying? The concentrated attack against Christians by the Beast previously in Revelation now *includes* an attack against other *peoples*, people who *don't* believe in Jesus.

In trying to understand all this we must not lose sight of what or rather *who* is behind these symbols. The Beast is made in the image of the Dragon, Satan. It is the Dragon who calls up the Beast out of the sea (13:1). If we think of that big picture, then one point we can glean from this is … Satan is a cruel master.

The beast and the ten horns you saw will hate the prostitute. They will bring her to ruin and leave her naked … Satan and his powers set up the prostitute's false salvation for you, but he hates her and the attention she gets. He sets her up only to kill her. So Satan turns around and attacks his own followers. Satan loves to use his people and these enticements draw them, but there is no loyalty with Satan. He actually *hates* those who follow him. He doesn't just hate believers—he also hates *unbelievers*. He hates even the very things and people he uses and brings *them* down to ruin. He is like the classic pimp. The prostitute's employer, who uses the prostitute, he lives off her, but he actually *hates* her and despises her. Up until now, Revelation has concentrated on Satan's Beast and kings attacking Christians. Now this vision is saying Satan is actually attacking *his own*! How does this work practically? 'People' in power who don't follow Jesus are now fighting against … *each other!*

One example of one of the heads of the Beast (which has escalated attacks on Christians in the last generation) is extremist Islam. When we talk about more Christian martyrs than any other time in history, militant Islam has played a big part in that. The militancy has increased, churches have been burned, Christians have been jailed by blasphemy laws, and many have been killed for the faith. But what have we seen happening even in recent years? I find it amazing that many of the victims of suicide bombers are actually Muslims. The Islamic State is one manifestation of the Beast, but suicide bomb attacks are often Muslims killing fellow Muslims.

And what about the strange things going on with Satan's Beast such as governments which have previously oppressed Christians, the likes of Egypt, Libya and Syria? In the last few years we see them turning on themselves. Governments are overthrown, or governments turn on their *own people*. Not *only* against Christians! Satan seems divided against himself (Mark 3:26). He is attacking his own. That is what is predicted here in this text. *The beast and the ten horns you saw will hate the prostitute. They will bring her to ruin and leave her naked; they will eat her flesh and burn her with fire.*

Governments in the West legalize the prostitute, literally legalizing prostitution, sexual immorality, and make great money from the gambling industry and other manifestations of the prostitute's false salvation. But then they *hate* to have to clean up the mess she leaves in her wake. This is chaos. A world like this is a world that has gone nuts, turning against itself. How can you make sense of this? Well, actually it does make sense. It is being played out according to the script ...

> For God has put it into their hearts to accomplish his purpose by agreeing to hand over to the beast their royal authority, until God's words are fulfilled (17:17).

All along it was God's plan. The curtain is pulled back. This is the 'behind the scenes'! It all seemed so out of control, but look at this! **For God has put it into their hearts to accomplish his purpose** ... This is like that dual-purpose colliding in God's sovereignty when we read about Pharaoh and his willful hardening of his heart, and yet *it was the Lord* who was hardening his heart, working it all for *his* purposes. The sin is in the heart of man and Satan, but the Lord controls the whole action.

Idols and everything that Satan sets up for you to follow are actually set up to futility by none other than God himself ... all is meaningless and ruining itself, but it turns out it was ultimately God who was the one who made it that way. God will be God and will not let idols win. Jesus wins! God has directed all the idols to futility. Where have we heard that before …

> For the creation was subjected to frustration, not by its own choice, but by the will of the one who subjected it, in hope that the creation itself will be liberated from its bondage to decay and brought into the freedom and glory of the children of God (Rom. 8:20-21).

This world is all planned for the final glorious freedom of the children of God. There is a plan. It's all working ultimately for you if you are on the side of Christ … but against you if you are not. The Lord subjected this creation to futility because of sin, until he brings everything into judgment. He has also subjected evil, idols and Satan's work to futility. It's one of the hallmarks of history where ideologies and idols that are said to be the answer, and offer a new salvation, eventually implode and collapse. And people end up hating them. Whether it's the idols of fame and fortune, or ideologies like Nazism, Communism or Socialism, every false salvation will destroy itself. But it's not just Satan's Beast who brings them to ruin. They are just pawns carrying out the very words of God.

This explains why the world is going crazy. It explains how much of Revelation talks about the people of God being under persecution and attack, and yet why there is so much violence and attack also against those who are not Christian. There is a method in this madness. God wrote the script. He *put it into their hearts to accomplish his purpose by agreeing to give the beast their power to rule, <u>until God's words are fulfilled</u>*.

We can think of the idols and failed promises that in the end people find repulsive. Make anything into an idol and in the end, you will hate it. Good things are turned into idols. I have seen it with single people who idolize marriage and when they get married, the idol doesn't satisfy and becomes a greater heartache than the loneliness they felt before. I saw it in the entertainment industry. In many ways, the entertainment industry is united in opposition to Christ and his ethics, but it is also an industry where people devour *one another*. Everything is corrupted and the hate turns in on itself. People hate each other with bitterness. We wanted a world without

God, so God has given us up to ourselves. But his plan will not be thwarted, he ... *put it into their hearts to accomplish his purpose* ...

How do you figure this? The Beast and his kings will destroy Babylon. And it's all because God is the controller of all things to bring this about. He *put it into their hearts*. This is like in the OT when the Lord used nations to punish evildoers. But he didn't excuse the actions of the nations he used. God used Babylon to punish Israel, then held Babylon accountable for their attacks. You can't outsmart God and say, 'It wasn't my fault', or 'God made me do it.' God is not the author of evil. Evil is in the heart of the perpetrator, but God uses man's evil plans for his purpose for good things like justice, salvation, refinement and judgment until what? ... *until God's words are fulfilled* (17:17). It is all part of the plan of God, even part of God's plan to save your soul. Even the futility of the world speaks to some who are not yet saved and moves them to turn to the true salvation in Christ. And if you are one of his, but have lost your first love, if you have been enticed by the idols of the prostitute, God will bring all those things to futility until you say, 'meaningless, meaningless, all is meaningless', and he draws you back to the only true God.

So it was God's plan to give the power to the Beast. It is all written in the word of God. *Until God's words are fulfilled.* Jesus wins!

But what does this mean to us? The idols you get enticed by... are a big fat lie. Satan drives the Beast and he is a cruel master indeed. If you love ruling yourself and you don't hate your sin, if you think pleasing yourself is satisfying, any idol will please ... but only for a time, and then ... it's like a hard drug addiction. He is always drawing the victim in further, always requiring more and more to get high, but cruelly leaving the addict more and more empty and broken until finally he kills you off completely. Satan is a cruel master. He sets you up for a fall. The idols are truly like the hard drugs. They are the *ice*. They are *ecstasy*. They are *heroin*. They promise. They please. They give highs. And they draw you further and further and then dump you, to ruin. Futile. That is what any idol will do to you.

So what is the prostitute offering you with her idols? Success? Financial security? Immorality? Porn? Material things? Achievement? Vindication over rivals? All idols are going to be ruined and you will hate them. *They will bring her to ruin and leave her naked; they will eat her flesh and burn her with fire.* They are not only futile and turn out to be a big fat lie, but worse ... you are fighting against the living God! <u>*For God*</u> *has put it into their hearts to accomplish <u>his purpose</u> by agreeing to give the beast their power to rule, <u>until God's words are fulfilled</u>.*

Heaven and earth will pass away but the Lord's words will never pass away. This was written that you might be blessed (1:3), and see that what you were chasing in futility will come to ruin. How could you miss it? He put it in writing. Right here in the book of Revelation.

Jesus is the only true fulfillment. You have been part of that futility until you believe the gospel, the good news. Forgiven yes, but more than that. The gospel is about kingdoms. Who is king? Who is king of your heart? Jesus or an idol? Which king do you serve? Who has the complete affection of your heart?

Study Questions

1. Which people does the prostitute control?

2. Explain some of the arguments as to *when* the prostitute is ruined.

3. Why does the Beast turn against the prostitute?

4. Give examples of how the Beast hates the prostitute.

5. How can God control the action of those with evil intent without doing evil himself?

6. Why do the ways of this world turn out to be futile?

7. Give examples of things that are good but can be turned into idols.

8. Does the knowledge of the futility of idols affect your outlook on anything in your life?

9. Are you at a point where you are content in Jesus? What areas do you need to work on?

7
The Fall of Babylon
(Revelation 18:1-4a)

Revelation presents two polar opposites. There is the beautiful woman. She is pure and radiant. In Rev. 12 she is clothed in splendor. In Rev. 21 she is the beautiful bride. There she is also a city. She is the New Jerusalem. She is the bride of Christ—the church.

We have also been introduced to 'the other woman'. She is unholy and unclean, seductive and dressed in finery. And she also is a city. A city called Babylon. She is the opposite of the church—she offers an *alternative salvation*. She entices with her idols and immorality. She was manifest to the first readers as the city of Rome with all its idols and indulgences. And throughout the church age she makes herself enticing, even to us even today in the 'city' where you live.

Rev. 16 said she was judged. Rev. 17:1 introduced the action replay of her judgment. Now in Rev. 18 we really get the zoom-in close-ups. The first camera angle in 17:16 gave the wide lens. Here is John's next piece of film footage.

> After this I saw another angel coming down from heaven. He had great authority, and the earth was illuminated by his splendor (18:1).

John hears and sees this angel with **great authority**. Some say this could be Christ because this angel's presence lights up the earth, the kind of description usually reserved for God or Jesus. But 18:1 says this is **another angel**. So it must be an important angel who is delegated authority to represent Jesus with that great authority and glory.

> With a mighty voice he shouted: 'Fallen! Fallen is Babylon the Great! She has become a dwelling for demons and a haunt for every impure spirit, a haunt for every unclean bird, a haunt for every unclean and detestable animal' (18:2).

Like other 'great voices' (7:2, 10; 10:3; 14:7, 9, 15; 19:17) in Revelation that have introduced some great pronouncement, **a mighty voice** says, **'Fallen is Babylon the Great'**. What is so amazing about this? It's past tense! Babylon is fallen. Not *will* fall. Although it hasn't happened in time yet. In 18:21 it says she 'will be thrown'. So why is this speaking in the past tense? Fallen, fallen. It's because it is a done deal. We see God's panoramic view. God doesn't have to look into the future. He sees history all at once like a mural on a wall, and this is the view he is giving John. And John is giving it to us! What is it? She has already fallen! Fallen! Fallen is Babylon!

The certainty of this fall is underlined by the very symbol of the woman. Babylon! Babylon of old symbolized everything that raised itself up against God. The pride, the lust and the idolatry. We know Revelation has constantly given us OT historical references as forerunners to describe the last days. What happened to the first Babylon? God brought old Babylon down with a crash. History *will* repeat itself with this Babylon. This is what we have seen throughout Revelation. The plagues of Egypt repeated in the seven bowls. Sodom and Egypt in Rev. 11 were figurative. We also had wilderness wanderings. It's all happening again. History is like this great prophetic script of what is going to happen in the future. It happened before with the original Babylon so long ago …

> Look, here comes a man in a chariot with a team of horses. And he gives back the answer: 'Babylon has fallen, has fallen! All the images of its gods lie shattered on the ground!' (Isa. 21:9).

See the similarity with 18:2 … *With a mighty voice he shouted: 'Fallen! Fallen is Babylon the Great! She has become a dwelling for <u>demons</u> and a haunt for every <u>impure spirit</u>, a haunt for every unclean bird, a haunt for every unclean and detestable animal.* Isaiah says Babylon is filled with idols and Revelation reveals more. Behind those idols there is demonic power. But what we see in this 'fall' in 18:2, in the aftermath, is her total desolation. Now we *know* she is fully aligned with the Beast, with demons and unclean spirits. This is Revelation. Revealing what was behind her all along. Behind her seduction, behind her power, behind her idols are … demons!

It's one of the great themes of Revelation. The power of evil vs. Jesus and the overarching goal and theme of Revelation is that all principalities and powers of the Beast, the False Prophet and the Dragon himself must give way to this fact. Jesus wins! It might have *seemed* like they were powerful and winning. It *seemed* like it ...

> 'For all the nations have drunk the maddening wine of her adulteries. The kings of the earth committed adultery with her, and the merchants of the earth grew rich from her excessive luxuries' (18:3).

Adulteries! Sexual immorality! False religion! Idols! But there is more. Materialism and economic excess, as the **'merchants of the earth grew rich from her excessive luxuries.'** This was one of the challenges for the first readers that was part of everyday life. To buy or sell you had to have the mark. Not an outward mark, but you had to accept membership in the trade guilds which demanded pagan rituals, emperor worship, etc. If you want the work you have to accept the woman into your home, the great city, Babylon. Go along with her and you can buy or sell. Deny her and you could miss out. We saw how this worked out practically for the churches in Asia Minor. The church at Smyrna was one of only two faithful witnesses among the seven churches with no rebuke from Jesus. And they were what? Materially poor. 'I know your poverty'. But Jesus' assessment—you are rich and will receive a victor's crown. In contrast, the church at Laodicea was materially very rich. But Jesus' assessment—you are pitiful, *poor*, blind and naked. I'm about to spit you out of my mouth. They were giving in to Babylon. They had plenty to buy and sell.

This is more of the same message to the same people here in Rev. 18. It's written to them. It's a warning to those tempted to give in to Babylon. You might think you are gaining your security and all you need to take care of yourself, but look where the woman you committed adultery with ends up. And you will end up with her. You don't realize you are wretched, pitiful, poor blind and naked.

And down through the ages, the church at Laodicea has not been the only one to compromise so they can buy or sell. As we have noted before, Christians in every age have been challenged in varying degrees as to honest living vs. compromise with Babylon. It affects you financially, your ability to buy or sell. It happens today in your workplace. Working honestly? Business deals where truth is stretched. Cheating the boss on time, tax avoidance, cash-only jobs, and under the table deals. Once you compromise, it becomes the norm. Greed and dishonest gain become intoxicating … *For all the nations have <u>drunk the maddening wine</u> of her adulteries. The kings of the earth committed adultery with her, and the <u>merchants of the earth grew rich</u> from her <u>excessive luxuries</u>*.

But who says we are rich with luxuries? Have you checked that global rich list yet? On the minimum wage you are in the top 1½% of the richest people in the world. And we complain about not having enough money to enjoy all the good things! But here is the picture of the end. All those things you worked for and placed such importance on, idolized, and even gave priority over God—fallen! Fallen is Babylon the great! It's like literally pulling out the rug from under your feet. Shoomp. Pulled out, and underneath is a dusty old termite ridden floor. And she is left exposed in her ruin. That's what is going to happen to those things you put your hopes in. Then you see the shallow and pathetic nature of them. Exposed!

All those times you coveted. Gotta have better. 'Just a little bit more.' This is what it all ends up like. But surely not in the church? There have always been times when the church has this temptation with economic greed. In the Middle Ages Thomas Aquinas once called on Pope Innocent II (who was not so innocent), when the Pope was counting a large sum of money. Referring to the apostle Peter's word to the crippled beggar, the Pope said to Aquinas, 'You see, Thomas, the church can no longer say 'Silver and gold have I none'.' Aquinas replied, 'True, Holy Father, but neither can she now say, 'Rise and walk'.'[8] The church loses her way! Materially! The great city of Babylon becomes our delight. We don't want her money! Just the things it buys.

What about now? Has there ever been a time in history when the evangelical church is more focused on economic prosperity? We even openly have a 'prosperity gospel'. Become a Christian and have all the money you want. God wants you to be rich. But money is the root of all kinds of evil. It's so intoxicating. It's one of the deadening factors to faith in the Western church. Our security is in storing up from what the Beast provides. We don't have to live by faith. And we don't have to worry about asking for daily bread because of our

---

[8] Cited by F. F. Bruce, *The Book of Acts*, Revised Edition (Grand Rapids: Eerdmans, 1988), 77–78

relationship with Babylon—she will take care of us. We can buy and sell. One of the things that was brought home to me on my first visit to India was how sheltered we are from reality in the West. I was expecting poor and homeless people; we also have those in the West. But in Australia, with a tiny population of 25 million people, most citizens can show up to the government offices the next fortnight and be given money to survive. India has 1.3 billion people and if you don't work, that's it! No government welfare. And yet the Christians we met in the villages would show up any time, any day or night of the week, walking miles just to worship God. They came and were hungry for God's word. In the West we can't even show up to church once a week on time.

Babylon makes us dull in sensitivity to God's word. We scoff. 'How can prosperity gospel preachers justify themselves in the face of Jesus' words that the son of man has no place to lay his head?' But how can we be so dull to the sensitivity of Jesus' words, 'When did I not feed you? When did I not clothe you? When you did not do it to the least of these you did it to me.' We get drunk on her wine. God gives us money so we can provide for ourselves and what else? Ephesians 4:28 says it's so we can 'share with those in need'. Share? I'm saving up for myself! Okay I'll give a bit out of my surplus. But I need my overseas trip and I might not have enough for 'tomorrow'. But Jesus said do not worry about tomorrow.

When everyone around you is drunk on her maddening wine, it makes it more justifiable living in a land of plenty. But can you see the demonic ploy behind materialism? That's why it creeps up on you. If you are playing with sexual immorality, pornography etc. and you are unrepentant, you can be certain you will fall with Babylon and you can hardly say you were surprised. But with her economic enticements, it creeps up on us because the Lord doesn't begrudge you providing for yourself a house, car and good things for your family. But if we think the money we gain is ours and not given by God for God's use in his kingdom, we have been enticed. How much is enough? How much should I give to the poor? It's subtler than other sins.

So what is John seeing? Can you see it? Can you see this Revelation? Let's read it again and try to figure out who this message is for. John gets film footage of the future and this is another time machine episode. You get to look into the future. Fallen! Fallen! Past tense. It's already happened ... **She has become a dwelling for demons and a haunt for every impure spirit, a haunt for every unclean bird, a haunt for every unclean and detestable animal.** This is the picture of the barren desolation when God is absent. This is all that is left. It's like an eerie torturous haunt. Vultures and evil spirits.

John the apostle has seen pictures of heaven. What did he see? He saw lots of people rejoicing for joy in the presence of the Lamb. On the other hand, he saw people on the Day of Judgment running in terror from the wrath. John sees the future. He might not have had time to notice what you were wearing, but in one of these pictures he saw you. Either in those heavenly scenes with people singing from every tribe, nation and tongue, or in the crash when he saw the woman fallen and those fallen with her. Can you see yourself in the crowd? Which one? What if you could really see yourself in the future like John is seeing you here? Would that make any difference to you?

You hear about people who come close to death, and for some it turns their lives around. They don't even get a picture of the future. They just come close to it. But Revelation gives you this picture. You can't say God has left you guessing. Revelation gives us pictures of certainty of the future. Right now, you are either already fallen with Babylon. Finished. Done deal. Or rejoicing. So can you see your face in the crowd? You're in one of them. In the crowd rejoicing—or in the great crash of Revelation 18?

In 1:4 it says to the first readers of Revelation that the whole book was addressed to all seven churches. So did they all read the whole book? Of course all the churches read the whole thing on the edge of their pews. And what was the refrain addressed to them in the individual letters to each church? *'Whoever has ears, let them hear what the Spirit says to the churches.'* This phrase was not an interesting aside. Repetition in the Scriptures highlights importance of something. And the repetition to each church is— *listen!* If you have ears to hear, this is a warning. If you are in those first churches, or if you have felt the enticement from her, if you are in danger of getting caught up with her—look at her future. She is coming down. Even before it happens, you get to see the end of the movie. This is the certainty. 'Fallen, fallen is Babylon and those following her!'

I remember a man who took his friend to the cemetery and said, 'This is where you and I are going soon, but we will be there a lot longer than on this earth. Gotta get it right this side.'

Revelation gives you a picture of two possible ends after that grave. You get a crystal ball! People hanker for a crystal ball. They visit psychics. (I'm not recommending it. God says not to in Deut. 18:10-11.) But this crystal ball is certain. It's from God. It might not be as popular as the local psychic. 'I have your reading for you.' Wow what is it? 'Yes, your future is here. You got smashed at the bottom with the city you followed. You, your idols with you. Fallen. Fallen. Fallen is you!' Not going to that psychic again.

So is this Revelation all bad news? Is it all doom and gloom? No, it's not. Do you know why? This fall hasn't happened yet! This is good news! You get a look into the time machine in advance. You get the answers to the exams in advance! You get told in advance how to *avoid* this crash. How?

> Then I heard another voice from heaven say: '<u>Come out of her</u>, my people, so that you will <u>not</u> share in her sins, so that you will <u>not</u> receive any of her plagues ...' (18:4).

Come out! **Come out of her!** Come out from your idols. It's not too late! It hasn't happened yet. **Come out of her!** Now! Don't look around at what other Christians are doing. They need this same message. Many who call themselves Christians are living during the week as though God is not looking. They have their favorite addictions, some obvious—alcohol, pornography, bad language and anger. Some addictions are not so obvious. Pride, reputation, coveting a salvation that is 'the other woman'. The city offers them all. It promises the world's salvation. Sex, relationships, economic security, and enough to buy the things I want. But the message is, it's all gonna crash. 'Come out!'

The Preterist says this is speaking only to Christians in the first century. The Futurist says this speaks to no one in church history but only to some in a future seven-year period. Both of those could be possible, but what if this is a call to you? What if this is a call to all Christians of all eras? 'Come out' began as an OT call, and it is the same call God's word makes to all Christians, the same call the apostle Paul made to the church ...

> What agreement is there between the temple of God <u>and idols</u>? For we are the temple of the living God. As God has said: 'I will live with them and walk among them, and I will be their God, and they will be my people.' Therefore, '<u>Come out</u> from them and be separate, says the Lord ...' (2 Cor. 6:16-17a).

Same call. Same idols. **Come out!** What if 18:4 is not just for some tiny part of history or the future? What if this word is written to you? 'Come out of her,' lest you share in her sins and plagues. What if God knew in advance that Satan would offer an alternative salvation, the other city—the 'other' woman? And what if the Lord knew that you would be in danger of her seduction? So he gave this book of Revelation and addressed it to the servants of God and said: Blessed are all who read this *and take it to heart.* He also said, 'Look out! You are getting taken in. Come out of her!'

The lifeguard at the beach looks down from his tower and sees you and your children heading into the water with a great white shark coming in. You can't see the danger. From his vantage point he sees clearly. What does he say? 'Come out! Come out!' And what do you say? 'Oh, don't be a spoilsport.' That is what is going on here! This is good news. This is God's vantage point. He sees the future! And he sees where you are headed with those idols of Babylon. Fallen. Fallen.

In fact, this is even greater. Here is something to take home with you. When he says, 'come out', who is he asking to come out? Did you see those beautiful words? This is not the Judge standing there with an axe. Look again. **Then I heard another voice from heaven say: 'Come out of her, <u>my people</u> ...'** *'My people'!* It's a personal call! How great is the love the Father has lavished on us, that we should be called children of God! It's for those who are his. 'My people'. Whoever has ears let them hear. There are millions of people around you who have no ears. Their eyeglasses keep slipping off their heads. It's not for the world. They are not listening. It's a call of a loving Father to those who are his very own children, 'My people'. 'I will be their God and they will be *my people*' (Jer. 31:33, Ezek. 37:27, Heb. 8:10).

Come out! Yes, it will cost you to come out. You might have to give up some things. Take up others. You might 'come out' through tribulation, without so much money to buy or sell. You will have to deny yourself and take up your cross. But look who is calling you. This is the love of a Father who has a plan for you, his child, and sees the danger you are in. 'Come out of her, *my* people.'

Do you know what it cost God to call you one of 'his people'? Look at Babylon and the crash she deserves and all those who follow her. An almighty *crash!* It took God sending his Son to experience that crash! *He* took the fall. Big time! *He* went to ruin. *He* became sin for us. *He* was crushed and fallen with an eternal weight of hell's judgment so you could become one of *his people*.

If God went through all that for you personally so you could be one of his, do you think he is going to call you out into something bad? He has promised. My people. I will be with you.

This is not a written road map of *when* it's going to end, but the certainty that it *will*. Your life does not go on. There is an end. Which woman? Which salvation? Who is it that calls you to *come out of her?* The One who gave us his Son for you that he could call you one of 'my people'.

Then I heard another voice from heaven say: 'Come out of her, my people, so that you will not share in her sins, so that you will not receive any of her plagues ...' (18:4).

Study Questions

1. Is this text repeating what we have seen of Babylon? If so, why?

2. Babylon of old is already fallen. How is this Babylon fallen?

3. What do we learn from this text about the power driving Babylon?

4. Give examples of how her economic strength could be enticing.

5. How does this apply to the Western world church?

6. Why might hers be a subtle temptation?

7. How can this picture in Rev. 18 be of inspiration to you?

8. To what people in history is this call directed?

9. Give at least two ways this call to 'come out' is a call of love.

8
Come Out of Her
(Revelation 18:4b-8)

Last time we saw the people of God being told to come out of the evil city, Babylon. The church advances to the ends of the earth over the past 2000 years, and during this same time the 'other woman' continues to advance with her counterfeit alternative salvation. She is the prostitute. The unholy city. So yes, she was there with John in the form of the city of Rome. And she continues to offer herself in the form of the city you live in right now.

So what does it mean to 'come out of her, my people'? Some have taken it to mean remove yourself from the world, hence we have a history of things like monasteries. Professing Christians trying to 'come out' of the world. The trouble with that is much of Revelation and indeed the Christian faith is about the fact that we are to be witnesses *in* the world. Just as those witnesses in 11:3-7. Just like Jesus is the faithful and true witness and those who follow him hold to the testimony of Jesus (12:17). Where did we get the phrase, 'In the world but not of the world?' It comes from Jesus words …

> My prayer is not that you take them out of the world but that you protect them from the evil one. They are not of the world, even as I am not of it (John 17:15-16).

So here in Revelation when we are told 'come out of her', it means morally. In our previous chapter, we looked at the apostle Paul's words *Come out from them and be separate, says the Lord. Touch no unclean thing, and I will receive you'* (2 Cor. 6:17). It's a moral 'come out'. It was the call in Paul's day to the Corinthians. If you are living in this world, then this woman of seduction is real and seeking to be in your life now! And God calls you now to come out of her!

But there is a tightrope to walk. An error we could make on one of two sides. Either we fail in our witness *in* the world, or we are too much *of* the world. It's not always easy to balance this. How do we shine a light in this dark world and yet not be a part of the darkness? The answer might sound obvious, but the only guide (rule) to walk this tightrope is the Bible. Mature Christians can forget that. I have seen all kinds of things decried as 'worldly' just because they are not part of a Christian stereotype or 'tradition'. Maybe they are worldly, but did you find that specifically in the Scriptures?

On the other hand, there are many things that are not actually bad in themselves but are used in a worldly or idolatrous way. Sport can be worldly. So can music. Yet they are given by God and spoken of positively in the Scriptures. And we are to be witnesses who shine. We want Christians to live, work and play in any and every sphere of life and vocation where they don't become part of Babylon. So play your sport, but watch how you play, or whether it encroaches into idolatry. Play your music, but examine if the lyrics cut across Scripture. Use these things to engage with non-Christians. Enjoy your games and social media with your friends, but give all these things the Ephesians test. God gave us a manual in Ephesians 5:1-20 as to when we need to 'come out of her'—sexual immorality, bad language, and dirty jokes. Idolatry. Look it up in the manual!

As Christians, we should stand out in the way we engage in activities, but don't lose sight of the whole point. Use these things to be a witness in a dark world and the testimony you bring!

There will always be a tension between being a witness and 'coming out of her'. Christians are prone to error on one side or the other (apart from you with the perfect balance). Ask yourself: Which of these two errors am I are more likely to lean towards? Am I failing to be a witness in the world? Or am I failing to come out of the world? (If you fail in both I can't help you!)

I remember attending a wedding where the clergyman (with full garb vestments), was getting his photo taken with a beer in his hand at the wedding ceremony (before the reception), and all the drunks were lining up to get a photo with the priest. The Bible would say he is free to drink, and he was certainly engaging in the world, but was that wise in that scenario? Or was it a stumbling block to others? So there are all kinds of ways we can be *of the world* by misusing our freedom too.

It can get confusing at times, so remember our bottom line is our chief end and that is to glorify God. And our guide to do this is the word of God. This might sound obvious, but there are times when even evangelizing should not be done if it means compromising truth, propriety or the glory of God. The call is to come out of her.

> Then I heard another voice from heaven say: 'Come out of her, my people, so that you will not share in her sins, so that you will not receive any of her plagues; for her sins are <u>piled up to heaven</u>, and God has remembered her crimes' (18:4-5).

When people see some horrible evil, they can think God is absent or distant, but this text tells us God is not absent. He is not only watching but is keeping a record, and there comes a point when his patience runs out. This text says there is a specific amount of sin and when it is **piled up to heaven**, *that* is when God **remembers**. Of course, he never forgot, but that is when he will act. It's like the tower of Babel (Gen. 11:3-4). It's also like Sodom. The sin and cries have reached up to God (Gen. 18:20, 19:13). It's filled to the brim. It's like God's sending the Israelites in to destroy the Canaanites only when their sin had reached the full measure (Gen. 15:16). Just like today, people think they are getting away with things and others complain that God is letting people get away with evil. But all the time it is 'piling' up until a point where God says 'no more'...

> Give back to her as she has given; pay her back double for what she has done. Pour her a double portion from her own cup (18:6).

Justice in full! The original Greek grammar allows for it to mean 'double it back on her'. This is confirmed by the next verse, that she gets precisely what she deserves ...

> Give her as much torture and grief as the glory and luxury she gave herself. In her heart she boasts, 'I sit as queen. I am not a widow; I will never mourn' (18:7).

This is taken straight from historical Babylon (Isa. 47:7-8). This is the typical 'punishment fits the crime' kind of language that the Bible uses. It was pride that was her crown. She was so proud. Self-glory. That is what she enticed with. And we need to pause on that.

This is her cry: **In her heart she boasts, 'I sit as queen. I am not a widow; I will never mourn.'** This is the heart of the great city, the great prostitute, and the great alternative salvation to the church. This is what she was about, and therefore this is at the heart of what she uses to tempt you. Most people who ever live will share in her luxuries, adulteries and maddening wine, but they will also share in her punishment and plagues. Most people will spend eternity receiving (along with her) all the fullness of what they deserve. But what will be at the heart of their crime? Precisely the sin of Babylon. Pride. Boasting. I will be okay. I don't need a thing. I will never mourn. It was the first weapon this woman's great father, the Dragon used. It was the original sin. Pride. 'You will be like God.' And, 'You will not surely die.' You will never mourn! You won't be brought down. This is the one thing (more than any other) that people delude themselves with in relation to God. They have no fear of facing God with their sin because they think they don't have enough sin to worry about. *I will never mourn.* 'I am a not a bad person. I have lived a good life. I am not as bad as some.' Boasting. They don't need a Savior.

This pride even explains where all the religions come from. If Christianity is the only way, why are there so many other religions? It's because they are all manifestations of Babylon's pride. On one hand people can't deny God exists, so they think worship of God makes sense, but on the other hand they flee from a God who demands they have to empty themselves of all pride. How do you put these two things together? Religion. All kinds. But with one doctrine that covers them all. It doesn't matter if it is clothed in religion or irreligion. It all comes down to this: 'If I do enough good things [religious or otherwise] and be nice to people, that will make me good enough for God. I might need God's help, but I can do it. I don't need a Savior to take away my sin.' *I will never mourn.* They have been enticed by the seduction of the other woman and her pride. But what follows is the shock. And it only takes one day. There is a day when all that 'progress' you were making comes to a screaming halt.

> Therefore in one day her plagues will overtake her: death, mourning and famine. She will be consumed by fire, for mighty is the Lord God who judges her (18:8).

Now that doesn't look good. It's all over **in one day.** If that is where it all ends for those following her, why doesn't everyone who reads this conclude, 'Man, this is terrible. Better come out from this woman. I should walk with Jesus and avoid this!' Isn't this a no-brainer? Why wouldn't everyone listen to this kind of warning and run to the Savior? But if you show this to your skeptical friends, these chapters of Revelation from 17:3-4 with a woman dressed in enticing clothing sitting on a Beast, they'll think you are loopy. Even if you explain, 'This is apocalyptic literature. It's meant to symbolize real and concrete things! This book describes most prophetically the world we live in.' But still they dismiss it easily! Is it because it lacks credibility? Or is there some other factor?

Which is more credible? That Jesus didn't give people enough 'evidence'? Or that human beings are so prideful they are ready to be taken in by the self-centered, materialistic, idolatrous seductions of the other woman herself?

Is faith in Jesus just some religious leap in the dark? If anyone really could stand outside this in an unbiased way, which one of these makes more sense? Jesus (who gave this Revelation) is a deluded/deceiver, *or* human beings deceive themselves out of their own pride? Look at the two possibilities and ask if this were a mere intellectual question, which side has more credibility? One side says the world popped out of nothing. Human life is meaningless and there is no purpose. Morality, good, and evil don't exist. There is really no meaning to love and beauty. Relationships with family and loved ones are as the Buddhists say, just an unworthy delusion and a meaningless meeting of travelers through time.[9] Ships in the night. Life is meaningless. It's a meaningless drive for survival that is driven by what? Nothing! Because we popped out of nothing for no reason, with no meaning behind our existence. That is one possibility shared by the side of unbelief. Or? The other?

Jesus is not some random ancient figure who performed a few random miracles thousands of years ago. Jesus did *not* just appear in a vacuum. He came after centuries of prophecy. Prophecy that defies all skepticism. Hundreds of predictions of a Messiah, down to details of where he would be born (in Bethlehem), the family line of this birth, and the time of his birth. His crucifixion described with details,

---

[9] Buddhist Scriptures, Ed. Edward Conze, (London, Penguin Books: 1959) p.91

'They pierced my hands and my feet' (Ps. 22:16). His dying for the sins of his people and his resurrection were predicted along with another 300 prophecies. In fact, Professor Peter Stoner did a mathematical study on the probability of anyone fulfilling just eight of the more detailed prophecies by mere 'chance' and it came to the mathematical probability of one chance in 10^{17}. He put that into perspective by saying this figure means the likelihood of Jesus just getting 'lucky' fulfilling these predictions is like laying silver dollars two feet deep across the whole state of Texas, with only one silver dollar marked. Then you blindfold a man who can travel as far as he likes across Texas, but he only gets one pick and it has to be the right silver dollar the first time. That is the same probability of someone fulfilling the prophecies of Jesus by chance.[10] And that is only the beginning. Jesus doesn't just miraculously fulfill all the prophecies. He turns out to be the most famous miracle worker who ever lived, the most famous human ever on earth. We still date our calendar from his entry into the world. He happens to be the only one in history who claimed to be God in the flesh and have it taken seriously on a worldwide scale. And more, his teaching has reached the ends of the earth and has influenced more of the world than anyone who ever lived. But this is the cruncher—his unique teaching on the human condition is the only thing that makes sense of this world. Contrary to the true atheist position which says there is no such thing as moral evil, right and wrong, but only survival of the fittest; rather Christians know there are such things are right, wrong, love, beauty and relationships.

But something has gone terribly wrong. What has gone wrong? Pride! This explanation of the human condition explains the trouble in the world. Why is it that no amount of education, technology or even religion can help us? Humans are consumed in pride. Self-righteously they cry 'peace not war'. Stop fighting. John Lennon sang about peace, but he was a wife beater.[11] Pride. The problem is with others!

---

[10] Peter W. Stoner and Robert C. Newman, *Science Speaks* (Chicago, Moody Press: 1976) pp. 106-112

[11] Lennon even admitted this himself to David Sheff in his series of interviews for Playboy Magazine in 1980.

This is Jesus' assessment of the human condition. It's Revelation's assessment. It's the heart of the woman who enticed humanity. So there are two alternatives. Either Jesus is the deluded/deceiver *or* human beings are deceived and deceiving themselves because of their own pride. 'I will boast. I will sit high. I will not mourn.'

Which is more credible? Jesus is wrong? Or human beings are filled with pride? We all know deep down life is not just survival of the fittest. We know there is such a thing as right and wrong, love, value and morality, but we never seem to be able to make it work because of our self-centeredness. We have been deceived so much in our pride that rebellion against the Creator means we seek fulfillment in *anything or anyone* other than the one who gave us life and breath and everything in it.

Humans are so committed to this that they embrace this woman, this city, and all her wares, and subsequently reject the truth, even in the face of God coming into the world in person. God did show up in person, confirmed by all of what was predicted before he arrived. Then he proved his divinity by doing things that had never been done before or since. Healing the blind, the crippled and even raising the dead. Imagine if someone could raise the dead today as Jesus did. Right before your eyes people who had died come to life. Would everyone believe it? No, they wouldn't. Not if it also meant humbling themselves. They would find some other excuse or explanation just as many did in the first century. Those who saw Jesus' miracles firsthand rejected him for that same reason. Pride.

Jesus sets down a record with his entrance into history that is so powerfully attested with the different witnesses that one scholar could say: Based on the witnesses through the number of manuscripts and their being so close to the date of the events and people, the record of Jesus is more attested than any other person or event in the history of the world prior to the invention of printing.[12] This same 'lucky' Jesus who picked the right silver dollar in Texas the first time sent forth a message that he said would go to the ends of the earth. And 2000 years on, all that he predicted about this world has come true. One in three people who walk the face of the earth claim to believe in him. Many more are influenced by his teaching

---

[12] Henry Morris, *Many Infallible proofs*, (Green Forest, Arkansas, Master books, 1974) p.22

indirectly. Much of the world stops each year to celebrate the time he came into the world and the time he gave himself up to save this world. Yet some people still claim that he never existed. Who is biased? Those who are for Jesus or those who are against him?

The only way you could explain such bias is in our text. They follow the heart of the other woman 'I will sit as queen. I will never mourn'. They will never be dependent. They will never submit. They will never be held accountable. Where is God with his justice anyway?

But then ... *in <u>one day</u> her plagues will overtake her: death, mourning and famine. She will be consumed by fire, for mighty is the Lord God who judges her.* The very thing that they say they hate about this God, that he doesn't bring justice to evildoers, happens. All her pride will be brought down and she will receive her penalty. But wait! So will all who follow her in their pride! That was the call to 'come out of her', so you won't share in her plagues! But along with the woman they said, 'I will never mourn'. I will never have to give an account.

Just as the text told us, it will be all so richly deserved. Most of all because it's a rejection of God's love. It's a rejection of forgiveness. It's a rejection of God's Son who gave himself up for the sins of all who believe. He took this judgment for all who would have the *opposite* of pride. That is, those who would humble themselves under Jesus as Lord and Savior. For those who don't, pride will cost you eternally ...

Therefore in one day her plagues will overtake her: death, mourning and famine. She will be consumed by fire, for mighty is the Lord God who judges her (18:8).

Study Questions

1. Where do we get the phrase 'in the world but not of the world'?

2. In which of these do you think you might be more prone to error—to be a witness in the world or to be too much of the world?

3. How would you respond to the criticism that God indiscriminately punished people in the OT?

4. What is the main enticement of Babylon and where does it fit with the gospel?

5. What makes people think they are on neutral ground when examining the truths of the Scriptures?

6. What would you say to someone who says Christianity is not credible?

7. What is the primary thing about Jesus' teaching that distinguishes him from all others?

9
The Great Crash
(Revelation 18:9-19)

If you were sitting in the church in Laodicea in the first century and you received this book of Revelation from John, surely you would get excited when you realize you have a personal letter addressed to your very own church from Jesus himself. Your city, Laodicea, was famous for its wealth and self-sufficiency. Let's recap the background.

Laodicea was well known as a major banking and finance center. The rich folks lived there. It had the usual trappings of a wealthy city, with theatres, a stadium, and gymnasiums with baths. In AD 60 there was a massive earthquake that brought devastating damage to Laodicea and other cities. Sardis and Philadelphia were also hit, and the Emperor provided financial assistance to rebuild the cities. But Laodicea not only refused financial help, it even gave aid to neighboring cities to rebuild. As the Roman historian Tacitus records, Laodicea recovered itself from earthquake.[13]

That is the city you live in. And in this personal letter from Jesus himself, he says to you, 'You say: I am rich; I have acquired wealth and do not need a thing. But you do not realize you are wretched, pitiful, poor, blind and naked' (3:17). Materially rich, but spiritually poor! That gives you a jolt.

Then, as you read the rest of Revelation, you get through to Rev. 18, where you read about this seductive woman. What is her primary means of seduction? Her riches and self-sufficiency! In 18:4 you read, 'Come out of her!' Then you read she is coming down! Being burned. And worse. Those who followed her are coming down too!

Do you think Jesus is trying to tell you something? You begin to question yourself. Have you been enticed by her too? Those in

---

[13] Tacitus, Annals of Imperial Rome, 14:27

government got caught up with her values and now those kings are crying. They had followed the woman who said she would 'never mourn'. Now *they* mourn.

> 'When the kings of the earth who committed adultery with her and shared her luxury see the smoke of her burning, they will weep and mourn over her' (18:9).

In the first century, **the kings of the earth** literally made their wealth and prosperity from the backs of slaves. Exploitation. It was the chase for money, comforts, luxuries, and status. Gotta have the right clothes and latest upgrades. Even for the average worker, idolatry was connected to the ability to buy or sell with the trade guilds and their pagan rituals. But now they see **the smoke of her burning**, which reminds us of Sodom's judgment and also of the Beast's demise (14:9-11). This might suggest this is the same judgment for both the Beast and Babylon. All the things you prized in Laodicea ... now you see them individually going up in smoke. The leaders, the kings, and their whole city are in ruin *when they see the smoke of her burning.* Those who looked to them are now ...

> Terrified at her torment, they will stand far off and cry: 'Woe! Woe to you, great city, you mighty city of Babylon! In one hour your doom has come (18:10).

The fear of the onlookers is such that they are **terrified at her torment**. Don't get too close to her. It might be you next. In 18:4 the warning was to 'come out of her *so that* you wouldn't share in her plagues', the judgment she deserves. But at this point it's too late. They are in awe of how quickly this has happened. It's like when the Berlin Wall came down. It stood as a great symbol and literal separation from the West and solidity of 70 years of Communism. But the wall just comes down. It was all over. All so suddenly. **For in one hour your judgment has come.**

> 'The merchants of the earth will weep and mourn over her because no one buys their cargoes any more— ...' (18:11).

Notice what they are really lamenting over? Are they lamenting over Babylon? 'Poor, poor Babylon?' No. Rather it's that they have lost their meal ticket. Their cash cow. Their source of wealth has just been decimated and lies in ruin, so they lament at the loss of their income source as **no one buys their cargoes any more**. They are the same people who had no trouble buying or selling before. The same people who would compromise in any way with the Beast to get what they wanted, now *they* can't buy or sell. All the goods are doomed with the city!

> ... cargoes of gold, silver, precious stones and pearls; fine linen, purple, silk and scarlet cloth; every sort of citron wood, and articles of every kind made of ivory, costly wood, bronze, iron and marble; ... (18:12).

There are the metals and alloys listed here that make our 'good stuff'. You can see everything from our cars and white goods, to the hardware for our technologies. These are the kinds of minerals and metals that feature heavily in the stock markets. The investments, the costly woods, the fine furniture, the best in cabinet making and bench tops. Here is the classiest in buildings and every kind of good thing. And if you look at the fine linen and gold, precious stones and pearls, these are some of the very things the prostitute Babylon was dressed in (17:4)! She is enticing. She is the alternative salvation to Jesus. The things of this world. She has it all! Every conceivable material thing of value. Every kind of the best foods, toiletries, cosmetics and the best in wine ...

> ... cargoes of cinnamon and spice, of incense, myrrh and frankincense, of wine and olive oil, of fine flour and wheat; cattle and sheep; horses and carriages; and human beings sold as slaves (18:13).

Listed here are livestock and the food chain as well as investments and big business in trade. Here you have the trappings from every sphere, every industry, commodity and every kind of production. Did you notice even people? **Human beings sold as slaves!** Labor exploitation. This is still speaking into our day. There are approximately 46 million slaves in the world today.[14] But that doesn't include the many more people in countries where they are virtual slaves to a system that gives them no freedom. People used by others. Babylon has legalized prostitution — literally and figuratively.

---

[14] https://en.wikipedia.org/wiki/Contemporary_slavery

These trappings of luxury and wealth would be familiar to the apostle John who received this Revelation in the ancient world in the Roman Empire. They represented luxury and were often part of the excesses of the rich and their idolatrous extravagances. To the first readers of Revelation, the city of Rome represented this city of 'Babylon'. But most of these items mentioned are the precious commodities of trade and investment today or in any era. Babylon entices throughout the church age offering an alternative to the pure woman, the church.

But most of these things are not illegal or immoral. For most of them we might ask, 'What is wrong with that?' Manufacturing, art and business? Some of those things we need to feed and clothe ourselves. What makes *them* part of Babylon? When John Calvin said our hearts are idol factories, he meant we turn anything into an idol, even good things, always wanting more. Coveting. More. Better. Like Nebuchadnezzar, the figurehead of the original Babylon, these 'things' took the place of caring for the poor. Where your heart is, there your treasure will be.

Basically, Babylon has control of industry and arts, commerce and trade, and the picture here is that every single part of it is coming down. All of it looked so beautiful. All the music that was heard, all the beautiful stuff is now a haunt of demons. Now the great crash has come. Babylon seemed so in control of the nations (she sat by 'many waters' i.e. peoples), but now she controls nothing, and the nations are in shock when it comes to the crash ...

> They will say, 'The fruit you longed for is gone from you. All your luxury and splendor have vanished, never to be recovered' (18:14).

The fruit you longed for? What were the things you longed for? It wasn't putting God first. It was idols. And where is that fruit now? Gone! What is the message here? Jesus put it this way: What would it profit a man if he gained the whole world but forfeit his soul? (Matt. 16:26). What did you do with the resources God gave you to use for his kingdom? All those goodies. Did you see them in there? Did you see all your good stuff that was so important to you? Did you see the costly wood that made your nice furniture and homes, that fine material that made your nice clothes, the wine, oh yes, the wine, the finer things in life, the food sources, the trading, and the investments. Your superannuation retirement plan! Look at the long list of things. But where are they now? Crashed. Vanished, never to be recovered!

> The merchants who sold these things and gained their wealth from her will stand far off, terrified at her torment. They will weep and mourn and cry out: 'Woe! Woe to you, great city, dressed in fine linen, purple and scarlet, and glittering with gold, precious stones and pearls!' (18:15-16).

The beauty is superficial and has no lasting value. Underneath, it is all a big lie. She offers you an alternative salvation to the pure woman. But the shock is that it all comes down so quickly!

> '<u>In one hour</u> such great wealth has been brought to ruin!' Every sea captain, and all who travel by ship, the sailors, and all who earn their living from the sea, will stand far off. [Commerce, trade and investment via shipping.] When they see the smoke of her burning, they will exclaim, 'Was there ever a city like this great city?' They will throw dust on their heads, and with weeping and mourning cry out: 'Woe! Woe to you, great city, where all who had ships on the sea became rich through her wealth! In one hour she has been brought to ruin!' (18:17-19).

The popular idea is that Babylon here is a future rebuilt Babylon of old. But the OT predicts that Babylon will never rise again. And this verse says the ships here are coming in and going out of Babylon. But Babylon is in the middle of the deserts of modern-day Iraq. It's hundreds of miles from the nearest seaport!

Clearly this is symbolic. Just as Revelation has been consistently using symbols, this is a metaphor for all that Babylon of the OT represents in our day. It can be seen in any city of our day that offers these same kinds of seductions of idolatry. It offers the hopes and security in things and investment priorities in our life. It is the *other woman*. The alternative salvation. All the way through, Revelation has been using historical OT events and places to show that what goes around, comes around. In Daniel 4 'Babylon the Great' is ruled by King Nebuchadnezzar, who was suddenly brought low because of his pride. Nebuchadnezzar built his city on the same site as the tower of Babel. Babylon had one of the great wonders of the ancient world, the hanging gardens of Babylon. But Nebuchadnezzar was judged for his pride and brought down so quickly because he refused to acknowledge God as sovereign and show mercy to the poor. So too, this 'Revelation' great city Babylon epitomizes all that any great city of the world represents. Materialism at the expense of the poor (see Ezek. 26:16-18).

And those who indulged her wares now lament over her, but they are not repentant. Lots of worldly sorrow, but too late for godly sorrow. No turning to God here. That day has passed. It's Judgment Day.

Why is John the apostle receiving such a graphic description even down to the food and items of everyday use, as well as investments ruined on that day? As mentioned earlier, many of these things are even good things in themselves. But, they are on this great list with this drawn out description of how they are brought to ruin, with the picture of people crying. Everything you had is ruined.

But why such detail of all this? How do you envisage the Day of Judgment? Isn't it centered on punishment for the wicked but joy for the believers? Yes, it is. But first, just pause on this. This moment might last but a second, but you are getting the still frame. Hit the pause button. Soak in what this photograph looks like. The Master film director is giving us the slow-motion replay of the crash.

See if you can find yourself in there. From those in power, kings, to those who worked with her, merchants and workers. Those who loved her goods. This is Revelation saying take a look at what you put your hope in, what you get your satisfaction from, your comfort and security. Pause for a moment right now on what pleases you. Is it the things of this world? Now pause on this and see how it ends. Babylon promoted the idea that value is about 'pleasure for me'. Status and security in what the world has to offer. Luxury and comfort that knows nothing of suffering for good, nothing of giving to others, nothing of living for God and using our time and resources for his kingdom and for those in need. It knows nothing of living by faith.

The scariest part is that this is written to you. Which of these things did you put your hopes in? Can you see it's not going to last? And our response is, 'Yes, but we still have to live in this world and we have to eat and clothe ourselves and live in a home, etc.' Yes, all of that is true, but where are you really putting your investments? Not only financially, but your time and your hopes? Where is your heart?

Which woman? The salvation of Jesus or the other woman?

Look at the things we think we need and work for so much to keep us secure and to leave a big nest egg for our kids. A life lived for the kingdom is a far greater investment to pass on to your children. Look how quickly the worldly kingdom comes down. That is the shock here. Babylon and her wares were here to stay. Hey, I have to live in this world. It's not going anywhere. But look how quickly it all is destroyed. 'Gotta live for the moment' but now that moment is so quickly gone and brought down and you are left lamenting. Terrified! It's the speed that is such a shock … **In one hour she has been brought to ruin.** It's like Haman in the book of Esther. One minute plotting things for his glory and the execution of Mordecai, the next minute he has a hood over his head, whisked away to his own execution. In one hour the whole thing turns around.

This is what is amazing when high profile celebrities are brought down. Rolf Harris is one of the most successful Australian entertainers of all time. He had hit songs reaching no. 1 in the Top 10 hits in Australia, UK and the US. He had his own successful long running TV program. As an artist he even painted the Queen (probably used British paints). He received Queen's honors and the commendations MBE, AO, CBE. He had success from a young age. He was even Australian Junior 110 yards Backstroke Champion and State Champion in various other swimming events. He was celebrated as a national treasure. But in his old age it took only 'one hour' and it all came down. The *moment* his verdict was announced of sexual assault of underage girls, it was not 'that year' or 'that month' or 'that week', or the next board meeting. The very hour he was pronounced guilty they tore down his image all around the world. He was immediately removed from the ARIA awards hall of fame list. Art galleries immediately took down his paintings and owners of expensive artworks were burning his paintings! His artworks that had sold for up to $50,000 were burned for nothing. His hometown in Perth had his star in the street pavement. They smashed up the concrete! His old school had his paintings hanging. They took them down. In one hour, ruined!

Rolf had a lifetime of success and adulation. In a moment, 'in an hour' it was all brought down to shame and contempt. There was weeping and mourning from those who put their trust in him and admired him. And his reputation and success can never be recovered. What does this life of 'success' add up to for him? It all adds up to worse than nothing. Humiliation. Punishment.

This is a picture of the shame and *speed* with which a lifetime of hope and things of value become worse than nothing. Where did you put your time, money, hopes? That is what it will be like for everything invested into this world. The great city.

If you knew when the stock market crash was coming and that everything you owned was going to become worse than worthless, what would you do? Would you be like the shrewd manager who went and quickly put things in order before he was about to lose everything? His job and home! You've heard of the great stock market crash of 1929, the crash of 1987, and the Global Financial Crisis of 2007-08. Well, I can predict with accuracy an even bigger crash that is coming—the crash of Revelation 18! You might want to know when it is going to happen, so you can get your money out. The trouble is, I can't tell you exactly when. But it is absolutely certain that it will happen. And when it hits it will be sudden. It seemed to take so long, but all of a sudden, it's upon you. And here is a picture of the 'pause'. It's the moment that everyone looks on in shock and terror at what they put their hopes in, and see them lying in ruins.

When it happens, it will seem like the same way Rolf Harris thinks now. Or Harvey Weinstein or Bill Cosby or any other celebrity who loses their standing. What does a whole lifetime of making good ground add up to now? What was all that achievement for? Nothing! On this day, in that very hour, people will actually be crying over the very people and things they used to worship and idolize. Think of your favorites. Think of the things you consider of importance. Lying in ruin. And because you put your hopes in them, you will be all the more terrified and shocked. It seemed like things were just going on and 'I have to live in this world' was the excuse. But when it all comes down, it will happen in a flash!

This is a picture of final judgment. It is a complete woe to the great city Babylon, the other woman, and there you are looking on her ruin and it's all too late. But wait! Remember Rev. 18 is not all doom and gloom. This is written in advance for us! Its written to say, 'Don't end up here lamenting!' You live in a time *before* this final judgment, *before* this great city is ruined. You have insider trading! You are warned of the stock market crash coming and what to invest in. And there is hope for us. Jesus the bridegroom of the true woman gave himself up for her, the church, for true believers. Invest in Jesus. Put your time and resources into the kingdom that lasts. Jesus' death on the cross stands in total contrast to Babylon. Instead of pride, Jesus *gave himself* up for his people. He did this so that they, in turn, would not live for themselves, but live as his church for him and for others. What went on at the cross was to take away your judgment in advance so that you could be free. Free from judgment and free from slavery to the things that will crash. Today is the day *before* the crash. It's written in advance to warn you. But the delay in judgment will not last forever.

They will throw dust on their heads, and with weeping and mourning cry out: 'Woe! Woe to you, great city, where all who had ships on the sea became rich through her wealth! In one hour she has been brought to ruin' (18:19)!

Study Questions

1. Why might this text be of particular interest to the church at Laodicea?

2. What is the sin of the 'kings of the earth'?

3. Give two precedents for the 'smoke of her burning'; and how might this help ascertain the woman's relationship and time frame.

4. What is it that onlookers are most concerned about?

5. How does this relate to the ability to 'buy or sell'?

6. How might these commodities relate to our present day?

7. Which of your 'good things' could become idols?

8. Is this how you would picture a description of the Day of

Judgment? What is it trying to convey in relation to Judgment Day?

9. In what way is this text good news and how can it be used to re-evaluate our lives?

10
The Tribulation Timeline
(Revelation 18:20)

Fallen, fallen is Babylon the great! Woe! Woe! The call early in Rev. 18 was, 'Come out of her my people' before it's too late. But now it's all too late. We saw Babylon falling and the shock, even terror, of those who indulged her. She is the direct rival and antagonist to the true woman, the holy city—the church. She also *persecuted* God's people. Back in 17:6 we learned that she was drunk on their blood. She said in 18:7 'I will never mourn'. Oh, but she does mourn. And so richly deserving is her punishment that now the people of God are told to rejoice over her downfall.

> 'Rejoice over her, you heavens! Rejoice, you people of God! Rejoice, apostles and prophets! For God has judged her with the judgment she imposed on you' (18:20).

There will be a time when God will answer all believers who have asked, 'Why, O Lord?', and believers will rejoice. Not only is there appropriate punishment for evil, but note this: It is the *victims* who suffered and even died who are now given the experience and rich blessing of God's perfect conclusion to the matter. God was right after all. You *can* rejoice. That disaster, that war, that suffering you thought could never be reversed—God did it! Now in heaven you see. God was right after all. Not only was he able to put everything right, but you are also called to rejoice! Not in vengeance, but rejoicing because the glory of the Lord has been vindicated. Babylon treated the saints in such evil ways, persecuting many, even to their deaths. But the question is, when did she do all that? That's the great debate over the book of Revelation. All Christians agree Babylon emerges during the time of the tribulation. But when is the tribulation? Remember the main views.

TRIBULATION and coming of Babylon

PRETERIST	IDEALIST	HISTORICIST	FUTURIST
Up to AD 70	Throughout church age	Babylon is Church of Rome	7 years in future

The Historicist sees Babylon as the Church of Rome during the last 2000 years. The Preterist has the woman Babylon as the Roman Empire (or first century Jerusalem), with the tribulation occurring up to the fall of Jerusalem in AD 70. The Futurist often has a revived literal Babylon appearing in a future seven-year period of tribulation. The Idealist (which I go with), has the tribulation beginning in the first century and continuing through the church age up to the Day of Judgment. So what has this to do with our text? Let's read it again carefully...

Rejoice over her [that's rejoice over Babylon of the tribulation] **you heavens! Rejoice, you people of God. Rejoice, apostles and prophets! For God has judged <u>her</u> with the judgment she imposed on <u>you</u>.'** The original Greek language has the sense of literally, 'God has given judgment on her for the judgment she passed on you.' Other translations say the same thing with different wording. For example, the King James Version ...

> Rejoice over her, thou heaven, and ye holy apostles and prophets; for God hath <u>avenged you on her</u> (18:20 KJV).

It's the same sense of God bringing justice to Babylon for what she did to you. This text is drawn from Jeremiah 51:47-49, which confirms for us that same meaning as in 18:20. In Jeremiah, Israel was told to rejoice over the fall of ancient historical Babylon *for what she did to God's people*. In fact, that meaning of our text is also confirmed in 18:6 which says *Give back to her as she is given*. So why am I laboring the exact meaning of this verse? Because it actually helps settle this great argument we have within the Christian church as to when the tribulation occurs. Did you notice it?

Rejoice over her, you heavens! Rejoice, you people of God. Rejoice, apostles and prophets! For God has judged her with the judgment she imposed on you. The Preterist view might be the only one of the four major views left standing after a careful reading of this verse! The Preterist says that the tribulation occurs *before* and concludes in AD 70. Our text says the *apostles* (who were definitely there in the first century pre-AD 70) experienced the tribulation! The apostles in heaven are told to rejoice because God is paying Babylon back for what she did to *you*. It's what she did to God's holy people *and* apostles in the tribulation! So the Preterist is still left standing (no wonder credible guys like RC Sproul have taken the Preterist view). The only question left is this: 'Is there any other view left standing after this verse?' I have agreed all along with the Preterist that the tribulation and Babylon are alive for those first readers in the first century, but I also said Revelation speaks to the seven churches with seven as God's number of completion, hence Revelation is addressed to *all* God's servants who read it and take it to heart (1:1, 1:3). So it also speaks to all God's people. Therefore, I agree with the Preterist that at the very least Babylon had to begin in the time of the apostles because they are mentioned … *Rejoice, apostles and prophets!* But I would go further and say it also speaks to all the people of God throughout the rest of the church age.

The Futurist might argue that *the people of God* refers to Jewish Christians, but I would say it means the same as it means in all the NT, where *the people of God* (saints) refers to all Christians. But we might still end up disagreeing over that. And Christians debate about whether NT prophets only applies to the first century or up to today. Again, that is an endless debate. But unlike *people of God* and *prophets*, we can't debate the *apostles*. The definition of an apostle in its technical sense (as it is used in 18:20, especially when in conjunction with NT prophets i.e. *apostles and prophets* – see also Eph. 2:20), is given to us in Acts 1:22 when the church chose an apostle to replace Judas. The qualification to be one of the twelve apostles was one who had been with Jesus before and after his resurrection. Even the apostle Paul, the former enemy of Christ, was an eyewitness of Jesus after his resurrection. By definition, apostles are only there in the first century.

So what are the apostles doing there in heaven rejoicing over what Babylon had done to *them* in the tribulation? *Unless Babylon and the tribulation began in the first century!*

The Futurist says Babylon does not manifest until a future seven-year period of tribulation, when Babylon got drunk on the blood of the saints. But even Futurist John MacArthur says 18:20 is speaking about martyrs during the tribulation.[15] That much I agree on. So what do the *apostles* have to do with tribulation martyrs? A quick survey of history and tradition ...

Apostle Peter: crucified. Early church historian Eusebius records that apostle Peter thought himself unworthy to die in the same way as his Lord, so he asked to be crucified upside down. They accommodated him.

Peter's brother, apostle Andrew: Hippolytus records that Andrew was crucified on an olive tree at Patrae (Patras), a town in Achaia.

James the apostle, brother of John, son of Zebedee: beheaded with the sword. Read about it in Acts 12.

Doubting Thomas? He didn't doubt in the end: he became a missionary to India and gave his life for Jesus, firstly receiving spear thrusts (with pine spears), tormented with red-hot plates, and burned alive.

Philip: some Jewish enemies had him tortured, then crucified in Phrygia, where he had ministered.

Matthew: beheaded at Nad-Davar.

Bartholomew (Nathaneal): flogged then crucified.

Simon the Zealot: crucified.

Thaddeus (Judas not Iscariot): beaten to death with sticks. Other sources say arrows.

Matthias: stoned to death hanging on a cross.

In addition, the apostle Paul was beheaded under Emperor Nero. John the apostle wrote this book of Revelation from the prison island of Patmos where he was exiled. He was the only one of the 12 who is said to have died a natural death. Well someone had to write this down because it is his fellow apostles that he is speaking of here ... *Rejoice over her, you heavens! Rejoice, you people of God! Rejoice, <u>apostles</u> and prophets! For God has judged her* [Babylon] *with the judgment she imposed on <u>you</u>.* And the woman Babylon has been persecuting *people of God* ever since the first century up to this day.

The letters to the churches spoke into the lives of those Christians in the first century, so the tribulation was alive for them, and here is the evidence. The apostles also experienced this period of trial. This

---

[15] John MacArthur, *The MacArthur Study Bible*, (Nashville: Word Publishing, 1997) p.2018

3½ years, or 1,260 days as it was called back in 12:5, is a figurative time of trial based on many trials of that length in Israel's history (see Vol. 2, ch. 2, on 11:2). But 12:5 told us the tribulation or the time in the wilderness, the 1,260 days, *began* from the time of Jesus' ascension. *The male child was snatched up!* That's the time of the apostles. Then comes the 1,260 days or 3½ years. All views agree that this 3½-year tribulation reaches to the end of the last days, but it clearly says in 12:5 it *begins* from the time of what? The apostles! (Jesus' ascension.) The tribulation then stretches to the end. John called it the *last hour*. You are in it now! If John can figuratively talk about the past 2000 years as the *last hour* or *last days*, he can also figuratively talk about it as 3½ years (OT typical time of trial).

This would mean that John and his first readers are also going through the tribulation. And what is Revelation all about? Who is it written to? John said at the beginning that he was writing to all the seven churches (1:4). For what purpose? This old man John, is in a cave imprisoned on the island of Patmos and says ...

> I, John, your brother and <u>companion in the suffering</u> and kingdom and patient endurance that are ours in Jesus, was on the island of Patmos because of the word of God and the testimony of Jesus (1:9).

Your *companion in the suffering*. It's an interesting choice of words. In Christian circles, the word *tribulation* has become a technical term or catchphrase, but it's a word in Greek that can be translated as *suffering* or *persecution*. We know the word from the gospels when Jesus talks about the time of tribulation at the end. This Greek word is used five times in Revelation. It can be called a *tribulation*, or a great *tribulation* (7:14), or it can be *persecution*, *affliction* or *suffering*. The Futurist argues that the *great* tribulation is distinct from the general use of the word tribulation on the basis of the adjective *great*. But Jesus himself puts that theory to rest because he used both *tribulation* and *great tribulation* interchangeably to mean the same thing in his speech on the end times in Matthew 24:9, 21, 29. But which word do you think John uses in 1:9? Our older translations are helpful here. *I, John your brother and companion in <u>the tribulation</u>* ...

It's the same word. What are John and his readers doing in the tribulation? The same thing our text says in 18:20. The people of God, *apostles* and prophets have been going through the tribulation from the first century. Suffering is a legitimate translation in 1:9, *I John your companion in the suffering,* but most other English translations say, *I, John your companion in the tribulation* ... So it's written to a people in tribulation with John (as one of the apostles, 18:20) also experiencing it. Isn't this what we were told right from the start about this book?

> The revelation of Jesus Christ, which God gave him to show his servants what must soon take place (1:1).

Those who say we should take Revelation literally usually don't take this plain statement literally. It's for God's *servants* from the first century. What follows in Revelation *must soon take place!* Soon for them! It's upon all of us who read this. Revelation was addressed to the seven churches. It was alive for them and for everyone who has read it since. As we are also told at the start ...

> Blessed is the one who reads aloud the words of this prophecy, and blessed are those who hear it and take to heart what is written in it, because the time is near (1:3).

It's a blessing to all who have read it in the church age because all of it is relevant and *the time is near* because it is upon us all! The tribulation began at the time of the apostles and continues throughout the past 2000 years. That is how it can be near and soon to all who read it! This book is a blessing to all!

The Futurist rapture view has the tribulation *not* in the church age because before or during the 'seven-year' tribulation the church is raptured off the earth. This means Rev. 4-19 is not for the church. The Futurist makes the point that the church is not mentioned during these chapters, though as we noted earlier (Vol. 1, ch.11), *the people of God* are mentioned all through, so are the *redeemed* and those who *follow* and *obey Jesus.* Again we ask, 'On what grounds can you say those saints are *not* the church?'

The book of Revelation started by addressing the whole book to the churches (1:4). And how does Revelation finish? The same way. The end of the book sums up its teaching and says the whole of Revelation is written *for* the churches.

'I, Jesus, have sent my angel to give you this testimony <u>for the churches</u>' (22:16a).

Why did Jesus send his angel? To strengthen *the churches* going through the tribulation! *I, John your companion in the tribulation.* Futurists often ask, 'Would God let his bride go through this horrific tribulation described in Revelation?' Answer: Look at the rest of the NT and ask the same question. I will translate the same Greek word used for *tribulation* literally as *tribulation* in the following texts. There are many others, but here are a few ...

> 'I have told you these things, so that in me you may have peace. In this world you will have <u>tribulation</u>. But take heart! I have overcome the world' (John 16:33).

> ... strengthening the disciples and encouraging them to remain true to the faith. 'We must go through much <u>tribulation</u> to enter the kingdom of God,' they said (Acts 14:22).

> Not only so, but we also glory in our <u>tribulations</u> ... (Romans 5:3).

> For our light and momentary <u>tribulation</u> is achieving for us an eternal glory that far outweighs them all (2 Cor. 4:17).

> You became imitators of us and of the Lord, for you welcomed the message in the midst of severe <u>tribulation</u> with the joy given by the Holy Spirit (1 Thess. 1:6).

Isn't this the same message the NT has taught us about trials?

> ... though now for a little while you may have had to suffer grief in all kinds of trials (1 Pet. 1:6).

> Consider it pure joy, my brothers and sisters, whenever you face trials of many kinds, ... (James 1:2).

> In fact, everyone who wants to live a godly life in Christ Jesus will be persecuted, ... (2 Tim. 3:12).

In 2 Cor. 11, the apostle Paul had his list of tribulations that outdoes anyone! He says at one point he despaired even of life itself (2 Cor. 1:8-9). Does the bride of Christ have to suffer? Absolutely! How could we miss it? The NT is filled with this fact.

I have always maintained end time views are secondary and we still enjoy unity on things of first importance. So you might ask why have I bothered going into detail with this verse and how it relates to the different views of *when* the tribulation occurs. The reason is this: It's the pastoral importance of this text. If this text is plainly teaching that the apostles were punished by Babylon, then this woman Babylon has been enticing and persecuting throughout church history from the time of the apostles. And what does that mean? It means you are in the tribulation right now, and helps you understand why you feel under attack, why there seems to be oppression, temptation, conflict, division in the world, in the church, in your relationships, and in your heart. It would mean this woman Babylon is far subtler and more deceptive than you have realized. You could be being enticed by the adulteries of her maddening wine right now and not know.

Instead of a fanfare tribulation with events so obvious, even tattoo marks on people's hands and foreheads to indicate who is with the Beast and who is not—what if Babylon is far subtler than that? What if she has slipped right into our midst now? You would need this Revelation to figure it out. Could she be that deceitful? How could we be in tribulation now, yet in many ways not even realize it?

Let's recap on her enticements. The metaphor. She is a prostitute. Sex. Sexual immorality. Metaphor yes, but not coincidence that it's the great shipwreck wreaking havoc in the church. People in the church actually think they can play with sexual immorality, including pornography, and think they are not being sold down the river of hell. Drunk on the maddening wine of her adulteries!

But even that is too obvious. The greatest seduction in Rev.18 we have seen is her enticement with material prosperity. She doesn't entice with money … just the things it buys! Your security and enjoyment are in the things of this world. Let's recap Rev. 18 so far and look at what comes crashing down in Babylon. The list of things includes everyday material 'stuff' we like to buy or want to have. Most of those things are actually good things we all need in some measure. Her enticements are not all the obvious sins like murder and adulteries, etc. What are you doing with the money God has given you? Look at this text and see what will happen! This is perhaps the scariest thing of all. How deceiving would it be if we have been deceived in the *middle* of the tribulation? How clever would the woman have to be that you don't even realize you are being deceived? And how seductive is this? What is the main thing that is spoken about in Rev. 18 with regards to the seduction of Babylon during the tribulation? Materialism. Yes sex, drugs and every idol. But the big one repeated in Rev. 18 is what did you do with your money and what do you treasure? It's the great day of the sheep and the goats; 'when did I not feed you or care for you?' When? I have no idea. And it all comes crashing down to the terror of those who look on. But to those who felt the weight of her seduction but didn't give in to her? In the future ...

'Rejoice over her, you heavens! Rejoice, you people of God! Rejoice, apostles and prophets! For God has judged her with the judgment she imposed on you.' This text also tells us full rejoicing is at this victory. It's Jesus' victory. Jesus wins. But there is no full vindication in this life. We are supposed to be afraid to say this. If I tell you straight out that we Christians are not living for anything final in this life, that Christian citizenship is in heaven and we are storing up treasures there, and rejoicing is only fully and finally at this victory when Jesus will wipe every tear, you might say, 'What? You should tell the people how you can have the good stuff in this life. Tell them about the wonderful plan God has for your life and it's all about you getting what you want. That will get more people in your church.' But it's all a big lie. 'Come to Jesus and be saved into a wonderful life.' No, come and be saved from the coming wrath of God and the crash of Rev. 18, because many who think they are saved are deceived by the seduction of this woman. And it gets worse. Come and be saved to *suffer* to walk through the *tribulation.*

Are you sure you want to follow Jesus? This life is filled with hardships. Yes, we rejoice now in the incredible grace that God has saved us, but often rejoicing through tears. Yes, God works all things for the good of his people, but not the good that Babylon wants to offer you. Yes, God does have a wonderful plan for your life, but it does include suffering. Remain faithful and you will *miss out* in this life on her luxuries and satisfactions she offers. You might even miss out on your ability to buy or sell if you forgo the easy money, the rorts, the cash-only deals, the shonky deals, or cheating on the boss.

And you will be discriminated for being a Christian. Be faithful to Jesus and *you will miss out*. Plus, anything you desire in addition to God is an idol from Babylon, and she will come crashing down. She is lying to you and she is infiltrating the church. We lament, 'What is to become of the church?' Answer: More attack! There is no vindication in this life! What, none? What? Live for the eternal plan? What? Set your hope on the grace to be given when Jesus is revealed? Live for the relationship with God now? Yes, but even that is not fully known until I am face to face? So wait for the full eternal bliss and rejoice in the victory that is finally in Jesus (18:20)? Yes. But it's not for just a moment. All the timelines of all the different Revelation views leave out the *eternity*, the other side of the final judgment. It's forever!

This is the secret of Revelation. This is the secret to being fulfilled in *this* life. We are pilgrims journeying through tribulation. This life is not home. When you live for the future and the final vindication of Jesus, and you know this Jesus who has loved you and given himself up for you so that you will be one day rejoicing (18:20), then nothing can touch you. No trial, no tribulation, no height nor depth can separate you from the love of God in Christ Jesus our Lord. You are free to enter into the fullness of this life, even through the trials, and see all God is doing in growing your relationship with him and enter into all that he has planned for you to serve him in this short time. You *can* rejoice now. That is why that theme of Revelation is repeated …

> This calls for patient endurance on the part of the saints who obey God's commandments and remain faithful to Jesus (14:12).

Why do you need so much patient endurance? Is there something wrong with you? No, you are going through the tribulation. Revelation uses OT historical times and places pointing to a greater fulfillment. What did Babylon mean to ancient Israel? Being in exile in Babylon. They were told don't leave Babylon until your deliverance comes. In the meantime, be in Babylon but not *of* Babylon. What an amazing part of the history of Israel to be used to describe our pilgrimage. We are in exile! Tribulation intensified by Babylon. Babylon was not home for exiled Israel. So too, we live in a city that is not our home! That's why Revelation is given. To let you know two things if you are suffering. Firstly, there isn't anything wrong with you! (This is how it was meant to be.) And secondly, hold fast, and be patient and faithful because Jesus wins!

The message of our text is this: If you hold fast with patient endurance and faithfulness, you will rejoice!

Rejoice over her, you heavens! Rejoice, you people of God! Rejoice, apostles and prophets! For God has judged her with the judgment she imposed on you.'

Study Questions

1. Can you give a time frame for Babylon and the tribulation according to the main four views?

2. Read Jer. 51:47-49. How does it confirm the meaning of 18:20?

3. How does the meaning of this text relate to the different views?

4. How does the apostles' martyrdom relate to this text?

5. What is the importance of the word *tribulation* as used in Revelation and Jesus use of it in Matt. 24?

6. If Revelation had never been written would the NT suggest the bride will go through tribulation?

7. How might our interpretation of 18:20 affect its pastoral application?

8. Could Babylon be subtle enough to entice us without us realizing it? Would that fit with Rev. 18?

9. How could ancient Israel's experience with Babylon help us see our world differently?

11
And Crashing with Her ...
(Revelation 18:21-24)

What a sight it must have been for John the apostle! He sees a boulder the size of a *large millstone*, which could be anything over half a yard (meter) in diameter or larger, because it's 'a boulder the size of a *large* millstone'. And this angel is so big he picks it up like a tennis ball and hurls it violently into the sea.

The imagery is like a terrorist on YouTube breathing out threats against the city you live in ... Then he picks up a massive rock from wherever he is in the Middle Eastern desert (even though he is really filming it from his backyard in the local suburbs), and he smashes that rock down into the water with a great crash! Well this is much scarier than that. The one making this statement is a *mighty angel*.

> Then a mighty angel picked up a boulder the size of a large millstone and threw it into the sea, and said: 'With such violence the great city of Babylon will be thrown down, never to be found again' (18:21).

As usual, Revelation's visions are drawing on OT precedents. When we looked at 18:20 last time we noted its connection to Jeremiah 51:47-49, which prophesied that Babylon would be punished for what she did to God's people. Following on from this we see another allusion to Jeremiah.

> Then say, 'LORD, you have said you will destroy this place, so that neither people nor animals will live in it; it will be desolate forever.' When you finish reading this scroll, tie a stone to it and throw it into the Euphrates. Then say, 'So will Babylon sink to rise no more because of the disaster I will bring on her. And her people will fall.' The words of Jeremiah end here (Jer. 51:62-64).

Again, we see Revelation consistently using OT historical places and events to fulfill prophecy in a far more profound and wider way. This new Babylon set itself up against God and this is what happens ...

> The music of harpists and musicians, pipers and trumpeters, will never be heard in you again. No worker of any trade will ever be found in you again. The sound of a millstone will never be heard in you again (18:22).

For those Christians in the first century who were reading this, following Jesus meant 'missing out'. Their ability to buy or sell has been severely affected because they wouldn't compromise. Babylon (Rome for them), controlled the market forces. She is the center of economic prosperity. If you really want to prosper financially, you have to work with her.

But now what do we read about Babylon? Before, she restricted the saints' work and trade. Now it's Babylon who has no worker and no trade going on in her. Before, it was those who stuck to the ethics of Jesus who missed out. Those who denied themselves in the kind of work they did and the entertainment they took part in, who missed out on the theatre and music in the ancient world because it went against God's word including sexual immorality. Likewise, now, it is the Christians who limit their entertainment as to what they watch on TV (the theatre was the ancient world equivalent). They restrict themselves to the music to which they listen. They limit themselves in the kinds of work and work practices they engage in. But now it's Babylon's turn. No work or music or entertainment to be found in *her*!

> The <u>light</u> of a lamp will never shine in you again. The voice of <u>bridegroom and bride</u> will never be heard in you again. Your merchants were the world's important people. By your magic spell all the nations were led astray (18:23).

Before she had lights, entertainment and fancy weddings. Before you saints were pressured by Babylon, but you didn't give in to her seduction, and because of this you missed some of the raunchy parties and fancy 'lights'. You missed some of the weddings! Maybe you missed out on your own wedding because you wouldn't compromise and marry a non-Christian. And now look at her. No **voice of bridegroom and bride** in her again.

There is a little word in the original Greek language that comes after the *bride will never be heard in you again*. It's a word that is often translated *for* or *because*. It has been left out of our translation, but it answers a question. Why are all these things being removed from Babylon? Why is she left desolate? *Because* **your merchants were the world's great men.** (This draws on Isa. 23:8 and 34:12.) *Because* they gave glory to themselves.

These are the great self-sufficient people of the world who made it big. They were the ones to whom you looked. They looked to themselves as the *important people*. These were people everyone celebrated and coveted. Success. Power. Money. The rich and the famous. And the celebrity, glamorous marriages were celebrated. Notice the musicians are listed there as well (18: 22). The great ones! *The important ones*. They had it all. They 'didn't need God'. 'God is for people who need a crutch'. The inhabitants were enticed by Babylon who had these great people, they were the *important* ones to admire and aspire to. Success. The glory of man.

But now when you look at the 'important ones' who make it in this world, it all seems so futile. Why don't people just see through it? The great ones seem as miserable as everyone else. They commit suicide and suffer depression just as often. Look at all the famous Rock stars who have either committed suicide or destroyed themselves with drugs. Wasn't the success enough? The famous are tormented and fail in their marriages as much or more than anyone. Why don't *we* see through it?

The answer is right there! **By your magic spell all the nations were led astray.** Babylon's sorcery! All the people were deceived by her magic spells and sorcery!

What is at the heart of this deception? *The glory of man*. It's the battle for supremacy in Revelation like the battle between Pharaoh and Moses. Who is God? Who is to be glorified? What is man's primary purpose? You would have thought it was obvious that God was God and he alone is to be glorified, but the deception is so great! God gives gifts and graces to people. He gives money and power to be used for his kingdom, but man keeps them for himself. But the theme of Revelation is that Jesus wins. The truth must come out. The true, living God will and must be glorified …

'You are worthy, our Lord and God, to receive <u>glory and honor</u> and power, for you created <u>all things</u>, and by <u>your will</u> they were created and have their being' (4:11).

It was God who gave us *all things*. He *created all things*. He is not looking for vainglory like we do. It is a simple matter of truth. God stands for truth. Acknowledge the truth. He gave us everything. He is God, not us. Isn't this fascinating? We little human specks try to lift ourselves up higher than each other and even higher than God. None of us are truly humble. It's ironic that the only one who is really humble is the God of this universe who came down and humbled himself (Phil. 2:5-8).

The Lord is God. It was by his *will* that each one is given gifts. Jesus gave gifts into the church. Each one is given gifts. Not everyone is given the same gifts. The Bible speaks about all kinds of gifts that people are given, including teaching, administration, serving, compassion, encouraging others, and contributing to the needs of others, etc (Romans 12). You have been given gifts. Why did he give you gifts? For the building up of his church! For his glory! Not for our self-glory. That's plagiarism to say, I've got this life/gifts for myself and it's for me. But this has been recurring throughout Revelation. Who gets the glory? The living God or Babylon? Look how this theme runs through Revelation …

> In a loud voice they were saying: '<u>Worthy is the Lamb</u>, who was slain, to receive power and wealth and wisdom and strength and <u>honor and glory</u> and praise!' Then I heard every creature in heaven and on earth and under the earth and on the sea, and all that is in them, saying: 'To him who sits on the throne and to the Lamb be praise and <u>honor and glory</u> and power, for <u>ever and ever</u>!' (5:12-13).

It's the song of 7:12 …

> 'Amen! Praise and <u>glory</u> and wisdom and thanks and honor and power and strength be to our God for <u>ever and ever</u>. Amen!' (7:12).

He alone is God. Babylon has been deceiving you! Stand for truth! It was the song of Moses and the Lamb …

> 'Who will not fear you, Lord, and bring <u>glory</u> to your name? For you alone are holy. <u>All nations</u> will come and worship before you, …' (15:4).

All through Revelation the question is raised—who will be glorified? God or the Beast and Babylon? People continue to say it will be them. '*I* will be like Babylon.' Babylon gave *herself glory* and boasted *I* will never mourn (18:7). *I* will not glorify God. And she enticed the nations to follow *her*. She was the alternative salvation and the people would not come out of her and glorify God. Even in the face of judgment they followed her and refused to give glory to God ...

> They were seared by the intense heat and they cursed the name of God, who had control over these plagues, but they <u>refused</u> to repent and <u>glorify</u> him (16:9).

The glory of God is not only the chief end of mankind. It is the chief end of eternity. Jesus wins! The Lord will be glorified as certain as this millstone smashing down into the sea is meant to show the absolute *certainty* of what will happen to Babylon. The counterfeit glories will not simply fade away. They will be smashed down.

We saw in our previous chapter from 18:20 that this seductive city Babylon has existed since the time of the apostles and throughout all the era of the church. So that means she is around now. But look at what 18:21 is saying. The great angel stands up with that great boulder and smashes it down into the sea and says, 'It's as certain as this. She is going to be crushed.' God will be glorified, not her!

The climax will come at the wedding supper of the Lamb in Rev. 19, where glory and honor will finally be given where it is due—to the Lamb, Jesus. This answers so much. It's the key to understanding life and where it is headed. You are either still stuck in the deceit of Babylon, going with self-glory and self-indulgence and self-lordship, or you are living for the praise of *his* glory. Or worse, you are lukewarm, neither hot nor cold and he will spit you out of his mouth. But Babylon keeps enticing. In the children's movie *Cars*, Doc teaches Lightning McQueen how to take the dirt road corner. 'You gotta turn right to go left.' Sometimes you have to go against what might seem natural to your own feelings in order to go with what you know to be true, to glorify God and have life to the full. Why? Because we have all the weight of the 'old man' but also the weight of the deceit of Babylon against us and ... *By your* <u>*magic spell*</u> *all the nations were* <u>*led astray*</u>.

If you are seeking self-satisfaction rather than the glory of God, then you are fighting against what you were created for and to what you were called. You are putting up a peashooter to try and fight against God's march to the ends of the earth that will end like this here in Rev. 18. Take a look at that millstone. Take a look at the *important people*. Take a look at everyone who exalts his or her own self. It's the great 'important people' who made 'good' in the world. The great ones are never heard again in this 'great' city.

It's also interesting that **musicians** are now excluded from Babylon (18:22). How many times have you heard, 'Hey, I don't mind going to hell, I'll be with all my buddies and all the great musos.' But sorry—there is no music in hell. The great 'important people' who received credit but never gave glory to the God who gave them their gifts can't play there! You heard them. All those great songs they sang, but you should have listened more carefully to the lyrics. The Lord didn't demand every song had to be explicitly about him, but were their lyrics and motives dishonoring to the Lord? Trampling on his holiness? Exalting man and his pleasure as the chief end? God was forgotten, the one who gave the very gifts that enabled this music to take place. In the end, it is removed from Babylon. What else?

> In her was found the blood of prophets and of God's holy people, and of all who have been slaughtered on the earth (18:24).

Their **blood** was not forgotten. It cried out from the earth and justice is not forgotten. Here is the final reason why Babylon is going down like a millstone into the sea. Because of her persecution of God's people. This verse reminds us that we are not talking about a single city, either past or future, but it crosses time as Revelation has been doing all the way through. It's **all who have been slaughtered on the earth**. So this is obviously going way beyond one literal city at one time, because it's all God's people, past, present, and future, who have been killed by Babylon. This could mean more than martyrs, as Jesus said whoever wants to save his life must lose it for my sake, so this could include all those who stood for Jesus and in some way received persecution, discrimination, or ostracizing from Babylon. They are not forgotten.

But what was so wrong with these things that Babylon enticed the people with? What is wrong with music and lights? What is wrong with successful business and workers doing their job? What is wrong with being a bride or bridegroom? Well, it was not the amount of money her important people made, or her musicians playing music, but it was a question of where God was in their lives. God is not against the rich or music. God doesn't tell the rich not to be rich, but rather he tells them to be generous (1 Timothy 6:17), and not to find their security in money.

Also, it must be noted that music, craft, marriage, and business are not exclusive to Babylon. Just wait until you see the new heaven and new earth! Music! We've seen throughout Revelation that there has been plenty of music, as well as bright lights, in the presence of the Lord. And weddings? Before we finish Revelation, we will see the ultimate marriage, the ultimate in music, and the ultimate in productivity in the new heaven and new earth.

So the problem was not in these things themselves, as though they are part of the sin of this world. The problem is that these things were given by God for his glory, but the very One who gave them was ignored. Worse. These things replaced the glory of God and were used to dishonor, even attack God. The people were deceived by Babylon and worshiped and served created things rather than the Creator who is forever praised. Amen.

When the glory of the Lord is not your chief end you will get hurt. You are going against what you were created for. That is why the 'important people' still hurt, have broken marriages, and are never satisfied with enough money, fame, or success. And the judgment is this: The weddings are coming down (18:23). The only marriage that is permanent and what we are to put all our hope in is the wedding in Rev. 19. Single people who have hope in earthly marriage to 'fulfill' their life need to look again at what happens here! People make marriage an idol. And if they can't have it, they are hurt. Married people make marriage an idol and they get hurt because their marriage partner doesn't turn out to 'fulfill me'. No spouse can fulfil the other because no one can take the place that should be for God alone. And when people discover that idols fail them, they are broken. Life hasn't worked out.

But when your chief end is the Lord, then things take their proper place. Marriage becomes a place to serve and please your spouse and reflect the ultimate marriage. Making money becomes something to provide for ourselves and give to others and a means to support the work of God's kingdom. Music and entertainment that doesn't dishonor God is to be enjoyed with thanksgiving, God has provided us with every good gift. The business and work in Babylon wasn't sinful in itself.

This section of Rev. 18 is like a song with a chorus. John the apostle is getting the music video as Babylon goes down, down, down. She is stripped of her glory. It's like one of those old Johnny Cash songs. After each verse comes the chorus ... *'never to be found again.' 'Never to be heard again'*... The angel hurls that boulder into the sea and it's like the slow-motion replay as the tsunami hits Babylon. Each verse describes the demolition. One wall at a time. *'Never to be found again.'* Look at the musical rhythm ...

Babylon is comin' down, like this millstone in the sea. *'Never to be found again'* (18: 21). Then the music stops. This is like when the cops arrive at a loud party. The music is turned off. The music is ... *'Never to be heard in you again'* (18:22). Pretty boring city with no music, but at least it survives. But then in 18:22 the trade also shuts down. The economy of the city grinds to a halt, *never to be found in you again.* At the end of 18:22 *The sound of a millstone* (no more grinding of grain, basic food production for bread) *will never be heard in you again.*

Finally, in 18:23, all work and commerce have stopped. And now she actually goes into darkness. Literally! The lights are turned out, *never to shine in you again.* What's left? Human relationships? None. The sound of couples marrying, *never to be heard in you again* (18:23).

So this is the slow-motion replay of her descent into hell, until she is in darkness and even the people aren't together anymore. There is no 'being with my buddies in hell'. Just darkness, *never to be heard again.* Babylon seduced you into turning good things like music, marriage, business, and career into an alternative salvation. What is supposed to be our salvation? The cross of Jesus! That is the greatest display of God's glory. We are meant to find all our meaning in that salvation. God came on a rescue mission for his enemies (Rom. 5:10). And he gave us the right to *become* children of God. To switch allegiances. How? Through the true salvation—the cross. Not only does it save us, but also it restores us to be whole human beings, to be what we were created for. For *his* glory. It enables us to follow the true King and to use all his good gifts as he enables for *his* glory.

But in the meantime, there is pain and forsaking things to glorify God. Often you have to turn right to go left. Why? Babylon is still persecuting you, seeking to deceive you with her *magic spells* into a false salvation. To entice you to find glory in *anything* other than Jesus, the true King who saved you. You are in the tribulation. Babylon is the Queen of the tribulation.

Study Questions

1. How can the references to Jeremiah help us understand this text? Does it predict old Babylon's reconstruction?

2. How would each of the things coming down in Babylon speak into the lives of the first readers?

3. How do we fall for Babylon's magic spells with regard to the 'important people'?

4. What is the theme of conflict in Revelation?

5. How can glorifying God be made difficult by Babylon?

6. What makes the things of Babylon evil, and how are they the cause of its demise?

7. How could each one of them be used for the glory of God?

8. How are we restored in salvation?

12
The Hallelujah Chorus
(Revelation 19:1-5)

When the Melbourne Cricket Ground Grand Final day crowd of 100,000 people hears the final siren, an amazing roar goes up! Now imagine that, but a multitude of times over! But even then, you haven't even begun to understand this ...

> After this I heard what sounded like the <u>roar</u> of a great <u>multitude</u> in heaven shouting: 'Hallelujah! Salvation and glory and power belong to our God, ...' (19:1).

Have you ever heard the Hallelujah chorus from Handel's *Messiah*? John the apostle got to hear the original—live! We learned in 18:20 that all who had been hurt by the evils of Babylon in the tribulation, all the apostles, prophets, and people of God throughout the church age were told to rejoice. And this is their response: A great multitude! And listen to the noise they make.

In Rev. 18 it was all doom and gloom. Weeping and lamenting. It was all to do with the fall of Babylon and the demise of those who followed her. But this is all rejoicing. The cry is **Hallelujah! <u>Salvation and glory and power</u>** **belong to our God** ... Babylon promised a false salvation and boasted of her glory and power. But God is finally shown to be the only one who deserves praise for salvation, glory and power. And his justice is vindicated.

> '... <u>for true and just are his judgments</u>. He has condemned the great prostitute <u>who corrupted the earth</u> by <u>her adulteries</u>. He has avenged on her <u>the blood of his servants</u>' (19:2).

She is punished as the one **who corrupted the earth by her adulteries**. But the judgment comes particularly because of what she did to God's people. Precious in the sight of the Lord is the death of his saints (Ps. 116:15). God did care about what you were going through.

Now you saints have finally made it to the end of the race! You felt it. You felt the maddening wine of her adulteries. She tempted you sorely, but you fought the good fight. And now you are free! So you praise God! This is why there is this Hallelujah chorus. The evil of sin is exposed, and the rightness of judgment is seen. God was right all along ...

> And again they shouted: 'Hallelujah! The smoke from her goes up for ever and ever' (19:3).

None of the things with which Babylon enticed you lasted. The 'city' is not eternal—only her punishment. And the punishment fits the crime. The very people who have blasphemed God for not caring or doing enough about evil will regret ever saying such a thing. Look how much God cares about the evil. **The smoke from her goes up for ever and ever.** Note that no one disagrees with the severity of the sentence. The elders and the four creatures in heaven cry 'Amen'!

> The twenty-four elders and the four living creatures fell down and worshiped God, who was seated on the throne. And they cried: '<u>Amen</u>, Hallelujah!' (19:4).

Everyone is in agreement. The Lord was right. His justice does fit the crime. There is no one saying 'it's too little', or 'it's too much'.

It's hard to imagine the exhilaration of heaven. What will your first response be? Well it seems we know because we have the film footage of the future here and the great multitude in heaven are shouting, *Hallelujah!* Hallelujah is a Greek transliteration of simply 'Praise Yahweh'. Yahweh is the personal covenantal name of God. It's not just a generic word for God, rather he is the God of his people. That's the first thing you do when you get to heaven. Praise God. 'Hallelujah!'

But praise God for what? What do you praise him for first of all? *Salvation!* And out of that praise for salvation is also praise for his glory and power to carry it out ... *Salvation and glory and power belong to our God ...*

Salvation is the Lord's from beginning to end. His glory. Not

Babylon, or the Beast, or the Dragon, but God has all the glory. It was not a works salvation. The Lord receives all the glory. Salvation doesn't belong to the church and its sacraments. Baptism and the Lord's Supper can't save your soul. It is all of God's work from beginning to end. He chose us in him before the creation of the world (Eph. 1:4). He sent his Son into the world to go to the cross to pay that eternal price. Salvation belongs to our God.

And how did you come to hear about this? God did that too. *Salvation belongs to our God.*

> From one man he made all the nations, that they should inhabit the whole earth; and he marked out their appointed times in history and the boundaries of their lands. God did this so that they would seek him and perhaps reach out for him and find him, though he is not far from any one of us (Acts 17:26-27).

Millions of people born into this world have never heard the gospel. The work of mission is a desperate one indeed. But God placed people where they would *seek him*. He placed *you* in your nation and even *marked out* the time and boundary of where you should live. In other words, he determined the exact time and place you live. And in that time and place, he placed you in the path of Christians, or put you in a Christian home. He brought good things, or even pain in the time and place you lived. Why? So *that you would seek God* and *find him*. It was God all along. Salvation belongs to our God.

And even then you couldn't and wouldn't believe, so he had to send his Holy Spirit into your heart so that you could believe.

> ... he saved us, not because of righteous things we had done, but because of his mercy. He saved us through the washing of rebirth and renewal by the Holy Spirit (Titus 3:5).

You must be born again by God's Spirit. Why? Because *salvation belongs to our God*. The Son of God went to the cross, then seeks you.

> 'All things have been committed to me by my Father. No one knows the Son except the Father, and no one knows the Father except the Son and those to whom the Son chooses to reveal him' (Matt. 11:27).

No one seeks God (Rom. 3:11), and no one knows God except *those to whom the Son chooses to reveal him*. You didn't seek him. He seeks you.

Salvation belongs to our God. Then, once he began that work in you, he wasn't going to just start something and leave it to you.

> ... being confident of this, that he who began a good work in you <u>will carry it on to completion</u> until the day of Christ Jesus (Phil. 1:6).

God completes it. *Salvation belongs to our God.* So you journey in this walk with Jesus. You fought against wild beasts. The Beast himself and the 'other woman' (Babylon) tried to entice you. It was like walking through the valley of the shadow of death. At times, you despaired even of life because you had to ...

> — continue to <u>work out</u> your salvation with <u>fear and trembling</u>, for it is <u>God</u> who works in you to will and to act in order to fulfill his good purpose (Phil. 2:12b-13).

All along you were **working it out** in **fear and trembling**, but it turns out it was *God* working in you. *Salvation belongs to our God.*

It's God who gave up his Son. The more you get to understand this, the more you realize how much you didn't understand and why there is not enough time in all eternity to finish this Hallelujah chorus. Romans 5:6-10 says very rarely will anyone die for a righteous man, but God demonstrates his love for us in this—he died for us while we were sinners! *When we were enemies* he reconciled us. Who would give up their life for enemies?

What about that smoke that goes up forever? If that is what you so richly deserve, then what must Jesus have gone through to take it away? Through the *eternal Spirit* the eternal Son gave himself up (Heb. 9:14). The smoke rose up forever ... in Jesus! Gehenna—outside the camp. In the darkness. Eternal redemption. The cross. *Salvation belongs to our God.*

If you are truly a believer, this was for you. Not everyone makes it. In fact, Jesus said:

> 'Enter through the narrow gate. For wide is the gate and broad is the road that leads to destruction, and many enter through it. But small is the gate and narrow the road that leads to life, and only a few find it' (Matt. 7:13-14).

This has always been the case. The world became populated from

Adam's time but there was not much worship of the true God. By the time of Noah, God had to destroy the entire population of the world (except Noah's family). How many people were on the earth then? Some say a billion. Others say it could have been seven billion. We don't know. How many were saved on the ark? Eight people! Out of the whole world! That's what I call a narrow road! And there is Noah in this picture in Rev. 19. Noah is one of them singing the Hallelujah chorus now, but not even all his sons made it!

How narrow is this road? Read on in the OT. It's depressing reading if you are looking for God's people to be the good guys. Even the good guys are bad guys. Do you want to talk about a narrow road that only a few find? God chooses one tiny nation out of the whole earth. And most of those Israelites were traitors to the living God. They worshiped other gods and did evil. Two guys make it to the Promised Land out of the whole wilderness generation. Then look at all those kings. A new king would rise up, and what? He did more evil in the eyes of God and led Israel astray. One king after another, and on and on. Only a few were faithful. It was a narrow road. Forget the other nations, only a few (a remnant) of those Israelites are singing that Hallelujah chorus now. It was so pathetic that Israel's kings were finally destroyed. Until ...

Another king came. A faithful king. The true King. Jesus. And *he* is the one who said, 'Narrow is the road that leads to life and only a few find it.' But he wasn't saying that to the Romans or pagans. He said it to the believing community. And sure enough, most of them (God's so-called people), rejected him! The Pharisees and Sadducees, the 'believers' mostly rejected him. Just how narrow is that road? At least we know that 11 of the original 12 apostles made it. They are there singing the Hallelujah chorus.

Then read the letters to the churches in the NT. They are filled with troubles and unbelief. Then read the letters to the churches in the book of Revelation. Only two of the seven churches receive a favorable report. The rest — Jesus is about to spit them out of his mouth or worse! And on through church history. Forget those outside. Worry about the church. How is it looking? It's a mess. For 1000 years in the Middle Ages the whole power base of the church didn't even teach the gospel! They banned the Bible! But there were a few lone voices who were burned out at the stake for standing up for God's word. And what of that small number? They are there now singing the Hallelujah chorus. Even in the dark ages God always had his people, because the gates of hell did not prevail against his true church. But narrow is the road. How narrow?

Then came the Protestant Reformation. Phew. Times of refreshing. But how long before heresy and Protestant liberalism crept in? The church denies the Bible. No wonder by the 20th century people looked to the Charismatic movement to pick up the ball after the traditional denominations dropped it. But look at the contemporary church today. It's like the Church of Rome in the Middle Ages with the Bible hardly being opened (in the church!), and when they do, for many it's to give a gospel of prosperity or feel good message. They wouldn't dare tell you a message like this, 'Narrow is the road!' It's narrow, *in the church!* Most don't make it. Jesus said, 'Many will come to me on that day saying, "Lord, Lord …", and I will say, "I never knew you, away from me you evildoers."' It would be funny if it wasn't tragic, that people who can't even bother to worship God in church regularly (which is the foretaste of those worshiping in the great Hallelujah chorus), could think they are on the narrow road. They have to be kidding. There's enough worry *inside* the church, forget those outside. How many are really born again *in* the church? How precious it is to be one of the few! How precious to have this salvation that belongs to God alone!

The Lord has been adding his few, little by little, throughout history. But what are only a few in any one era builds up throughout time, until that stadium is filled with that multitude …

> Then a voice came from the throne, saying: 'Praise our God, all you his servants, you who fear him, both great and small!' (19:5).

In John's vision of the multitude he sees the individuals. He is able to distinguish one from another. Some are **small**, others are **great**. In Rev. 5 he could even see their ethnic distinctions (every tribe, nation and tongue). As John's eye line panned across this great crowd in heaven, he saw all who are there. The only question is … did he see you there?

It's a question we have asked before in heavenly scenes in Revelation, and indeed one of the very reasons this book was written to the saints. It was to get them to see the finish line and encourage them to press on through the tribulation. If you know Jesus, then John would have seen you in that crowd. Did he see you? John was probably too busy looking for himself like we always do in a group photo. But the big question remains—were you there in the picture? Are you converted? How do you know if you are on that *narrow road* that leads to life? Is this great salvation *your* salvation? Can you say salvation belongs to *my* God! How do you know you have this salvation? It's when the Spirit of God does a work in you whereby you really believe. You believe in this love and salvation that belongs to God, and you see the cost of what Jesus did. It will change the way you think. The old stuff with which Babylon enticed you becomes garbage to you. Here is the evidence. You rejoice over its demise from Babylon *and her sin* in Rev. 18 when it all crashes! That's how much you hate sin and love the Savior.

A great illustration that I believe originates from the Prince of Preachers, C. H. Spurgeon, is where two plates of food are placed a few feet apart. One is a plate full of sumptuous gourmet food, the other, a plate of rotting smelly, putrid, garbage. You set a pig free near the two plates and the pig goes for the garbage every time. That is natural for the pig. Then Spurgeon says, imagine if you had the power to magically transform that pig into a human. The *instant* the pig was chowing down on that garbage, suddenly, it's a human who is eating that putrid garbage. That person would spit it out and probably throw up what they had eaten.

Likewise, when we are truly children of God, when God has purchased us by the blood of Jesus, when he has saved us and is at work in us, we will occasionally put our head back in the slop bucket. But when we do, we will spit it out and wonder why we ever liked it. If you're still eating garbage and loving it, you have to wonder if you've ever truly been converted. Because when you know Jesus, *you believe!* You've seen by faith what Jesus did on the cross to pay for evil. Your evil! God sees sin as grievous and now so do you. Now you love the cross but hate the sin.

So the question is not whether you admit you are a sinner. Not whether you do good deeds. The question is not even whether you are sorely tempted. It's not even if you are afraid of hell and want to escape it. That doesn't prove you are saved. But does sin taste like putrid garbage to you? Do you glory in the cross of Christ and acknowledge that he went through that torment of eternal smoke rising up in his body for you, so you can no longer live in that sin?

Do you really *believe* in Jesus? Do you glory and Hallelujah in this salvation that belongs to God? If you do, then John saw you there in that Hallelujah chorus. Even though you will continue to sin, you are there in that chorus and you will long for the day when you will sin no more, when all sin is cast down. You'll rejoice when it is cast down. But if you are not at a point where you hate sin and love the cross, then you are not saved.

The amazing grace is that this word was given to you in advance. We are still in 'today'. We are not in Rev. 19 yet. While there is life there is hope. Call out to God day and night to give you a new heart until he answers! Pray for a heart for Jesus and what he did at the cross. A heart that will one day be so lost in the wonder and love of this great salvation so that this will be you there …

After this I heard what sounded like the roar of a great multitude in heaven shouting: 'Hallelujah! Salvation and glory and power belong to our God, …' (19:1).

Study Questions

1. What is this great rejoicing in response to?

2. What indication is there that there is agreement in heaven on the fairness of a punishment that goes on forever?

3. Give several ways that could explain that salvation belongs to God.

4. Give some points of Bible history that show how salvation is a narrow road.

5. Give reasons why John's vision of heaven includes individuals.

6. Did John see you there?

7. How do you know you are in that hallelujah chorus?

13
The Wedding
(Revelation 19:6-9)

These are the very first words of the Bible ...

> In the beginning God created the heavens and the earth (Gen. 1:1).

So there was a beginning to time. God was already there in the beginning when he created time and everything else. God is outside of time not in need of anything. Later in the Bible God reveals he is Father, Son and Holy Spirit. He is one God existing in three persons. People say God is love. But how can God be love or even know what love is, if there was no one to love throughout all eternity before God created the world? Answer: God existed in three persons having dwelt in perfect love and harmony for how long? Forever.

You might picture God in that perfect harmony as sitting around for eternity *until* he creates the world, as though billions of years of eternity go by and then God thinks, 'I've got a great idea, I'll create a universe.' Well, it didn't happen that way. God knows all things always and is outside time. God always saw the future so there was never a *time* when God did not have this creation fully in his mind. Think about that. There was *never a time* when God had not planned this life!

So with no irreverence intended (because I can't explain it any other way), it's like the three persons, the Father, Son and Holy Spirit are sitting around a table together, looking into God's crystal ball (meaning God's own mind), and the future is already clearly there. It has *always* been there in front of God. God *always* had the creation in his mind! The Father, Son and Holy Spirit were not figuring out creation as if they had to draw up plans and get them through local council (if it was our local council no wonder it took billions of years). No! The plan was already *complete* in the mind of God.

ALWAYS! There was *never* a time when God had not planned the whole thing.

God didn't need us or anything else. He wasn't lonely. So what was the plan? What is the meaning of this life? Why did God bother? We look out on our world and it is not all good. We look at our own lives and wonder, what is this all about? What is the point? What was it that the Father, the Son and Holy Spirit were planning? What was *the* plan? And the answer is: *A wedding*. The Father planned a wedding for his Son.

The concept of marriage and a wedding is the language that is used in the Bible. It climaxes at the end of the Bible, near the end of Revelation. The Bible comes to completion with a wedding. In fact, the whole Bible is really the story of a wedding.

A lot of planning goes into a wedding. Once the date is set you have to find a venue. The Bible starts with God in the beginning creating the venue for the wedding. *In the beginning God created the heavens and the earth.* Like any great wedding, it is not just about the venue, but it's about a romance. There is a love story that leads up to the wedding. Well, the Bible has a love story that leads up to a wedding. It's the greatest love story ever told. The greatest wedding. Again, this is the way the Bible itself describes it. Long before we get to Rev. 19 this wedding concept has been used in the Bible. We might think marriage and weddings are something man made up for practical convenience. Or that in Rev. 19 the human construct of marriage is being used to describe God's plan. But it's the other way around! God gave humans marriage, the most intimate relationship between two people, *to point to* the ultimate meaning of life. It's the ultimate wedding that God planned before the world was created. It was planned before any human marriage took place and before God gave marriage to humanity. One of the very first stories in the Bible is about a marriage in Genesis 2. That is when God gave marriage between a man and woman (in the beginning), but we must not miss the 'big picture' wedding theme of the whole Bible.

Throughout the OT God speaks of himself as being in a relationship with his people and likens it to marriage, as God calls himself the *husband* of his people. For example, ...

> For your Maker is your <u>husband</u>, the LORD Almighty is his name, the Holy One of Israel is your Redeemer; he is called the God of all the earth (Is. 54:5).

> ... 'for I am your <u>husband</u>. I will choose you—one from a town and two from a clan—and bring you to Zion (Jer. 3:14).

> I will <u>betroth you</u> to me forever; I will betroth you in righteousness and justice, in love and compassion (Hos. 2:19).

God is the husband and his people are the bride. This love story of God and his people continues into the NT. Jesus refers to himself as the bridegroom. John the Baptist also referred to Jesus as the bridegroom. And when the apostle Paul instructs married couples, he concludes with this.

> 'For this reason a man will leave his father and mother and be united to his wife, and the two will become one flesh.' This is a profound mystery—but I am talking about Christ and the church (Eph. 5:31-32).

The apostle effectively says, 'I'm telling you how to live in your marriage, but also I'm actually telling you about something bigger than that. A profound mystery. *The* marriage, between Christ and his church.' Human marriage wasn't the starting point. It is only a symbol that points to the meaning of life. The PLAN. The wedding God planned from eternity between Christ and his people.

There are other texts that use this description of God's relationship with his people as a marriage, so by the time we get to Rev. 19 and the wedding described there, it's not just arbitrary or a new metaphor. The Bible climaxes in the last book of the Bible with *the* plan. *The* wedding banquet!

At a wedding reception when the wedding couple are introduced to the wedding party ... 'Ladies and Gentlemen please welcome Mr. and Mrs. ...!', people are cheering. It's a great celebration. Well, for this heavenly wedding party it's like nothing you have ever heard or imagined. Those invited to this wedding banquet can't contain themselves. Nothing compares to the cheer going up for the introduction of this wedding party ...

> Then I heard what sounded like a great multitude, like the roar of rushing waters and like loud peals of thunder, shouting: 'Hallelujah! For our Lord God Almighty reigns. [Great rejoicing in anticipation of what? THE wedding!] Let us rejoice and be glad and give him glory! For the <u>wedding</u> of the Lamb has come, and his bride has made herself ready. Fine linen, bright and clean, was given her to wear.' (Fine linen

> stands for the righteous acts of God's holy people.) [Even the wedding dress is pictured.] Then the angel said to me, 'Write this: Blessed are those who are invited to <u>the wedding supper</u> of the Lamb!' And he added, 'These are the true words of God' (19:6-9).

The Bible continues right up to the end of this last book (Revelation) picturing not only the beauty of this wedding, but picturing the intimacy of this marriage …

> I saw the Holy City, the new Jerusalem, coming down out of heaven from God, prepared as a <u>bride</u> beautifully dressed for her husband. And I heard a loud voice from the throne saying, 'Look! God's dwelling is now among the people, and he will live with them. [But look at this marriage relationship of love between husband and bride.] They will be his people, and God himself will be with them and be their God. He will wipe every tear from their eyes' (21:2-4).

What a marriage. What a picture of love. Wiping every tear. Right up to the very last words of the Bible, it's the *bride* who essentially says, 'Come on, let's have this wedding celebration. Come on, you are all invited to join this wedding' (22:17).

So our text in Rev. 19 describing this wedding is the meaning of life and the meaning of our existence. Human weddings are meant to be pointing to this. It was God's plan all along. People search for the meaning of life, and what is it—42 or something? No. The meaning of life is a wedding. This is the reason God created the world. God is *glorified* in that wedding.

Perhaps it's no coincidence that human beings are fascinated with marriage and weddings. It's as though we are made in the image of God and this fascination has to come out. Cultures that have never heard of the Bible have marriages and weddings. Why is that? It can't be just for sex or to have children. People have both of those without marriage. Even our current society's obsession with same-sex marriage makes no sense even from an unbeliever's point of view. Before same-sex marriage was passed in Australia, we already had laws providing civil registration for same-sex relationships, including all the legal and financial benefits of married couples. Why do people want to bother trying to redefine and hijack marriage? Why not just live together? It's as though there is something deeper in the human heart desiring marriage, even when it's being distorted. Why this longing for marriage? Many who are single desire to be married. Some who are married struggle with a difficult relationship and long for an improved marriage. Many divorced people want to try again to get it right. Everyone seems to be focused on the happy marriage. Movies portray this ideal where the romance culminates with 'and they lived happily ever after'. I would like to see the sequel to some of those movies ... just how 'happily' and how 'ever after' are they? Unfortunately, in this fallen world, marriages don't always fulfill peoples' hopes. About half end in divorce. Many of the rest that survive are troubled, unhappy and even torturous. What happened to that wedding day when everyone was so happy, even cheering? Like this cheering like the *roar of rushing waters and like loud peals of thunder, shouting: 'Hallelujah'* (19:6)!

Many marriages don't live up to it. And yet that doesn't stop the human pursuit of a happy marriage. It's as though we are longing for something about marriage that no human spouse can live up to. Even those of us who enjoy all the blessings of the happiest marriages know that our happy marriages alone don't make us complete. What is it that we long for? It's this scene here ...

> Let us rejoice and be glad and give him glory! For the wedding of the Lamb has come, and his bride has made herself ready (19:7).

The wedding. It's deep down in our being because we were created for God and this wedding. It's the blessing that we long for ...

> Then the angel said to me, 'Write this: 'Blessed are those who are invited to the wedding supper of the Lamb!' (19:9).

Remember that God, Father, Son and Holy Spirit saw the plan for this wedding in eternity. Always. And God looks down the corridor of time to this wedding. But that is not all he saw. He saw the wedding *preparation*. He saw the bride. He saw himself as the bridegroom. And how does he (the bridegroom) look?

> Let us rejoice and be glad and give him glory! For the wedding of the Lamb has come, and his bride has made herself ready (19:7).

He looks like a lamb! So who is the bride and bridegroom? It is the same as what the apostle Paul said ...

> Husbands, love your wives, just as Christ loved the church and gave himself up for her ... (Eph. 5:25).

The bride of Christ is the church. All who have trusted in Christ, men, women and children, Jew and Gentile. The true people of God is the bride. And the bridegroom is Jesus, the Son of God, for whom the Father planned this wedding. But you can't appreciate how wonderful this wedding is unless you know how expensive it is and all the preparation that went into it. This was the most expensive wedding ever.

And when did he choose his bride?

> For he chose us in him before the creation of the world to be holy and blameless in his sight. In love he predestined us for adoption to sonship through Jesus Christ, in accordance with his pleasure and will. (Eph. 1:4-5).

He chose his bride from before the creation of the world. He looked into that crystal ball and saw his bride. How was she looking? A beautiful bride? No, she looked ugly. She was an adulteress. She was unfaithful. When adultery happens most people say it's over, but what if you knew in advance your spouse was going to commit adultery? Would you go through with the wedding? The Lord saw this adultery, and the consequences of his bride's infidelity was disastrous! He saw that this was her eternal destruction. She could never make it to the wedding. She could never wear that white dress. The consequence was she was stricken with a terminal cancer, an eternal cancer called sin. But worse ... the bride didn't even realize she was walking around with this cancer, even though it was dotted throughout her body.

If you are one of those who make up the bride, then every lie you've told is adultery and has caused you to develop dots of cancer in your body. Every foolish word? More adultery, more dots. Every bad thought you have ever had? Adultery and more cancer. Spots inside throughout. And those spots are sitting inside waiting to kill you, eternally. Death is just a door to receive the great medical examination of all that is riddled inside you. And we are stuck in these cancerous bodies and the X-ray will show it all up on that great day! We desperately need a transplant! The bride is desperate and in eternal trouble.

But now, if you want to see the love of a bridegroom—behold the man nailed to the cross! What was he doing there? Giving up his life for his bride! Taking the cancer in his body. He gave himself up to become the great transplant. The substitute! He was taking the eternal death, hell on the cross for his bride! And you thought humans made up marriage and love stories? This is the greatest love story ever told. It's the whole plan of life!

The wedding was always planned, but the cost was also planned. Looking into that crystal ball, the Father could see the Son. That's why he is depicted in this future wedding as a lamb! A lamb is a substitute sacrifice. A transplant. That is the cross. Remember this?

> ... all whose names have not been written in the Lamb's book of life, the Lamb who was slain from the creation of the world (13:8).

Did you get that? Slain from the creation of the world! The Father and the bridegroom looking into that crystal ball from the creation always had this plan to save his bride for the wedding. The cost of the wedding!

Because God is so transcendent, because he is not in need of the creation, because he existed eternally apart from creation, we tend to think that somehow God's existence in eternity was *removed* from the creation plan, long *before* it all. But this wedding was always at the forefront of God's *mind*. FOREVER! There was *never* a *before* when this wedding was not in the mind of God. That means there was never a time when God did not have in the forefront of that crystal ball the plan to slay his own Son! Doesn't that chill you? Slain from the creation. That is always who God was and is. The loving Father who gave up his Son, and the Son who have himself up, all for the love of his bride. The cost of the wedding, the cross, was not just in time. It's always been there in the mind of God! It's an eternal work to save the bride forever. He always had this plan that once you got through this short life, he would be with you in that wedding banquet, forever.

Why would he do it? Because he loved his bride. It's a love relationship. He had names that were written from before the creation of world! His church includes everyone who will come to the wedding. Jesus' church is his bride. His people. So this is why his true people meet together each week on the day he rose from the dead. He tells them to meet. Why? Because it's like a date with your fiancée in this relationship. Jesus meets with his bride in preparation for the wedding! Jesus promises spiritually to meet with them to celebrate the day he defeated their death (that's why it's called the Lord's day, Sunday, 1:10), when he paid for this wedding. They meet because they love him. It's a great love story. It's a great blessing ...

> ... 'Blessed are those who are invited to the wedding supper of the Lamb!' ... (19:9).

The Bible climaxes this love story with the wedding ceremony at the end, and the invitation to 'come to the wedding banquet'. We are not actually at this wedding yet. But what is amazing is that not everyone who is invited to the wedding will come. As Jesus, the bridegroom himself said of the wedding banquet ...

> 'The kingdom of heaven is like a king who prepared a <u>wedding banquet</u> for his son. He sent his servants to those who had been invited to the banquet to tell them to come, but they refused to come ...' 'For many are <u>invited</u>, but few are chosen' (Matt. 22:2-3, 14).

What a travesty to be invited and with no good reason reply 'no' and miss the wedding. Because if you miss this wedding, you miss it forever. Why are we here? Where is history going to end? It will end with a wedding, and there will be a great number of guests, but many who were invited refused the invitation.

For every one of us there will be one of these two endings, depending on whether you receive this invitation or not. Your destiny will either be Rev. 18, with cancer still in your body so that you crash to your eternal destruction in hell, or Rev. 19, because you trusted in Christ, in his transplant work, and followed him all the way to this wedding. If you do trust in Christ, you will see that he had planned it. No more tears. No more pain. Face to face, finally in exceeding joy. Now we see in part, then we shall see and know fully, as we will be fully known. This is the meaning of life.

Have you ever been to a wedding of a special couple that you know and love? You know that feeling of being happy for them. Love is in the air. Families join together. They sing and feast! But we also know many times the joy doesn't last in earthly marriages. But what if that joy and love and peace could stay that way—forever? That was God's plan all along.

This short time here on earth is when the bride will **make herself ready**. If you are part of the bride, this is the time when we 'make ourselves ready' for the wedding. All of what goes on in life here is not wasted. We need to explore these verses further next time. But this is what this short life is about. The *preparation* for *the* wedding. The preparations might seem like they take a long time, but suddenly the wedding is upon you.

But for now, we wait ... and wait... and when we get to that wedding banquet, do you think you will be bothered by having to wait for so long? It's not a mere 20-year celebration of joy and bliss, it's not 50 years, not 1000 years, not even 50 billion years, but forever and ever. You won't be complaining about that little waiting. Why? Because you will be with your true spouse. The Lamb slain from the creation. You will recline at this wedding feast with him! The Lamb! Jesus! You will rejoice and party along with Abraham, Isaac and Jacob, and Peter, John and James, and other believers. And all those troubles will seem like nothing.

That's why unbelievers would hate heaven, because they don't want to spend time with the Lord now. They don't want to worship him or talk to him through prayer or let him speak to them through his word. What a pain heaven would be for them, face to face with the one they didn't want to know who now dominates heaven. But heaven is about this wedding ... *being with your true spouse!*

So for those who really know him, the Father, the Son and the Holy Spirit looked into that crystal ball and always had this plan for you. This wedding. And here in Revelation we get a glimpse of it. You know how life is always about looking forwards? You look forward to when you finish school and get your driver's license. You look forward to your first job and to relationships—marriage. You also look forward to things you want to achieve, to making enough money to be comfortable, and to retirement. Have you noticed how we are always looking forwards? But *nothing* in this world ever 'arrives'. There is no true 'arrival' until you are at this wedding. The whole creations groans in expectation of this wedding.

Let us rejoice and be glad and give him glory! For the wedding of the Lamb has come, and his bride has made herself ready (19:7).

Study Questions

1. At what point did God plan the creation of the world?

2. Give reasons why God gave humanity marriage.

3. Why is marriage a 'profound mystery'?

4. Give examples in Scripture, leading up to Revelation, how the Bible refers to the ultimate marriage.

5. Why is it significant that the metaphor of the Lamb, not the Lion, is used here?

6. What is the significance of Jesus seeing his bride in advance through time?

7. How does this affect your view of God?

8. How does the contrast between Rev. 18 and Rev. 19 relate to the wedding invitation?

9. Give examples that demonstrate we have an inbuilt desire for this wedding.

14
The Wedding Preparation
(Revelation 19:7-8)

The meaning of life is this wedding! Jesus and his bride (his people). In this chapter you are given this picture of your future. There you are feasting and rejoicing at the wedding banquet. You are in the presence of the Lord. The struggle is over. There is no more temptation from Babylon to rise up and attack you. It's all gone! The long-awaited rest is here. This is the joy of heaven! Salvation belongs to our God.

It's the message of Revelation. You are meant to stand alongside John the apostle, who first saw this picture of the future, and see yourself there! You are meant to understand why you have been finding it so tough with the opposition. But now—look where you finish! Jesus wins, and this is what it looks like when he wins! This is why it's written. To tell you to keep on going. Look how it ends!

> 'Let us rejoice and be glad and give him glory! For the wedding of the Lamb has come, and his bride has <u>made herself ready</u>. Fine linen, bright and clean, was given her to wear' (Fine linen stands for the righteous acts of God's holy people.) (19:7-8).

G. K. Beale points out an interesting connection between these two verses and the two chapters of Rev. 18 and Rev. 19. The preparation of the bride who **made herself ready** is connected to both the **righteous acts of God's holy people,** as well as all that went on through the attacks from Babylon in Rev. 18.[16] Unbelievers ask (and maybe some of us ask), if God finally brings every deed into judgment, why does he have to allow evil to happen in the first place? As always, Revelation is revealing, and it pulls back the curtain for

---

[16] G. K. Beale, *The Book of Revelation*, (Grand Rapids, Michigan: Wm. B. Erdmans Publishing Co. 1999) p. 934

the behind the scenes look at what is going on. We looked at this in earlier chapters, but it is more fully developed here as we see Rev. 18 and Rev. 19 are connected in more ways than one.

Rev. 18 shows the judgment of Babylon. She is the alternative salvation, the counterfeit to the church, the great city and the great prostitute who persecuted the saints. She didn't take all the saints' lives, but she pressured every single one of them, for everyone who wanted to live a godly life was persecuted (2 Tim. 3:12). For some it was pressure in the home to put up with ridicule or just pressure to conform to family rather than Jesus. For others it was in the workplace, but they held fast and missed out on opportunities to buy or sell. For others it was loneliness instead of compromise or receiving the mark of the Beast, but they held fast to Christ. For others it was the waves of temptation that Babylon brought upon them. The glitter of the world and its lusts and material enticements were constantly thrust at them. They felt the weight. They went through many, many trials. It seemed like they constantly had the world, the flesh, and the devil against them. Trial after trial.

But Revelation is revealing something here. Our present sufferings are achieving for us an eternal weight of glory at the hands of who? Babylon! God was using Babylon, but for what purpose? God was preparing his people through all these trials. Preparing them for what?

The wedding! Remember that it was all a plan. A plan for *his bride has made herself ready*. She was being prepared! How? Well we have been looking at it in Rev. 18. There were the attacks, enticements and temptations of Babylon ... through many *hardships*. Now in 19:8 we also see the preparation comes through the bride's righteous acts. And through these righteous acts she receives her rich rewards.

Most Christians know Romans 8:28, 'all things work together for good'. But as we've noted before, the context of Romans 8:28 is suffering. Rom. 8:18, 'I consider our present *sufferings* are not worth comparing', and so ... 'God works all together for good'. But the context after this phrase is even more important to us. The Lord is working something in that suffering which is very specific. He is preparing his bride!

> And we know that in all things God works for the good of those who love him, who have been called according to his purpose. For those

God foreknew he also predestined <u>to be conformed to the image of his Son</u>, that he might be the firstborn among many brothers and sisters (Rom. 8:28-29).

The point of the suffering was to be conformed to the image of God's Son. The Son went through suffering. So while Babylon is the agent of evil upon you to suffer, the Lord was over it all for the sake of Christ. It was all about his kingdom and his glory, but also for your rewards in heaven, for his advancing of the gospel, *and* your transformation into the image of God's Son. So that you can make yourself ready! It was already flagged in the letters to the churches ...

> Do not be afraid of what you are about to suffer. I tell you, the devil will put some of you in prison to test you, and <u>you will suffer</u> persecution for ten days. Be faithful, even to the point of death, and I will give you <u>life</u> as your <u>victor's crown</u> (2:10).

You will suffer! Evil is behind your suffering, but the Lord says he is over it all, working it out for your rich reward. Even the victor's crown he will give you. We saw it also in 14:13.

> Then I heard a voice from heaven say, 'Write this: Blessed are the dead who die in the Lord from now on.' 'Yes,' says the Spirit, 'they will rest from their labor, for their <u>deeds will follow them</u>' (14:13).

Salvation is a free gift of God and no sin can be brought up against you, yet none of the works you labored to be faithful were wasted. They will be richly rewarded. They will follow you! It's the same principle here in 19:7-8. *Let us rejoice and be glad and give him glory! For the wedding of the Lamb has come, and his bride has <u>made herself ready</u>. Fine linen, bright and clean, was given her to wear. (Fine linen stands for the <u>righteous acts</u> of God's holy people).*

We need to connect these verses here. 'Made herself ready' *relates to* 'her righteous acts'. Does that mean she was saved by those righteous acts? We know it can't be. That would war against 'salvation belongs to our God'! So why do these fine linen garments given her to wear for the wedding (19:8) represent the righteous acts of God's holy people? They were given to 'make her ready' for the wedding. They are the things that she did that contributed to her purifying. They were not only refining her, but they resulted in rewards in heaven for all of her faithful service.

Many of those *righteous acts* were done in spite of opposition, in spite of temptation, in spite of hardship. And who do you think has brought all these trials and temptations that result in preparation for the wedding banquet? It's none other than Babylon! The city where you live. She attacked God's people. Outwardly and inwardly. Temptation. Marginalized. Spiritually and emotionally tormented them. But all the while she was being outsmarted! The Lord was using it all to prepare his bride. So she *made herself ready*. What a mind-blowing plan! That is why God let it all go on! It *was* a plan!

> 'Blessed are you when people insult you, persecute you and falsely say all kinds of evil against you because of me. Rejoice and be glad, because great is your reward in heaven, for in the same way they persecuted the prophets who were before you' (Matt. 5:11-12).

Rejoice and be glad! It's the same wording … **Let us rejoice and be glad and give him glory! For the wedding of the Lamb has come** … And the rewards? He has been preparing you for that wedding. It was God's plan. Did you notice that … **Fine linen, bright and clean, was given her to wear? (Fine linen stands for the righteous acts of God's holy people).** Notice those righteous acts are *given* to them. They are *given* salvation by Christ, but also *given* righteous acts to make themselves ready. The apostle Paul put it this way …

> For we are God's handiwork, created in Christ Jesus to do good works, which God prepared in advance for us to do (Eph. 2:10).

It's God *preparing* those works, but in Revelation it is revealed the works weren't just prepared, but *given* for the bride to 'make herself ready'. It was given for the richness of the wedding banquet. It was the Lord who prepared the fine linen for her. It was all a plan despite the evil motives and trials Babylon put you through. God was using it to make you ready for the fullness of the reward of the wedding banquet.

But what we are learning here in Revelation as the curtain is pulled back is that this is the bigger plan behind our trials. It was a wedding plan. Preparation had to be made. All of history comes down to this, this plan was always in the mind of God. Here the curtain is not only pulled back on history, but on *your* history. Yes, with Satan behind her Babylon was at war against you, and you went through much pain to maintain your witness. You didn't give up on Jesus despite the tears. You fought on in your secret life and public witness, and now you find that none of it was wasted. All along it was the master plan of God to transform and refine you and *give* you individual reward for those 'righteous acts'. They follow you. All those things you did and trials you went through were a preparation for the wedding.

So what are you going through now, in pain or trial? I can tell you. Preparation … for the wedding! You are entering into the sufferings and becoming like Christ. This also means that in this life you are growing in a more intimate relationship that could be achieved no other way.

Jesus said he is looking forward to this wedding when he will drink the wine anew with you on that day! So this 'preparation' is connected with *coming out* of Babylon and the *coming into* a more intimate fellowship with the Lord. The apostle Paul spoke of this …

> … As God has said: 'I will live with them and walk among them, and I will be their God, and they will be my people.' 'Therefore, come out from them and be separate, says the Lord. Touch no unclean thing, and I will receive you.' And, 'I will be a Father to you, and you will be my sons and daughters, says the Lord Almighty.' Therefore, since we have these promises, dear friends, let us purify ourselves from everything that contaminates body and spirit, perfecting holiness out of reverence for God (2 Cor. 6:16c-7:1).

This is our motive. We already have these promises of God, so we purify ourselves. And now we know it's all a plan. In this tent we groan, waiting to be fully clothed. The fine linen. Waiting for the wedding! God had a reason. God outsmarted the devil. God is such a genius. He was not simply letting evil go and eventually saying, 'All right that's enough, now it is time for Judgment Day.' It is far more profound than that. It's like the cross of Christ itself. Genius happened there. The very thing that the devil thought was his victory, God was using for his defeat and the victory of the bride. So too, Babylon was causing the suffering of God's people. All the while it was part of God's great plan to prepare them for the fullness of what they would experience in their joy at the wedding. The full 'blessing'.

> Then the angel said to me, 'Write this: '<u>Blessed</u> are those who are invited to the wedding supper of the Lamb!' And he added, 'These are the true words of God' (19:9).

When you take the Lord's Supper you not only look back at Jesus' work on the cross, but you also look forward to this wedding banquet ('until he comes'). But then you have to go back into your week with Babylon trying to drag you down and you forget again about that wedding you were so looking forward to. It all seems to drag on. When you read the stories of triumph in the Bible, like Abraham and Sarah rejoicing over having a child in their old age, and Joseph becoming the leader in Egypt, we say, 'Ah, yes God's plan.' But if you were Sarah waiting a lifetime for a child, or Joseph in jail year after year of the best years of your life that you can never get back, you might not be so matter of fact saying, 'Well, it is all God's work for good.' Or the man lame for 38 years or the man blind all his life before Jesus healed them ... we know it was for good, but what if it is you living through those years? And everyone just says to you, 'Don't worry, it will all work out for good.' What good can God possibly be doing and why so long, oh Lord? Well, this is explained in Revelation, but it can only be taken hold of by faith and it's this—none of our longest trials are wasted. They are all preparation for the wedding.

We looked at this in relation to the suffering church at Smyrna in Rev. 2:8-11. But we are given more revelation in this text so it's worth recapping. Atheist scholars have argued that if God was able to create a world without sin in the Garden of Eden, and bring perfection in heaven where people can't sin, then why didn't he make it all perfect from the beginning and skip the whole problem of evil in between? Thus, their argument is that God couldn't or wouldn't do that, so God is not powerful enough, not good enough, or doesn't exist.

But the atheists miss a big point. They assume a relationship with God and the heavenly rewards could be as rich and glorious if God's people had never been allowed to fall, and if God had never revealed his glory in the cross. They assume the *wedding* would be as exciting and enjoyable. But it couldn't. It had to have this *preparation*. For this wedding to be all that it is, man had to go through the fall. The Son of God had to go to the cross *and* you had to go through your preparation! Yes, the choice of man to sin was real. The evil of the fall was man's fault, not God's. Yes, God allowed that choice. But God was not outsmarted. He actually used that choice and the fall as a *preparation* for the wedding, and his rescue plan will heighten the experience of love and triumph in that wedding, and increase the richness of the reward—eternally.

This doesn't mean that God needs evil to show love. The message is that *despite* the reality of evil, God outsmarts the enemy and shows an even greater love. God has been *preparing his bride* throughout history through suffering, and your individual call to suffering and righteous acts, to bring about a love and relationship on a level that could not come about any other way. It's all a plan. A wedding plan!

Those who deny God because they believe he lets this world go on in evil are mistaken because they don't know the plan! We also note (again) that the sinless angels who will share heaven with us will *never* experience the joy of heaven and a relationship with God in the same way that redeemed human sinners will. They never experienced evil in themselves (sin), but neither can they experience the depth of the love of a God who would give his own Son for me, the sinner. This text shows us another reason they won't experience heaven in the same way. It's because they haven't been through the *preparation!*

God, in *making his bride ready,* is also showing that his love cannot be beaten. *Love will triumph!* Jesus wins. God doesn't just punish evil and Babylon—his love triumphs over evil and Babylon.

So that great question comes up again. If God knew that he would have to put up with so much evil and condemn many into hell just to save and bless some, is it really worth it? Well, the answer hasn't changed. Take a look at the cross! The cross says that God thought it was worth it. The cross removes the idea that God is just dispassionately working out a plan that could be one of many options. God is not playing a game with history. God sent his only Son into this evil world to take the full weight of punishment that his people deserved. There was no other way. Jesus asked if there was another way, '... *My Father, if it is possible, may this cup be taken from me*' (Matt. 26:39). But the Father's silence from heaven was deafening. No! There was no other way. And there is no other way God could make you ready for the wedding but through your trials.

What works is he doing in your life? Pain or hardship? Loneliness?

Enduring a difficult marriage? Health issues? Battling a temptation that never seems to leave? Have you understood how the Lord has been making you ready for the wedding? None of the people like Abraham, or Joseph, or the man lame for 38 years, or the man blind since birth probably understood *at the time,* through all those years of trouble, what God was doing. So you may not understand it either. But the question is … do you believe? Do you trust God?

This text is also showing us that there is more to come than just judgment for evil. Revelation is revealing that your works will follow you. The fine linen is being woven. You are making yourself ready for the wedding banquet. Do you believe it? Are you a *believer?*

We cry with the Psalmist … *How long oh Lord?* (Psalm 13). This is the cry of God's people as far back as 3000 years ago when King David cried it… *How long oh Lord?* The answer is still the same: As long as it takes! As long as it takes to make you ready for the greatest joyous ecstasy of the greatest wedding banquet.

The wedding preparation God has given you is not just about you either. His plan includes those who cross your path, such as the souls of your spouse, children, parents, and friends. The souls of the people who cross your path are at stake on how you take hold of the fine linen (works) he has prepared for you. 'You are my witnesses,' says the Lord. God has others planned for this wedding banquet and calls you to be a witness to them. That too is part of the righteous acts he gave you.

So this is what life was all about. A wedding banquet! The goal and culmination of life climaxes in a party! A wedding party! Think of those times of joy when you enjoyed a special wedding. Well, this one won't disappoint. When the bride appears and comes face to face with the bridegroom—sitting down to the wedding supper with him. And oh, what a bridegroom! Picture it from the imagery of Revelation. He will wipe every tear from their eyes, and he will be with them and be their God. Jesus said many will come from the east and the west and will take their places at the *feast* with Abraham, Isaac and Jacob in the kingdom of heaven. And all the *preparation* was worth it.

'Let us rejoice and be glad and give him glory! For the wedding of the Lamb has come, and his bride has <u>made herself ready</u>. Fine linen, bright and clean, was given her to wear.' (Fine linen stands for the righteous acts of God's holy people). Then the angel said to me, 'Write this: Blessed are those who are invited to the wedding supper of the Lamb!' And he added, 'These are the true words of God' (19:7-9).

Study Questions

1. What is the overall reason this wedding banquet scene is given to readers?

2. How are 19:7 and 19:8 connected?

3. What is the connection between Babylon's evil in Rev. 18 and the wedding in Rev. 19?

4. The Lord has individually 'given' you righteous acts for individual reward. How does this reflect in your life now?

5. In what ways is God 'making her ready' for the wedding banquet?

6. How can you respond from this text to someone who says that God cannot exist because of evil?

7. Does God need evil to show how good he is?

8. Why won't sinless angels experience joy in heaven in the same measure as the saints?

9. What overriding factor shows that God's unfolding history is not arbitrary or random?

10. The Psalmist cries, 'How long, O Lord?', but what must happen to signify the answer to that question?

15
Marriage
(Revelation 19:7-9)

We have found the meaning of life. A wedding planned from the beginning which climaxes in Rev. 19. Scholars like William Hendriksen have noted a similarity in the Bible story compared to an ancient world marriage.[17] John, the apostle, sees this beautiful wedding banquet, but in John's day, marriage had a certain procedure. The first thing was the announcement of a betrothal. The betrothal was considered as binding as marriage. (That's why in the gospels Joseph felt he needed to divorce Mary even before they were married, before Joseph understood how she became pregnant. They weren't yet married, but they were *betrothed*.) During the betrothal time the groom has time to pay the dowry to the father of the bride and gives the bride time to *make herself ready* (19:7). After the betrothal interval the groom comes with his friends to the bride's home to collect her, then takes her back to his home. Then you have the wedding banquet which lasted for seven days! ('Seven' makes it sound like a nice, 'complete' banquet.)

We can follow this line of thinking to understand the Bible's marriage story which climaxes here in Rev. 19. First the betrothal—the bride was chosen. She was *chosen* from before the creation of the world (Eph. 1:4). Then the wedding was announced. We know it was announced from the OT to the NT. The Messiah was prophesied. Then the Son comes, which is betrothal time when the Son pays the dowry price. What was the price for this wedding? It was the greatest price of all. The cross! The price was paid! It is finished! Then the bride *made herself ready* through the righteous acts of the saints (19:7-8). It's a life of faith and transformation which prepared God's

---

[17] William Hendriksen, *More than Conquerors*, (Grand Rapids Michigan: Baker Book House, 1967) p. 214-215

people (the bride) for the wedding. Then the bridegroom returns home, and that is where we are up to now. The wedding of the Lamb has come!

> Then the angel said to me, 'Write this: Blessed are those who are invited to the wedding supper of the Lamb!' And he added, 'These are the true words of God' (19:9).

Some people get confused here and say those invited to the wedding party must be different from those who are the bride, because a bride is not just one of the guests. That's true, but this is a vision. The bride of Christ is not one person but *all* the people of the church. If we want to press it literally we get into all kinds of trouble. The bride is millions of people, so does that mean Jesus is a polygamist? No. This is just a beautiful picture of the closeness of Jesus and his people. A meal together in the ancient world is a sign of closeness. This supper is like having a close intimate dinner with someone you have always wished you could meet and be with, but it turns out even better than you could have imagined. **Blessed are those who are invited to the wedding supper of the Lamb!** This is a beautiful picture. Can you picture sitting down to a meal with Jesus? Yes, reunion with others you know, but primarily it's about being with Jesus!

Notice the way the King of kings is described at his wedding. We are so used to it that we forget how strange this is. The bridegroom, Jesus, is described as the *Lamb*. This kind of takes away the romance a little. And here is your husband ... a lamb. But it's not odd because it reminds us of the center of all history *and* the central point of heaven. The cross of Christ! This is how much I have loved you! Slain from the creation of the world (13:8). You will see much more of this love when you see face to face.

This text is also the perfect wedding that our marriages are meant to reflect. So can we learn anything from this in relation to our earthly marriages? As we have noted, the Bible connects earthly marriage with the heavenly one. So the perfection of the ultimate marriage should teach us *principles* about our earthly marriages.

First of all, we have noted this picture is interesting for its choice of symbol from the point of view of a husband. A Lamb. Not a lion. Perhaps we husbands were hoping that the symbol of the husband who leads his wife might have at least been portrayed in his victory as a warrior, as Jesus is depicted later in Rev. 19 riding a white horse! Now that's us fellas! Soldiers. Macho-men. Riding in on your horse. But at the wedding banquet Jesus is described as a lamb. The Lamb who laid down his life for his wife.

> Husbands, love your wives, just as Christ loved the church and <u>gave himself up for her</u> (Eph. 5:25).

It's not the emphasis we husbands or 'would be' husbands are looking for. We are looking for the bit about wives submitting to their husbands. So if Jesus, as a husband and leader, was a lamb, does that mean all this stuff about husbands as the head over his wife cancels itself out and there is no real leader? No, the role remains, but husbands be careful, because you will be held accountable as to whether you gave yourself up for your wife as Jesus did. So leadership decisions have to be with your wife's best interest always. That's the way Jesus leads his church. As a lamb, giving himself up for his bride.

So this picture of Jesus as a lamb counters any idea of domineering headship. Who *is* the boss? A lamb that lays down his life for his wife. People who say the biblical roles are against equality miss the whole point. The roles in marriage are given to reflect Christ and the church, so it doesn't mean men are given the role as head of the family because they are superior or more suited to headship (in many marriages they are not!). That is not the point. The roles are not something created by domineering men (despite those who have abused their role). Marriage was invented by God to reflect the ultimate marriage here in Rev. 19, not to determine who is superior. And you see this picture in that *blessed are those invited*. It's a picture of bliss and serenity, of unity and love. So if you're married you could ask, 'Is my marriage progressing like this?'

The sacrificial leading of the Lamb who is the head is complemented by the submission of the bride. This picture in Rev. 19 is our destiny as believers. This is the meaning of life, and earthly Christian marriage is all about reflecting this meaning! So how is it going? Are you reflecting what your marriage was created for?

When an engine is badly out of tune it can splutter and backfire. Marriages get like that if you are out of tune with the Lord in how you are living. If you are having trouble in your marriage do a checklist. Husband, if you are not giving yourself up for your wife, and wife, if you are not submitting to and respecting your husband, then you are not living in tune with your role as given by God. So don't be perplexed as to why things are not what they should be. You are out of tune with God's created plan for marriage, which is to reflect Jesus and his bride and this beautiful picture here!

Rev. 19 is a wedding that is the restoration and pinnacle of the whole Bible story. It's a wedding that was planned from the creation, as was your marriage—that includes if you are single and going to be married one day. God gave you *your* spouse. We need to look at the sovereignty of God. Eph. 1:4 said he chose us in him! God chose us! From before the creation of the world. That is speaking of our salvation. But can't you see what that tells us about God? It's a plan. God chose! He is sovereign over all things. So God also chose *your spouse* from before the foundation of the world. We have to see God's eternal plan in our lives. So husbands need to stop looking to the left or to the right at other women. Husband love *your* wife (the one God gave you). Not just when she lives up to her role. And wife, leave out the hypotheticals as to what your husband *should be*. Wife, respect *your* husband. The one God gave you, not the hypothetical he doesn't live up to. This means that you don't just respect him when he is worthy, but respect him as *your* husband with his limitations now. So don't compare your spouse to anyone, or even a hypothetical of what they 'should' be. Enter into God's plan.

For single people, the hypothetical is just as deadly. Living in the hypothetical when God has said in his providence 'now is not the right time for marriage', is following another god of your imagination. Pastorally, I have found there is one thing worse than a miserable single person who wishes they were married. It's the miserable married person who wishes they were single! Look at the sovereignty of God in your life. If you are single, God has given you that for now. So enter into God's plan for *now!*

Now we can look at the blessedness of the wedding banquet in Rev. 19. It's because the bride is united to Christ. Something would be terribly wrong if you could squeeze unbelievers into this wedding banquet! And so, in our reflecting *this* marriage, the Lord commands a Christian not to marry a non-Christian. We are to reflect the unity in Christ of this marriage. The apostle Paul tells the Corinthians not to be unequally yoked with an unbeliever (2 Cor. 6:14). Paul even tells widows that if they remarry, they should only marry in the faith.

> A woman is bound to her husband as long as he lives. But if her husband dies, she is free to marry anyone she wishes, but he must belong to the Lord (1 Cor. 7:39).

As if to underline this, when Jesus says, 'What God has joined let man not separate', Matthew and Mark write Jesus' words using a Greek word (translated *joined*) that is so rare in the NT it only appears in this and one other place. The other time is when the apostle Paul uses the same word for *joined* when he says we should not be unequally *joined* or *yoked*. It's as though Paul has in mind Jesus' words on marriage when he says not to be unequally yoked.

So it's also wrong for a Christian to date a non-Christian, as it puts one or both in a manipulative position or temporarily uses the other. If the relationship develops it's either, 'Since you didn't become a Christian I have to dump you.' Or the Christian gets so emotionally involved they find it hard to get out at all. But even if we didn't have these direct commands in Scripture that our marriage partner must belong to the Lord, surely this passage in Rev. 19 would tell us on a practical level that it only makes sense. To be a part of the ultimate wedding, we have to be united with Christ and with others of faith. But if you are already unequally yoked, joined with an unbelieving spouse through no fault of your own (such as you were converted after marriage or you were never taught properly), you can probably testify how being unequally yoked can cause all kinds of confusion for your children (praise God he even covers that, 1 Cor. 7:14).

But whether you are married or single, the picture we should see in Revelation is this ultimate bliss and blessedness (*blessed are those who are invited into the wedding banquet*). This is a picture of heaven, and we need to be reminded we are not in heaven yet. The happiest earthly marriage cannot give completeness. There is always something incomplete in this life until we reach *this* wedding. That is why this book of Revelation was written. Despite the tribulation you face, there is an end to it. Jesus wins! Look at the blessedness.

The closest thing to heaven on earth is a deeper relationship with the Lord. If you are not able to find fullness in him, you will never find it in earthly marriage. In fact, if you don't find that fullness in the Lord, then marriage can make things worse. That's why many married people struggle. They set up marriage as an idol. Christ plus marriage for completeness is like Christ plus anything. It can't work. When you discover your marriage partner can't supply that completeness and happiness, you discover two defective relationships. Your dependency on Christ alone was not what it should be, and the marriage will be a disastrous disappointment because your spouse didn't fulfill you either.

So am I saying marriage is not all it's cracked up to be? Is the answer to the great theological question *What is the great tribulation?* — marriage? By no means! Marriage is a beautiful blessing, as long as it's kept in perspective and not turned into an idol. The magical answer to fulfillment is not married life or single life. The answer is to find our all in Christ!

We need to keep our text of Revelation in perspective. This is a picture of home for the believer. The picture of unending joy. Blessed are those who are at this wedding banquet. What we have now is a fallen world, and we sinners are on a pilgrimage to the Promised Land. *Everything* in this life is imperfect. The apostle Paul said there are advantages and disadvantages in both married and single life (1 Cor. 7). Many Christian people don't ever understand this. Instead they continually look to the greener grass. 'If only I was married it would be better for this, this and this.' Or, 'If I was single I would be freer to serve the Lord in this, this and this.' One of the big mistakes people make is to think that when Paul talks about the gift of singleness, he means people who have that gift are happy about it all the time, free from the weight of temptation or loneliness. Or when Paul talks about love in marriage, he means that calling should be continual blessedness. But the apostle Paul talks about advantages and disadvantages on *both sides*. Unless you accept this, you will always be grumbling and looking to all the advantages of the other side, cast down by the disadvantages. So you never enter into the blessings and advantages of what God has called you to now! Always coveting the advantages of the 'other side', forgetting that it also has disadvantages. Why do we miss this? Because we are not home yet! We need to finish the race to get to *the* wedding banquet to find that perfection. We are betrothed to Christ and yet we are not at the wedding banquet yet. In the meantime, God is working in us for our salvation, and uses all our relationships to refine us and *make us ready* (19:7). This includes single people. All of us are in relationships which test us. But this is most profoundly worked out in marriage. We work out our salvation in our marriages.

Husbands do what? Give yourself up for your wife as Christ did. That is not just a clever way of putting things. It's meant to replicate your salvation. Christ gave himself up for you, but also, it's what you do in coming to Christ. You give yourself up to the Lord when you are saved. But you also do this throughout your life. You offer your body as a living sacrifice (Rom. 12:1). He already bought our salvation, but it's our salvation being *worked out* as husbands (Phil. 2:12). You are 'making yourself ready' (19:7-8) for *the* wedding, *the* salvation, your entrance into glory. Laying down your life is working out your salvation. It's what you were called to do if you are a husband, and God called you to a particular wife to carry this out. 'Oh, but my wife is a hard nut to crack. Why do I have to lay down my life more than other husbands?' Well, actually, it's not just about your wife, it's about you. God chose your wife for you because of what *you* needed in *your* salvation. You see it in 19:7-8 when it says those in the wedding banquet 'made themselves ready'. How did that happen? It's the fine linen that stands for the righteous acts of God's people (19:8)! Through your righteous deeds! Including in your marriage! It was all part of your preparation for *the* wedding.

So husband, laying down your life is not only about her shortcomings, in that you are to nurture her salvation by cleansing her, washing with the word and giving yourself up for her. Laying down your life is also about you! Marriage is so intimately tied to our salvation. We looked at the reason we were predestined, but now we can see it's directly related to our marriage ...

> For those God foreknew he also predestined to be <u>conformed to the image of his Son,</u> that he might be the firstborn among many brothers and sisters (Rom. 8:29).

That is a husband's plan of his salvation. Predestined, to be conformed to the likeness of Christ! How are you going to be conformed to be like Jesus? By doing what Jesus did so profoundly. *Giving yourself up* for your wife! God predestined your wife for you, not to wash the dishes, but so that you'd be conformed to the likeness of Jesus. To 'make yourself ready'!

What about wives? How is marriage about your salvation? How could you miss it? When it says wives submit to your husbands as to the Lord, wives are not simply submitting to the husband because you got the raw end of the deal. This is not just about your husband. It's about your salvation being worked out—*making yourself ready*. You are submitting 'as to the Lord' because it's all about your relationship with Jesus. Oh, but what if he doesn't lay down his life for me? What if the only time he lays down is in front of the TV? It's not just about him, but your salvation! What did we just say to husbands? Predestined to be conformed to the likeness of Jesus.

Wife, your husband was predestined for you in your journey to be conformed to the likeness of Jesus. What did Jesus do more profoundly than anyone ever? Submit! The garden of Gethsemane was the ultimate submission. 'Not my will but your will be done.' This is your *transformation into the image of Christ*. Wives submitting and husbands giving themselves up! All this time we've had all these hang ups about roles in marriage when in fact they were just two sides of the exact same coin. They are what our salvation is all about. How did you come to faith? How are we transformed? We *give ourselves up* and *submit to the Lord* who gave himself up by submitting to the Father. Both are conforming us to be more like Jesus!

So if you really take the Biblical roles seriously, if there is a major decision you have to make, like where to go on your holiday or what color to paint the house, and you just can't come to an agreement, who gets the final say? Well, taking God's given roles seriously it has to be the husband. And husband, what will that decision be? The one where you give yourself up for your wife! How easy is this!

And you thought the purpose of marriage was to make *you* happy. 'Hey this isn't working out. I have difficulties. Children. More difficulties. And I am not feeling complete and happy.' Don't be thrown as though you are supposed to feel happy all the time. You are not at *the* wedding banquet yet! There is something more important to Jesus than even your happiness. It's 'making you ready' for this wedding banquet!

When Judgment Day comes the redeemed sinner will hear, 'Well done, good and faithful servant.' And 'whatever you did to the least of these you did it for me.' Who will Jesus be speaking of when he says, 'When you helped the least of these you did it to me'? Your spouse! You saw each other at your worst and helped each other into the wedding banquet. There was not one moment of giving yourself up and submitting to each other that was wasted. It was all a plan for this wedding banquet.

And until that day, the refining process must go on. So, the fact that we marry a sinner might sound obvious, but if you miss this deep-seated worldview issue it will cause great heartache. Now you say, 'I know, I'm married to a sinner.' But even unbelievers can say that. But do you really know it? The test as to whether you pay lip service to that truth is how upset or annoyed you get at your spouse. Exasperated—by a sinner! Oh, but I know all that. No, you don't! Not if you find it such a big thing that you are dealing with a sinner who sins again and again. You have not accepted that you are married to a sinner. You get exasperated as though you should already be at the wedding banquet. No sinners there. But we are not there yet! This is a worldview issue. The world expects life and marriage should be like the future wedding banquet before we get there!

Another reason why people struggle in marriage is because they have the wrong idea about love. The world's idea of love is that of being owed. 'Hey, I do this for you, so you are supposed to love me.' Or, 'If I submit or give myself up, you should reciprocate.' But how does that idea of marriage compare to the wedding banquet of Rev. 19? What is so special and joyous about that wedding? It's that Jesus is the Lamb. He shows us what true love is. It's not something that is owed. Why did he love you? No reason except this. Grace. It's called grace. Grace is purely unconditional. Ask yourself this question. Have you forgotten grace in your marriage? It is freely given. It is not owed. Grace says that even though you are dealing with a habitual sinner, instead of being annoyed, angry or upset, you do what Jesus did. You offer grace.

If you are struggling in your marriage, the gospel of Jesus can restore it. How? First, understand you are to follow Christ unconditionally. Second, you need to understand what Christ has done for you—grace. And what he has prepared for you. See the end of this great wedding banquet that he has prepared you for.

Then the angel said to me, 'Write this: Blessed are those who are invited to the wedding supper of the Lamb!' And he added, 'These are the true words of God' (19:9).

Study Questions

1. Describe some of the traditions of ancient weddings that can be related to the biblical story.

2. How would you respond to someone who objects that those invited to the wedding must be different from the bride?

3. How can this text be helpful in addressing earthly marriage in the way the bridegroom is depicted?

4. Should Christians marry non-Christians? Why or why not?

5. Why should the blessedness of this wedding supper caution us about what to expect from earthly marriage?

6. What are the advantages and disadvantages in married vs. single life?

7. How do the God-given roles in marriage relate to our salvation?

8. What might indicate whether we have really accepted that we have married a sinner?

9. Have you forgotten grace in your marriage?

16
Jesus' Hidden Name
(Revelation 19:10-16)

John the apostle got so caught up in the moment of seeing these amazing things, like the wedding banquet, that he fell down to worship the angel next to him. But the angel quickly corrects him— *Don't do that!* Then he says, 'Get up and worship only God!' John's slip up in idol worship is not there by accident. Think about the context of the previous chapters. Babylon has fallen. She enticed with her idols. We say, how could Christians fall for worshiping statues, images or worship saints or Mary? But look at this. How could the apostle John fall for worshiping anyone but the Lord? The message from this episode in this little connecting verse is, 'If you think you are standing firm against idolatry, be careful lest you fall.' After John is rebuked for trying to worship the angel, it's as if the next scene says ...

'Do you want to see the one who *really* should cause you to be on your face worshiping?' Look at this new scene. Revelation has been going back and forth with the camera switching between judgment and heaven, then back again. So we are not dealing with a chronological sequence. Before Jesus was depicted as a lamb ... gentle, meek and mild, and the bridegroom rejoicing at the supper. But now this is something John has never seen before. This is a camera angle that John hadn't conceived of before. John looks up and what does he see? He sees *heaven open!* And there in heaven ... who is it? John knows who it is. The Word of God—Jesus! But this is not like 4:1 where John saw a *door* in heaven open and he gets a peek inside. This time *heaven* itself is now *standing open!*

When the disciple Stephen was being stoned to death, he looked up and saw heaven open with Jesus there. Heaven was right there above Stephen. It was not some distant place the other side of Pluto.

It was another dimension, so close that Stephen could clearly see Jesus. It just needed to be opened. Well now it's open for *everyone* to see!

> I saw heaven <u>standing open</u> and there before me was a white horse, whose rider is called Faithful and True. With justice he judges and makes war (19:11).

It's obvious from this description that the rider is Jesus. So why doesn't John just say, 'Hey, there's Jesus! We walked together for three years.' He doesn't say that because this is an awesome new perspective of the one he walked with. If you believe in Jesus—which Jesus? John sees Jesus in a whole new way.

Long before the movie series was made I read the book by J.R.R. Tolkien, *Lord of the Rings*. From the book's depiction of the character Strider, I pictured him to be a tall, gangly hobo who befriended the hobbits along the way. (That is the advantage of reading a book as opposed to watching a movie, you can paint pictures through your own imagination.) So I imagined Strider as a tall, travelling drifter, who looked kind of like an only slightly more dignified version of the cartoon character Goofy. So it really blew me away later in the book when this lanky hobo turned out to be none other than the great king Aragorn, who marries an elf princess. Maybe Tolkien was borrowing from this story of Jesus, the humble carpenter from Galilee who ends up as the conquering king. As the Johnny Cash poem says, a man who ... 'Never traveled more than 200 miles from where he was born. And wherever he did go he usually walked. He never held political office, never wrote a book, never bought a home, never had a family, and never went to college. Here was a man.'[18]

The apostle John walked with this man. John was out fishing when Jesus first called him. They travelled together for three years, often sleeping under the stars. John saw him vulnerable, tired, and hungry. John believed in him.

But which Jesus do you believe in? John never saw anything like this. Just like the *Lord of the Rings* character, a travelling drifter with no place to lay his head, who turns out to be a king. But not any king. The returning King. The conquering King. The King of the universe.

---

[18] *Here was a man* written by Johnny Bond and Tex Ritter

Do you know what John is seeing here? This is the picture of the second coming of Christ! He bursts forth from heaven! **I saw heaven standing open and there before me was a <u>white horse</u>** ... You didn't know there were horses in heaven, but it is a powerful symbol. The ancient world tradition was that a king returning from a battle victory rode a white horse down the main street of his home city with his army in tow. Now here comes the ultimate conqueror! The warrior. And how scary is this. He makes war. On the white horse, the **rider is called Faithful and True. With justice he judges and <u>makes war</u>.** His conquering is based on the name he is called—*Faithful and True*. This is one of the great aspects of his conquering. All the promises of God are 'Yes' and 'Amen' in Jesus. Before the end of Rev. 19, you see the promises going back to Genesis 3, the war against the serpent. The promise was that one born of the woman would crush the head of the serpent. Well, here he is! It took longer than you were hoping, but that doesn't matter now you can see firsthand he is *Faithful and True* to that promise.

There are also the promises of the OT to bring the Messiah who would deliver his people. The promise was of judgment to come on the Day of the Lord. Again, he is *faithful and true*. Here it is!

Through the years we put up with unbelievers scoffing at a world filled with evil who said, 'How can a loving God allow this?' But now we see *with justice he judges*. He said he would bring justice—now it's here. He *makes war!* He is proved Faithful and True. Now John sees him face to face. John believed all those promises. We believe them too, but sometimes it is hard to live by faith. The promises of God are that he will work all things together for good for his people. But sometimes we wonder how he can do it. How can he make everything that's happened in my suffering in the past work for good?

But take a look at this ... John sees it. He said he was coming back and here it happens! The conquering King. He brings his people with him for their reward. He proves *Faithful and True* after all. Unbelievers denied he could or would do it. Many believers were tossed to and fro by the tribulation of life. They despaired. But here Jesus is proved right. Now he is vindicated as *Faithful and True*.

But it gets even more awesome! Do you think you believe in Jesus? Which Jesus do you believe in? Is this the picture of Jesus you have?

> His <u>eyes are like blazing fire</u>, and on his head are many crowns. He has a name written on him that no one knows but he himself (19:12).

John had already seen the awesome sight of Jesus where his **eyes are like blazing fire** (1:14). The eyes of the Judge. The Day of Judgment is not just when every eye will see *him,* but when his blazing eyes will see *you,* and will look right into your heart. I thought it was scary enough when this girl I knew appeared one day wearing colored contact lenses! So what will it be like when the Judge of men and women appears with eyes like a blazing fire? He is the one who *with justice he judges and makes war.* Did you get that? This isn't gentle Jesus meek and mild anymore. He makes war! He is the most awesome warrior you have ever seen. He doesn't need human weapons. His eyes are fires of X-ray. He can see straight into your heart. He always could ...

> Nothing in all creation is hidden from God's sight. Everything is uncovered and laid bare before <u>the eyes</u> of him to whom we must give account (Heb. 4:13).

But now *you can see* those eyes that can see into your heart. Do you know what this picture in Revelation is teaching? These are symbols teaching us how Jesus will appear to us when he bursts forth from heaven on that day. A conquering king whose piercing gaze no one can escape. Heaven will be opened. Think about this. Jesus is poised right now like this in heaven waiting for this moment. It will happen unexpectedly—like a thief in the night. But meditate on this. Even now those eyes are looking from heaven into what is really in your heart now. He can see your struggles. But he can also see if you are secretly holding back a part of your heart from him. He can see if you are saved or if you are still lost. You can hide your secret sins from the world, but he sees it all so clearly through those eyes of fire, and one day you will see those blazing eyes face to face.

This verse also tells us he wears **many crowns.** He is King of all kings. John is seeing the Lord not as the carpenter from Nazareth, when he returns he will look like the King of the universe!

And **He has a name written on him that no one knows but he himself.** This could mean that no one but the Lord himself will ever know the name, or it could mean a name that *was* known only to him, but now Revelation is revealing it. For example, we are told no one but he knows the name written on him, but only a few verses later in this revelation *of* Jesus (1:1) we read the *name written* on him ...

> On his robe and on his thigh he has this name written: KING OF KINGS AND LORD OF LORDS (19:16).

Is this the name now revealed? It's **written** on him. In fact, he is given three names in this text, *Faithful and True* (19:11), *the Word of God* (19:13), and **King of kings and Lord of lords** (19:16). All of these reveal his true character. His true name. This is what 'name' means in the Bible. God's name is more than just a word. It is his character. It is *who* he is. Hallowed be your name!

John knows Jesus as much as any man who ever lived on earth. But when he sees him as the King of kings and Lord of lords, there will never be a full comprehension of the wonder of his name. He is the Lamb who became the great conquering King. The only one who can open the seals and carry out God's plan. Can anyone really know the fullness of God's name? He became a Lamb who was slain, but returns as a conquering king. Jesus really is incomprehensible. Before he came riding a donkey. Now he rides the conquering white horse. If a person's name is meant to capture their character, it's not hard to say Jesus' name is 'unfathomable'. Only he really knows it. Only God fully knows God. Only he knows the depth of his name. We might know the words of his name, but we will spend a billion years in eternity lost in the wonder, love and praise of who this great conquering King really is, this Lord of lords, and even then, we won't have even begun to understand the fullness of that name. Remember the wedding plan? The God who before the creation always saw himself slain? It was him! Who is this conquering king?

Do you believe in Jesus? Which Jesus? This scene is not the Lamb. This scene is Psalm 2. The kings of the earth rebelled. Be warned, be wise, but they didn't. And look who shows up! It's not Strider! Even when you know the words of his names you still don't fully know. Look at *this* name.

> He is dressed in a robe dipped in blood, and his name is the Word of God (19:13).

Another name! **The Word of God.** What an amazing identification. God is a speaking God. God communicates. And he did that most profoundly through Jesus, who is the Word of God. He is the final Revelation of God. By him all things were created (John 1:3). How? The creative power of the whole cosmos was in this *Word* of God.

> By the <u>word</u> of the LORD were the heavens made, their starry host by the breath of his mouth. (Ps. 33:6).

The power to create is in that word. How did Jesus stop the storm? His word! The whole *creation* is subject to his word. In the beginning was the Word, the Word was with God and the Word was God. But there is still more to this Word of God. His word created this universe but also sustains the universe …

> The Son is the radiance of God's glory and the exact representation of his being, <u>sustaining all things</u> by his powerful <u>word</u> (Heb. 1:3a).

Sustaining how many things? *All things!* How? *By his powerful word!* Have you thought about that? Do you think you believe in Jesus? Which Jesus do you believe in? How do planets and solar systems line up to enable life and an ordered universe? Some say by laws of nature. But why should there be laws? Did the planets just figure this out themselves? What keeps them sustained in laws so that we don't have chaos with planets colliding and the cosmos destroying itself? It's Jesus! That's how far the people of the earth want to deny this Word. They would rather say the planets figured it out themselves! One word from Jesus in heaven and the planets fall into *chaos!* He sustains the planets. He sustains *all things!* One word from him in heaven right now and your very next breath will be your last.

His word has power to save (1 Pet. 1:23). In fact, even heaven and earth will pass away but his words will never pass away (Matt. 24:35). *And now* we are told that same power of the Word is being unleashed. To do what? To judge! This is the day! If there was enough power in that Word to create the universe and sustain it, what hope do you think you have now when he uses that word to judge sinners? This conquering King wins! That's why it says … **He is dressed in a robe dipped in blood.** The robe in blood is not symbolizing his work on the cross this time. He is not the Lamb here. This signifies what he has come to do as *judge*. The Judge comes and will *spill* blood. We will see that the sword comes out of his mouth (19:15). He speaks and the world comes into being. He speaks and men are saved. He speaks and men are judged! All by the *Word of God!*

How powerful is the word of God? Now can you see how imperative it is to read it and be transformed by it! And be saved from judgment by believing it and trusting in it! Because what John sees is what we will all see. The Word of God personified. His name means so much more than John can comprehend. 'John, were you there when I created the universe by my Word?' How awesome is this one who is called the Word of God? Do you know Jesus? Which Jesus?

This is a picture of the end of history. This is a living word picture of what you will see when you see Jesus. Blood. Fire in his eyes. You can fool people to think that you really walk with him. You can even fool yourself. But when you see those piercing eyes, your heart is laid bare.

> The armies of heaven were <u>following him</u>, riding on white horses and dressed in fine linen, white and clean (19:14).

His armies are also on victorious white horses. Angels might be included in those armies, but this scene is connected with 17:14, where Jesus is also called Lord of lords and King of kings.

> 'They will wage war against the Lamb, but the Lamb will triumph over them because he is Lord of lords and King of kings—and <u>with him will be his called, chosen and faithful followers</u>' (17:14).

With him are his faithful followers. *All* the armies of heaven. Maybe this is what Paul meant when he said we would judge with Jesus. But we need to keep perspective because Jesus is the only one with blood on his robe to judge. But when this happens **the armies of heaven were following him, riding on white horses.** The only thing that counts on this day is which army you are with. This is *the* war! This also supports the interpretation that the battle of Armageddon is Judgment Day. There the nations were gathered for a *war* also. But what sort of war? We noted in Rev. 16 that in this war the humans lose the battle. Now we see the confirmation that the same 'war' mentioned here (19:11) is in fact the Day of Judgment. On this day there are only two sides. The world's armies where the kings of the earth take their stand—and Jesus' army that he marched to the ends of the earth. His soldiers put their pride, money, self-glory, and plans to one side to join Jesus' army to take his message of rescue to the ends of the earth. So often it looked like they were losing, but his soldiers knew this day would come. Now the conquering king comes in person and his army is with him. This day it's too late to swap allegiances. It will be revealed whose side you were on. There is no neutral ground. Were you part of his army, or did you desert? Did you go back to the old leaders of the flesh? Did you support Jesus' army with its battle? Did you spend that time seeking to be there for someone, or to build a relationship with a non-believer to share the gospel? Did you support a Bible study, a prayer meeting; or encourage fellow soldiers in their fight? Which army were you fighting for? Or were you too busy to join the army?

Jake Bilardi was an 18-year-old from Melbourne, Australia, who was recruited by Islamic State and committed suicide for their cause. This young guy went from being an Aussie atheist to an Islamic suicide bomber. Did he hear the gospel in between? They are all around you now. People who are hurting, confused, or suicidal. It looks like our army is losing, but then comes this time ...

> Coming out of his mouth is a sharp sword with which to strike down the nations. 'He will rule them with an iron scepter.' He treads the winepress of the fury of the wrath of God Almighty (19:15).

Here is that sharp sword as the word of God coming out of his mouth! This is partly from Isaiah 11:4, but primarily from Revelation's favorite Psalm ...

> I will proclaim the LORD'S decree: He said to me, 'You are my Son; today I have become your Father. Ask me, and I will make the nations your inheritance, the ends of the earth your possession. You will break them with a rod of iron; you will dash them to pieces like pottery' (Ps. 2:7-9).

It's the same in our text. **He will rule them with an iron scepter.** Now it all makes sense. Why do the nations rage? They plot in vain. If you didn't find your refuge in the Son, then he will terrify you in his wrath and rule with an iron scepter.

Also, **He will tread the winepress of the fury of the wrath of God Almighty.** The kings of the earth took their stand against the Lord and his anointed. They would not come under his rule. 'Let us break their chains. Release us from this king. We will *rule* ourselves.' And it all comes down to this: His robe is marked with blood. His eyes are like fire. The sword comes out of his mouth. He makes war. How does that reconcile with the Lamb, Jesus, who so loved the world that he gave himself up? Weren't you listening? Jesus *first* came riding a donkey proclaiming peace with God, but now after the ages, the King returns riding a white horse waging war. The day of grace allowing men to claim kingship and lordship over themselves and others has finished.

Didn't he warn us all this was going to happen? How many times have we read in all those parables from gentle Jesus, about the king who would return? The kingdom of heaven is like …? Like a *king* going on a long journey, one day the King returned to settle accounts. He told you! The kingdom of heaven is like a *king* who gathered the nations. Then the *King* will say to those on his right … and those on his left … all those parables. He told you! *He* was that king!

> On his robe and on his thigh he has this name written: KING OF KINGS AND LORD OF LORDS (19:16).

Every possible name that has been raised up to claim to be a king or leader or idol or important one, the great, the rich and famous, every ideology and power that has made the claim—now the truth is to be fully revealed! Now we know there is only one true King of kings and Lord of lords. Jesus wins. All those who want to win and be vindicated in this world are dashed. Right now, if you want to win in this life, if you want to get your pound of flesh, if you want your justice in this life—repent! There is only one who will win. There is only one who will be vindicated. There's only one King of kings and Lord of Lords. Stop trying to be king! Join *his* army!

What about all those who thought they had an answer. 'Yeah, if your Jesus is real then what about evolution? What about all that suffering? You can't answer that!' And they raged, arguing against him. But whose word turns out to be right? Yours? Or Jesus'? The Word of God wins!

So you think you believe in Jesus? Which Jesus? Do you still believe in Jesus like 'Strider'? Jesus riding on a donkey or walking along with his disciples? If you believe in Jesus as the Lamb of God, Savior and Lord of heaven, then 50 million years into eternity you still won't have come close to grasping or comprehending all the things known only to him. You haven't even begun to know! This is the conquering king. He *is* the King of kings and Lord of lords! Now you know in part but when you see face to face ...

On his robe and on his thigh he has this name written: <u>KING OF KINGS AND LORD OF LORDS</u> (19:16).

Study Questions

1. What was the point of including John falling down to worship an angel?

2. John already believed in Jesus, so why is this scene a 'Revelation' for him?

3. Why is Jesus called the 'Faithful and True'?

4. How does Jesus 'make war'?

5. Does Jesus literally have eyes like fire? What does it mean?

6. What does it mean when it says that only Jesus knows his name, if it is written for us in 19:16?

7. What are the different names Jesus is given in this text and what do they mean?

8. What is the significance of the armies of heaven 'following him'?

9. Does this text challenge you about being a part of his army?

10. Does this text challenge your perception of Jesus?

17
The War
(Revelation 19:17-21)

The rider on the white horse has arrived. He has arrived to fight a war! What war? In our previous text John saw this awesome sight with heaven opened and a rider on a white horse who wages war. But what kind of war is this? Now we find out ...

> And I saw an angel standing in the sun, who cried in a loud voice to all the birds flying in midair, 'Come, gather together for the great supper of God, ...' (19:17).

We notice there is almost a parody here. Satan has been mimicking throughout history and now the tables are turned. We have just finished the first half of Rev. 19, the great story of the glorious wedding supper. Well, if you are not invited to the wedding supper you get to go to another supper, but the menu doesn't seem quite as appetizing. **Come, gather together for the great supper of God ...**

> '..., so that you may eat the flesh of kings, generals, and the mighty, of horses and their riders, and the flesh of all people, free and slave, great and small' (19:18).

It's the same kind of ugly imagery we read in Ezekiel 38, 39:4, 11, 15, 17-20, describing the defeat of Gog and Magog. What has that got to do with Revelation? And why are Gog and Magog also mentioned in Rev. 20? Well, Revelation is doing what it has been doing all along, using OT places, names and events, such as Sodom, Egypt, the Exodus and Babylon, and applying them in a far more profound and far reaching way. OT history was all part of God's much bigger plan. And it doesn't get any bigger than this. Gog and Magog were real historical nations which pointed forward to an even greater fulfillment than just a judgment on the land of Magog. All nations!

I would have thought it was obvious that this text is speaking of the physical return of the King Jesus. But the Preterist disagrees. The Preterist interprets most of Revelation as occurring before AD 70 and says even this event is not the second coming of Christ. The Preterist points out that Jesus is to come back the same way he left, and he didn't leave riding a white horse! That's a good argument against anyone who takes the images of Revelation literally, but as I keep pointing out, Revelation itself told us to take these images symbolically. We have already noted the white horse was an ancient symbol of a returning victorious king. The Preterist says this episode is describing Jesus spreading the gospel, not his return. To me that leaves a lot unexplained in this text. Not least of all, this graphic language of bodies being eaten and enemies thrown alive into the lake of fire. That doesn't sound like people being saved through the gospel.

The Futurist agrees with my Idealist position that this *is* the second coming of Christ, but also says when Jesus comes back it is not for the final judgment of unbelievers, as that doesn't happen for another 1000 years. This battle you see here is against the armies of the world, then Jesus sets up his 1000-year reign on earth. The Futurist takes this vision to be literal (does that mean Jesus *is* literally coming back on a white horse?), and these are literally the armies of the world gathered together to fight Jesus, who returns for a literal worldly war with weapons, to fight it out. Jesus overcomes them and then sets up his 1000-year millennial reign on earth.

We have noted many times how the book of Revelation told us to expect symbolism from very first verse, where John writes that it's a Revelation to 'make known' (1:1) through signs and symbols. The reason I bring this up again is because it's the same root word used here in 19:20 for miraculous 'signs' that John wrote in 1:1 which is translated as 'make known'. So Revelation is teaching in these signs or symbols. If we ignore this and insist on taking these not as visions, but literally, it leaves us with great inconsistencies. To have armies gathering with a plan to fight Jesus before his return would work against everything Jesus said about his coming like a thief, unexpectedly. If the armies of the world were able to prepare in that way to fight Jesus, then the whole world waits in expectation to challenge Jesus ('Let's get our best army tanks and take him on'.) But unbelievers don't even *believe* Jesus is coming back, let alone know *when*. And then *believers* would all be able to plot Jesus' return. 'Hey look, the armies are gathering together. Get ready. Jesus is coming back.' But he will not come with your careful observation. Rather there is heavy symbolism going on here. That is not to say it is meaningless esoteric poetry. Symbols symbolize something! I hope to show here the reality is even worse! Symbols can be a means to describe the indescribable that has never been seen before.

So what is symbolized in this great supper of God? And how gruesome the symbol to **eat the flesh of kings, generals, and the mighty, of horses and their riders, and the flesh of all people**. Notice it wasn't just the great kings, but also the **free and slave, great and small.** It's like the buzzards are hovering to eat their fill. What does this suggest? Answer: You're a dead man! Total defeat. As Jesus said in Luke 17:37 *Where there is a dead body, there the vultures will gather.* This scene would have also stood out to John the apostle, reminding him of the OT where the devouring of bodies is the ultimate degradation in contrast to a proper burial. It's meant to signify the ultimate humiliation! He would have recalled Jezebel, the OT queen who was eaten by dogs.

As I have mentioned before, symbols are always symbolic *of* something, and the reality is worse. Most unbelievers probably wouldn't care if this was literal. They think when you die, you die, and the worms or birds eat your body. So what! You won't know it! But this is far worse than literally dead bodies being eaten! As we will learn from later parts of Revelation, this is conscious, eternal destruction. It's the war to end all wars.

> Then I saw the beast and the kings of the earth and their armies gathered together to wage war against the rider on the horse and his army (19:19).

What battle is this? This is the same scene described back in Rev. 16. This is the battle of Armageddon! The wording in the original Greek language for 'gathering together' is almost identical to the battle of Armageddon in Rev. 16.

> They are demonic spirits that perform signs, and they go out to the kings of the whole world, to gather them for the battle on the great day of God Almighty (16:14).

It's the same wording because it's the same event! In fact, the same wording is used in the later description of the end ...

> ... and will go out to deceive the nations in the four corners of the earth—Gog and Magog—and to gather them for battle. In number they are like the sand on the seashore (20:8).

There is Gog and Magog from Ezekiel again, connecting it with the same event as we have here in Rev. 19. Hasn't Revelation been giving us action replays all the way through from the parallels of the seals, trumpets, and bowls to the action replay of Babylon's fall, etc.?

There is another factor which even more clearly shows that the Rev. 19 war is the same Armageddon in Rev. 16 (and Rev. 20). There is a definite article in the original Greek language before the word **war**, so it literally says, '*the* war'. The article doesn't appear in our English translations because it would be incorrect English grammar. It would look like ... *their armies gathered together to wage THE war against the rider on the horse and his army* (19:19).

In the original Greek language Revelation was written in, that article indicates this is not just talking about any war, but THE *only* war which has already been introduced in Revelation. The *only* war already mentioned as THE war in both Rev. 16 and Rev. 20. The war called the Battle of Armageddon, and the battle against Gog and Magog. The great supper of God. The war. The battle. The end! This is it!

So what is the battle of Armageddon? We looked at it back in 16:16. It's the nations attacking Christ, but Jesus wins. So is this where the idea of the 'One World Government' comes in? This is the popular idea, but we have seen in Revelation the idea of the unifying of nations, kings and powers. But they were not unified as a government, or a single system, or a structure. But they do unite with a common purpose ...

> They have one purpose and will give their power and authority to the beast (17:13).

The kings, or powers of the earth, are of *one purpose,* and they unite and gather in that *one purpose,* which is to oppose Christ. So it doesn't necessarily mean they have to become one Government or a conscious world order. They can be entirely separate, even enemies, in government, ideology, religion or structure. Remember it doesn't matter if it is a closed Muslim country, a communist country, the Western media empire, the entertainment industry or any other entity. They are all powers united with *one purpose*—they are against the Lord and his anointed. Their master, the Beast, represents the worldly powers that the people look to, to win their battle, their powerful hero who has ruled on this earth. They put their hope in his power. The Beast legislates to squeeze out Christianity. But when they unite against Christ, it doesn't go according to their plans. Like a big fish gobbling up the minnows only to have an even bigger fish snatch him up, suddenly ...

> ... the beast was captured and with it the false prophet who had performed the signs on its behalf. With these signs he had deluded those who had received the mark of the beast and worshiped its image ... (19:20).

But the beast was captured! The Beast is suddenly caught playing out of his league, by an infinitely greater, more powerful slayer. **And with him the false prophet.** When we looked at the False Prophet back in Rev. 13, we looked at the many false miracles done in the name of Christ, even great signs from the sky, fire, etc. But in the times we live, there is much more we can see today of false miracles and signs in the sky than any other time in history. We must not forget that the False Prophet (Satan's second beast), is more ecumenical than just the miracles of Christian cults. He doesn't care if his work is inside or outside the church, formal religion or not. In fact, in our lifetime there has been a far greater intensity of the miraculous, including things coming out of the sky, which deludes people into rejecting Christ and into receiving the mark of the Beast and worshiping his image. There is a plethora of false miracles going on today like never before, such as the UFO phenomena! And the Beast has supported it, spending billions promoting it with SETI (Search for Extra Terrestrial Intelligence). Millions of people have claimed to have seen signs in the sky. Near Death Experiences (NDE) have multitudes convinced that heaven is for everyone without the need for a Savior. And there is a frightening similarity between a NDE and an OBE (Out of Body) and UFOs, and even illicit drug use. They all have a spiritual connection between them. Like never before, there is a barrage of the miraculous in the skies. How? Where is it coming from? The UFO experiences may well be real because they come from the *prince of the air* who is able to *transform himself into an angel of light* (2 Cor. 11:14). And all these strange phenomena are 'gathering together' for one purpose to tell us one thing—you don't need Jesus! That is the common message of the UFO experience. 'There is something bigger. You don't need Jesus.'

Does that mean we are closer today to the battle of Armageddon? Well, every day we are always closer to THE war! Closer to the day when *the beast was captured, and with it the false prophet who had performed the miraculous signs on its behalf. With these signs he had deluded those who had received the mark of the beast and worshiped its image. The two of them were thrown alive into the fiery lake of burning sulfur.*

The annihilationists love this. They say hell is not a conscious state and here is the evidence: Thrown into the lake. Eaten up by birds. You won't know a thing! But again, we are dealing with symbols painting a gruesome picture of which the reality can only be worse, because we get the confirmation later in 20:10-11 that their *torment* lasts *forever*. We are also told in 19:20 that they are thrown in while still **alive**. And it's not just the Beast and False Prophet who are caught, but everyone who was following them …

> The rest were killed with the sword coming out of the mouth of the rider on the horse, and all the birds gorged themselves on their flesh (19:21).

We know by now we don't expect Jesus to literally have a sword coming out of his mouth. It's another symbol. He will judge by the word that comes out his mouth! The sword of the Spirit. That word will cut men down on the day when they hear his word … 'Depart from me, you who are cursed, into the eternal fire prepared for the devil and his angels.' That is the same sort of idea Paul uses to describe Jesus' defeat of the lawless one …

> And then the lawless one will be revealed, whom the Lord Jesus will overthrow with the breath of his mouth and destroy by the splendor of his coming (2 Thess. 2:8).

The popular idea today is that the battle of Armageddon is only a lesser judgment, followed by 1000 years of peace during which unbelievers get another chance to repent, and only *then* is the final judgment of the wicked. But this text says he judges in *the* war. This is it! When Jesus comes back there will be no more second chances for anyone when the Beast, the powerful leader, is *captured* and is thrown into the lake of fire. All the Beast's followers, great and small, free and slave, are utterly destroyed. Their flesh is eaten! But what about those armies gathering to fight Jesus?

There is no mention of this war being like human armies duking it out, with Jesus finally gaining the upper hand. When this rider on the white horse arrives for this battle of Armageddon, as we have said previously ... it won't be a fair fight. With the *breath of his mouth he will destroy them*.

The white horse symbolizes conquering. The rider came once as the humble one riding a donkey, now he rides as the conquering King. Who will fall in behind the mighty King and be saved? He takes no prisoners. Well, actually, he takes *only* prisoners, only those who surrender and fall in behind him.

So I disagree with the Preterist that this is a picture of the gospel going forth. This rider has a bloodstained robe. This rider comes only for judgment, not salvation. And those who resist him? They think they have safety in numbers. 'Everybody's doing it!' They gather together, but the conquering King will return and it will be *devastating*. There will be no mercy this time. This is why judgment is described in such graphic terms here. Because it is so richly deserved. The invitation of mercy went forth to the same people. Did you see them in 19:18? It was not just the Beast and False Prophet, but the kings and the slaves, the great and the small. They were offered peace, but said no and rejected him.

Think about this rider. He is the King of kings. If you have complained about evil in this world, however grieved you were, the King was *infinitely* more grieved and angrier, but for the last 2000 years he has held back his anger in patience to give a day of mercy for all who would surrender to the King. But what most people did for the last 2000 years was gather together and *complain* about the length of time God was patient and merciful! Can you believe that? They *complained* about the length of time God was being merciful and long suffering. They used God's mercy and the day of grace as an excuse to unite in their armies *against* him. That was their favorite weapon. 'I could never believe in God because he doesn't stop the evil now.' God's mercy was their main weapon of choice to gather against him. And God *still* gave them more time to repent. More patience, more mercy ... but again, they only gathered against him. So, God holds off with more mercy. It just goes on and on ... no it doesn't! That is the message of this text.

There comes this war. The return of the conquering King! That is why it had to be so graphic. It was to show how richly deserved it all was. The same one who rode with peace of the cross was rejected. Now he comes only with judgment. Let's read the text again and see if you don't agree with me that this is finality. There will be no more judgment after this because there is nothing left to judge ...

And I saw an angel standing in the sun, who cried in a loud voice to all the birds flying in midair, 'Come, gather together for the great supper of God, so that you may eat the flesh of kings, generals, and the mighty, of horses and their riders, and the flesh of <u>all people, free and slave, great and small</u>.' Then I saw the beast and the kings of the earth and their armies gathered together to wage war against the rider on the horse and his army. But the beast was <u>captured</u>, and with it the false prophet who had performed the signs on its behalf. With these signs he had deluded those who had received the mark of the beast and worshiped its image. The two of them were <u>thrown alive into the fiery lake</u> of burning sulfur. <u>The rest of them were killed with <u>the sword coming out of the mouth of the rider</u> on the horse, and all the birds <u>gorged themselves</u> on their flesh (19:17-21).

Study Questions

1. What is the parody in this text?

2. What is the Preterist view of this event? Give points for and against it.

3. What does the Futurist see in this event and give points for and against that view.

4. Where does the concept of 'One World Government' come from? Give arguments for or against.

5. How could the False Prophet Beast be deceiving with miraculous signs in the sky today?

6. What is this war and how do the people gather against the Lord?

7. Does this text teach a final Judgment or partial judgment with Judgment of the wicked still to come?

18
The 1000 Years
(Revelation 20:1-2)

This is the big one. We have come across controversial passages in Revelation before, such as the two witnesses in Rev. 11 and the 144,000 in Rev. 7 and Rev. 14. But without doubt, Rev. 20 is *the* most controversial text in the whole of Revelation. And Revelation is still without doubt the most controversial book in the Bible. And the Bible is still without doubt the most controversial book in history. So surely this time we have the greatest controversy in history! How can we figure it out when geniuses have wrestled against each other for 2000 years? Well remember, you don't have to worry. You can trust me.

No! You know I don't want you to do that! If you don't see it in the Scriptures for yourself, don't believe it. But we won't all agree on this, because this is so difficult that even the most devout Christians have interpreted this differently. So this isn't a test of who is more godly, but perhaps a test of who can show love and charity in keeping secondary issues in proportion the way the Bible encourages us to. I hope you have memorized Paul's list of things of first importance because you might need them here. *These* are the things of first importance. Jesus Christ died according to the Scriptures and he was raised on the third day according to the Scriptures (1Cor. 15:3). Jesus crucified and resurrected is the foundation of our faith and forms the truth on which we stand together. It also becomes a test of whether you are a Christian. Rev. 20 is not on that list of things of first importance! And yet amazingly, some lose sight of that and see *this text* as a test of your Christian faith or how highly you view Scripture.

So even if you don't agree with my view, at least *disagree* with the famous dispensational scholar John Walvoord who says that if you don't agree with his view, it's the equivalent of denying the resurrection or the deity of Christ.[19] In fact, Christians have had different views on these 1000 years from the earliest times. Justin Martyr, around AD 150 rebuked a fellow Christian for using his millennial view as a test of orthodoxy, because as he pointed out even way back then, there were different views on this subject among born again believers.[20] So what's the fuss over? It begins in the first three verses ...

> And I saw an angel coming down out of heaven, having the key to the Abyss and holding in his hand a great chain. He seized the dragon, that ancient serpent, who is the devil, or Satan, and bound him for a thousand years. He threw him into the Abyss, and locked and sealed it over him, to keep him from deceiving the nations anymore until the thousand years were ended. After that, he must be set free for a short time (20:1-3).

And 20:4 continues saying Jesus reigns for these 1000 years! The controversial question is: when is this 1000-year reign of Jesus? Is it a literal 1000 years? There are three major views of this 1000 years or 'millennium'. The first (premillennial), has two main strands.

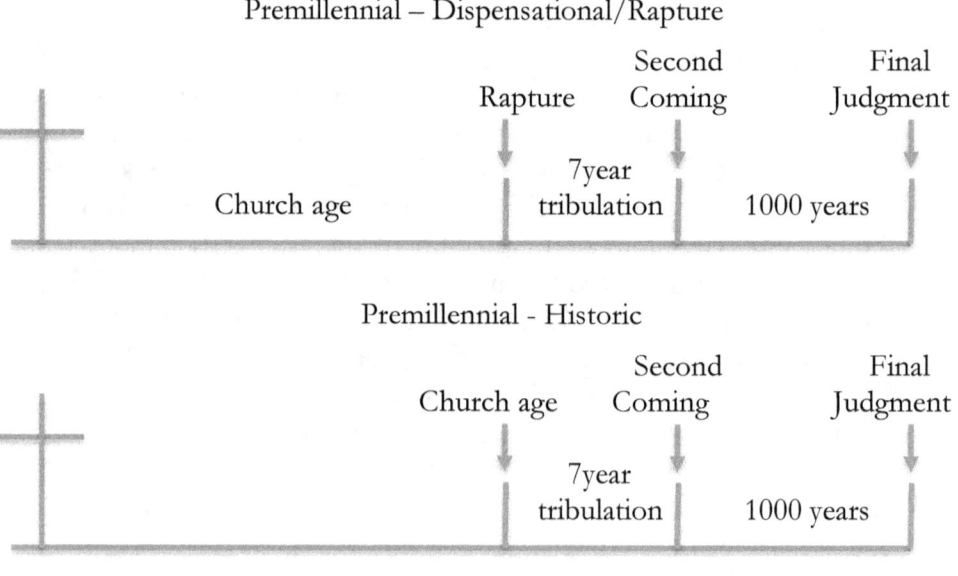

---

[19] John Walvoord, *The Millennial Kingdom* (Findlay, OH: Dunham Publishing Co., 1959) p. 16
[20] Justin Martyr, *Dialogue with Trypho*, Chapter 1, 30

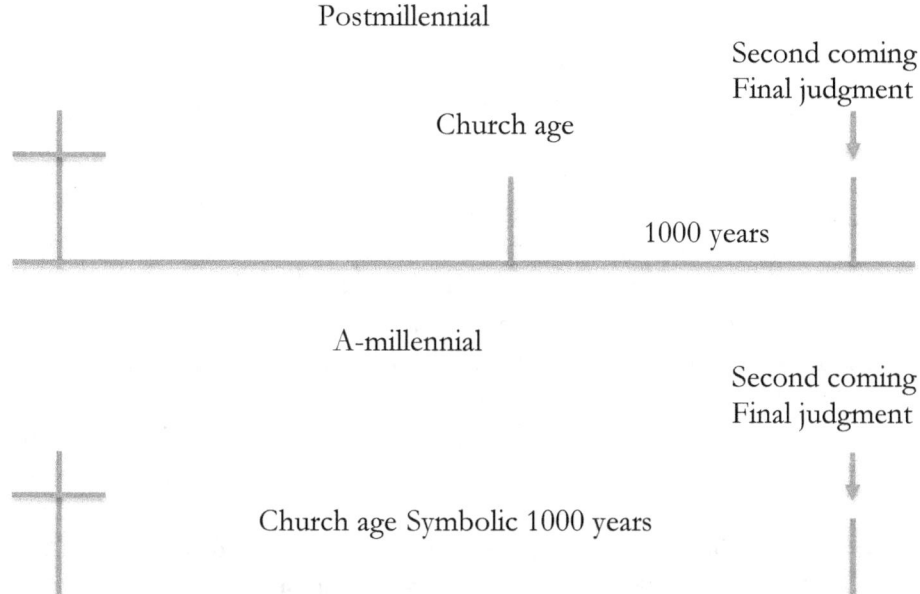

The most popular view amongst Christians over the last 100 years, since the publishing of the Scofield Bible (1909), has been the dispensational view of *premillennialism*. John N. Darby, founder of the dispensational view came up with the idea of the rapture in 1830. According to this view, at some time in the future, Christians are raptured from the earth. This is followed by a seven-year tribulation. (Some say the rapture occurs in the middle of the seven years.) After the seven-year tribulation, Jesus returns and sets up his kingdom in Jerusalem and reigns for a literal 1000 years. Jesus' return is pre (before) his millennial reign, thus premillennial. When Jesus comes back, he *then* reigns for 1000 years in Jerusalem, where the temple is rebuilt. And mostly Jews, who have been converted in great number, reintroduce sacrifices as a memorial to what Jesus has done. Satan is bound during this time so there is peace, albeit we note that sin still exists and people still die during this 1000 years while Jesus rules over the nations on earth from Jerusalem. After the 1000 years, Satan is released and he gathers the nations together for one final assault against Jesus, who defeats their armies. Then comes the final Day of Judgment of the wicked. This is also when the new heaven and new earth are established (after that 1000 years). So Judgment Day for the wicked occurs 1000 years after Jesus' second coming.

The historic premillennial view differs with the rapture view. This view goes back further through the history of the church (hence *historic* premillennial). It differs in that it has no rapture at the beginning (or middle) of the tribulation, and does not always see Israel and the church as being dealt with separately.

The next major view is *post*-millennialism. It's not as popular today but was the most popular view before premillennialism overtook it in the 20th century. In post-millennialism, the last 1000 years of the church age is a time when Satan is bound, so there is a golden age of peace with conversions and the advancement of Christianity like never before. Then Jesus returns post (*after*) the last 1000 years of this golden age. Because Satan is bound, things get better for 1000 years before Jesus comes back (many with the post-millennial view do not see the 1000 years as necessarily literal). But Jesus comes back *after,* 'post' the millennium, thus post-millennialism.

The last major view is amillennial. Amillennialism doesn't accept there is going to be any wonderful golden age of good times and peace for 1000 years at all—either in the church age or after it. Now what kind of spoilsport would believe that! (Apart from me, John Calvin, Martin Luther and a few others.) Amillennialism has no 'majority of the world' converted before Jesus returns (as in post-millennialism). There is no future '1000 years' of good times with mass conversions of Jews after Jesus returns. According to this view, this 1000-years is symbolic of what you are living now. It's the church age from Jesus' resurrection and ascension until he returns, and in the meantime, it requires patient endurance on the part of God's people.

So which of these views is the most natural way of reading our text? If this text stands on its own, isn't it natural to see Jesus reigning for a literal 1000 years in the future? That's one possibility. But don't forget the first three rules of Real Estate—location, location, location! It's the same rules to exegete (interpret) Scripture—location (or context, context, context). This text does *not* stand on its own. What is the *location* of this text? For a start, it's right in a piece of *apocalyptic* literature. John is seeing visions or images. It is right in a book that has told us from the first verse that it would teach us through symbols and signs. And what have we seen in Revelation?

Right from the opening chapter we've seen Jesus with a sword coming out of his mouth, then Jesus as a lamb, a lion and as a rider on a white horse. Satan as a dragon and Satan as a serpent. How can Satan be both a dragon and a serpent? They are symbols. He is powerful and aggressive like a dragon and crafty like a serpent. The symbols are sometimes explained, and at other times they are not explained. When they are not, it forces us to go back to the OT and read it as John did, as someone who was brought up with the Scriptures from childhood.

But crucially, we have also seen numbers used symbolically, especially the number seven. The Lamb Jesus has seven eyes and seven horns. Seven lampstands were actually seven churches. We know by now seven is God's number of completion, so the seven churches represent all the churches. The seven spirits of God symbolize the complete Spirit of God. The seven seals, seven trumpets and seven bowls are the complete judgments of God, and so on. Then there is the number 12, which symbolizes the number of the people of God, with the 12 apostles and 12 tribes. Finally, four is the number of creation, with the four corners of the earth and the four winds of the earth.

Now we come to Rev. 20 and we see a 1000-year reign. So far we have had numbers symbolizing and images symbolizing all the way through Revelation. Can you see why following along with the rest of Revelation to this point that we could at least consider this '1000 years' as symbolic? It would be strange indeed if the visions suddenly switched to literal numbers after the first 20 chapters of Revelation.

The premillennial view all hinges on this 1000-years being a literal future 1000-year reign of Jesus. I'm disagreeing with that and saying it's symbolic and it's happening now. Does this mean I am one of these people who say, 'You can't take the Bible literally! It's all just allegory and parables that can be interpreted in different ways'? No! I still take the Bible literally. When it speaks in poetry, I take it literally as poetry. When the Psalmist says the LORD *is my rock and my shield* (Psalm 18:2), I don't think of the Lord as a literal rock or a bamboo shield etc. It's poetic! When Jesus says he is a shepherd or a vine or a door, do I think he is literally a door? No. But I literally believe the metaphor that Jesus is the door. Not a wooden door swinging, but the metaphor that he is the way into life and heaven. I take it as a symbol because that is Jesus' metaphor context.

So then you might ask why I take the days of Genesis 1 as six, literal 24-hour days? The predominant theory of evolution says the earth is billions of years old, and I hold myself up for ridicule even amongst some Christians when I say they are six literal days. But I maintain that view. Why? Because Genesis is not written as poetry! It's presented as history. I take the genre and context into account. Jesus quotes Genesis as literal history so I take it as literal history. Genesis says, 'there was evening, there was morning, the first day.' That seems like plain language to me. Exodus 20:8-11 says the motive for keeping the Sabbath rest every seventh day is because we are to follow the pattern God gave in six days of creation work, followed by a literal day of rest. The word 'day' is often used to mean an age or longer period, but again, context, context, context. It's used in that sense when there is no numeral connected to it. Apart from the first chapter, Genesis uses the word 'day' 357 times where it is combined with a number and every single time it refers to a literal day, just as I believe it does when Genesis 1 says the first day or second day, etc.

So what about the number 1000 in this context of Rev. 20? Firstly, we have noted the overall context is a book that consistently uses numbers symbolically. Is this the only time 1000-years is mentioned in the Scriptures? Well, yes and no. Rev. 20 is the only time 1000 years is mentioned in relation to Jesus' millennial reign. That ought to be a caution to our interpretation. It's not mentioned in the rest of Revelation. Jesus never mentioned it in all the times he spoke about end times. He never said *anything* about a 1000-year reign. The apostle Paul never mentioned it even once. Nor did Peter or Jude or James or anyone! In fact, the 1000-year reign is never mentioned outside Rev. 20. That ought to make us at least careful that our interpretation fits with the rest of Scripture.

But this is *not* the only time the number 1000 is mentioned in the Scriptures. It's used a great number of times symbolically to indicate a great indefinite number. As a matter of fact, it's God's favorite number in the Scriptures for that purpose, and apart from that purpose, 1000 is *rarely* used as a literal number except where the context is obvious, for example, 'he paid 1000 shekels.' Otherwise 1000 is God's choice of a figure of speech to signify a great, indefinite number. It was there in the 2nd commandment …

> You shall not bow down to them or worship them; for I, the LORD your God, am a jealous God, punishing the children for the sin of the parents to the third and fourth generation of those who hate me, but showing love to <u>a thousand</u> generations of those who love me and keep my commandments (Exod. 20:5-6).

Is that literally? Will God show love to 1000 generations? But hey, if you are in the 1001st generation, that's it! After 1000, will he hate you? No! It's symbolic of a great indefinite number.

> May the LORD, the God of your ancestors, increase you <u>a thousand</u> times and bless you as he has promised (Deut. 1:11)!

Is that literal? No! It's a great indefinite number …

> He remembers his covenant forever, the promise he made, for <u>a thousand</u> generations, … (1 Chron. 16:15).

Literally? Does that mean he forgets his covenant after the 1000th generation? Where did that covenant go? Psalm 84:10 says better is one day in your courts than how many elsewhere? 1000! But hey, that 1001st day I'd rather be elsewhere? No. It's God's symbol of a great indefinite number. The Lord owns the cattle on 1000 hills (Psalm 50:10). Why doesn't he say 10,000 hills? Doesn't the Lord own the cattle on 100,000 hills? Why didn't he say the Lord owns the cattle on a million hills? Well, the number 1000 is God's preferred choice of symbolizing a great, indefinite number. Our favorite metaphor for that kind of number might be to say 'millions' or 'squillions', but for God it's 1000. So it's not literally that the Lord owns the cattle on a exactly 1000 hills so that you are left wondering, 'Man, I can't wait to get to those free cattle on the 1001st hill because the Lord doesn't own them.' Do I take it literally? Yes. But only in the genre of literature it's written. It literally is symbolic or metaphoric language.

How many more examples do we need? Psalm 90:4 or 2 Peter 3:8—1000 years is like a day and a day is like 1000 years. What, literally? Does that mean for God to see 2000 years he would need only two days? Of course it's not literal. The JWs get hold of 2 Peter 3:8 and start adding up all kinds of numbers of days in Scripture and multiplying them by 1000 years to calculate the end of the world. And every time they get it wrong. What happened? They got it wrong because they took the 1000 years literally instead of symbolic of a long period.

I am laboring this deliberately to show I'm not just pulling out an odd example. We could keep going on and on through the Scriptures to find 1000 used symbolically in Deut. 7:9, Job 9:3, 33:23, Psalm 105:8, Psalm 105:8, Eccl. 6:6, 7:28, Isaiah 30:17, 60:22, and Amos 5:3. You can look up a concordance and see how many I have left out. The number 1000 is God's choice to describe a large, indefinite number.

We have also seen 1000 used symbolically in Revelation. We read about 144,000 in earlier chapters. Remember 12 is the number for God's people, and the 12 tribes and 12 apostles multiplied comes to 144, but in the 1000s. So why is it in 1000s? Why exactly 144,000? Or why is the holy city in Rev. 21 measured as 12,000 x 12,000? Because 1000 is God's expression of the great indefinite number of God's people (12)—in the 1000s.

The reason I have spent so much time on this is because for most of the body of Christ today, everything hinges on you believing that the only legitimate way of looking at this has to be a literal 1000-year reign of Jesus in the future. Many even think if you don't take it literally you are not being faithful to Scripture. There are major theological seminaries that won't allow you to study with them unless you sign a declaration saying these 1000-years are literal and future. There is such a commitment to this having to be a literal 1000-years that John MacArthur actually says of the 1000-years that when 'year' is used in the Scriptures with a number it is *always* literal and is never symbolic.[21] Never? Does that include all those examples of the number 1000 we have just looked at, to the point of boredom, where 1000 is *consistently* used symbolically, whether describing years, generations, or days? It's time to look up that concordance and see it for yourself! In fact, it's more accurate to say, '*never* is there anywhere in Scripture when 1000 years is *not* used symbolically' (see Eccl. 6:6, Psalm 90:4, 2 Pet. 3:8).

---

[21] John MacArthur, *The MacArthur Study Bible*, (Nashville: Word Publishing, 1997) p. 2021

Even if you don't agree with me on this, I hope I have at least shown that to take 1000-years as symbolic is an attempt to derive an interpretation from Scripture, and is not taking a *lower* view of Scripture. And if this 1000-year millennium is in fact symbolic of a great, indefinite period, this opens up the possibility of the amillennial view that this 1000-years is a great, indefinite period of time that covers the long stretch of the history of the church before Jesus returns.

But what difference does it really make? In the gospel, it makes no difference. It's not a thing of first importance. All the Christian millennial views agree in the end, Jesus wins. The central message of Revelation still stands across all millennial views. Jesus is coming back and wins in the end. So does it make any difference at all when these 1000-years take place?

In a secondary way, it does speak to the issues of the thoroughness with which Jesus dealt with sin and how he will deal with it when he comes back. Will Jesus still have to deal with sin and sinners for another 1000 years, as the premillennial view says, during the 1000-years when sin and death will still exist? And when Jesus returns, does he bring salvation in the full sense? Will Jesus come back to bring complete victory and justice and bring full judgment, or will he hold that off for another 1000 years? And perhaps more pertinent to us is this: Are there any second chances after Jesus returns? Whether it's through the rapture and people left behind, or those who survive into a future 1000-years, will some unbelievers get a second chance after Jesus returns? Or is now the only day of opportunity? I'm amillennial, so yes, I'm a spoilsport. I believe this text would have us know there are *no* second chances! Today is the day to find Jesus, to evangelize the Jews as well as the Gentiles, and when Jesus returns there will be no other.

There is another issue about our view of Jesus' reign during these 1000-years that is relevant pastorally. The premillennial view means Jesus' reign only begins in some future 1000 years. But the amillennial view is that Jesus' reign is *now,* during the entire church age. Jesus wins, not only in the end, but Jesus is winning now. Jesus reigns over history! Jesus' kingdom is not only to come, it has *already* begun. He said to the Pharisees, the kingdom of God is upon you (Matt. 12:28)! And though evil rages, right now Jesus is still winning.

The ascended king on high is reigning now (1:5). He is marching his kingdom to the ends of the earth, and in your life now he is reigning! It means you can read history through this lens. Jesus is sending forth his Spirit doing his saving work now. Why is Jesus allowing Islamic State to kill people? Because many disillusioned Muslims will turn to Christ. If Jesus is reigning, why did he allow communist atheism to choke religion in the USSR and China in the 20th century? Because it created such a spiritual vacuum in that country that now the Chinese Government can't contain the conversion rate to Christianity. Jesus is reigning now! How can you be sure that God is working everything for your good even in pain? Because Jesus reigns now!

This means that you can re-read this book of Revelation as a book which is unfolding before your eyes. The tribulation and cosmic warfare are alive right now! You can know that despite the way things look, Jesus reigns *now* in this 1000-years before the end. Are you going through trouble? Jesus reigns. He wins and is winning.

The difficulty with my view is that I now have to be able to explain how the devil has been bound from deceiving the nations over the last 1000-years (or literal 2000 years). How can that all be happening now in this church age when he attacks so much? Next chapter please!

Study Questions

1. Give reasons why this is not a text that Christians should divide over.

2. Describe the main two variations of the premillennial view.

3. What is the post-millennial view?

4. What is the amillennial view?

5. What is there about the context in which the 1000 years appears that might help us understand it?

6. Is this the only time 1000 is mentioned in the Scriptures? How

might that help us to be able to interpret that period?

7. What difference might one's view make of what Jesus deals with when Jesus returns?

8. What difference does it make to one's view of Jesus now?

9. What difference does it make to the urgency of evangelism and need to repent now?

9
Satan Bound
(Revelation 20:1-3)

We have examined the three main views of the 1000-years of Rev. 20. The premillennial view depends on the events of Rev. 19 and Rev. 20 following one another chronologically. So in Rev. 19, Jesus comes back and fights the nations, and the Beast and False prophet are cast into the lake of fire. Then Jesus rules the nations for this golden age of 1000-years of relative peace. The trouble with this is that Rev. 19 closed with the most devastating end to all unbelievers. Remember the gruesome picture? Nations completely obliterated, every single person!

> '... Come, gather together for the great supper of God, so that you may eat the flesh of <u>kings, generals, and the</u> <u>mighty</u>, of horses and their riders, and the flesh of <u>all people, free and slave, great and small</u>' (19:17-18).

All people! And if that was not enough, 19:21 said of whoever was left *'the rest were killed with the sword coming out of the of mouth of the rider on the horse, and all the birds gorged themselves on their flesh.'* It's the Day of Judgment. It's all over. If you take it literally, every single nation and person is eaten up! Jesus is pronounced King of kings and Lord of lords. It is the complete victory! How could Jesus commence a reign over the nations after this war, when there are no nations left? Rev. 20 then says Satan can no longer deceive the nations. Of course! There are no nations left to deceive!

So if Rev. 19 and Rev. 20 don't naturally follow chronologically, how can we understand it? Well, we have been careful readers through Revelation, and Rev. 20 is doing what we have seen throughout. It is an action replay of what went on before, with new close-up camera angles revealing more detail. This has been the pattern in Revelation, and it enables us to explain how we reach final judgment and yet continue with more information of pre-judgment. We have seen this all the way through. At the end of Rev. 6 we read about Judgment Day! We saw the same thing at the end of Rev. 11, when the dead are judged. It's all over. But straight after that, Rev. 12 recaps the whole history again, beginning at Jesus birth ('the male child born to the woman'), then his ascension into heaven ('child snatched up to heaven'), through to the end of the age. We saw the fall of Babylon in Rev. 16 when God gave her the cup filled with his fury, but then Rev. 17-18 starts over again with the judgment of Babylon. It's an action replay with more details. We've seen replays with the seals, trumpets and bowls, repeating the action from different camera angles.

In fact, it just happens that judgment is repeated throughout Revelation. How many times is it repeated? What is God's favorite number of completion? Seven! We have seen judgment repeated seven times. Revelation follows the same pattern as its favorite OT book, Daniel. Daniel is alluded to often. It is the other great apocalyptic book. People of all views agree that Daniel sees different visions, but *not* chronologically. Rather Daniel *repeats* teaching on those four kingdoms over the same period of time with new detail (always building to the final end).

So if Rev. 19 left no nations for Jesus to rule over after their complete obliteration and every individual destroyed, what is left for Rev. 20? The action replay! Rev. 20 gives another camera angle of the same period leading up to the same judgment and victory of Jesus winning, but this time with a gospel focus. This is the assurance that we the readers of Revelation need. When it looks like Satan is winning, don't give up. Why? Read Rev. 20. We see that Jesus reigns over Satan in these 1000 years …

> And I saw an angel coming down out of heaven, having the key to the Abyss and holding in his hand a great chain (20:1).

What is the Abyss? We have learned previously it can't be hell because you can't get in and out of hell. **The Abyss** is Satan's realm, but Christ has the power to invade it, and he has the key to lock him in. The angel at the very least represents Christ as he is **coming down out of heaven** …

> He seized the dragon, that ancient serpent, who is the devil, or Satan, and bound him for a thousand years. He threw him into the Abyss, and locked and sealed it over him, to keep him from deceiving the nations anymore until the thousand years were ended. After that, he must be set free for a short time (20:2-3).

But wait a minute! If these 1000-years are symbolic of the church age, how can we say the devil has been prevented from deceiving the nations? Isn't that exactly what he has been doing during this time? Someone once said, 'Every generation thinks the world revolves around them.' We live as though people in the past are so irrelevant because they lived so long ago. But if you have a sense of history, if you think big picture of God's history and plan, for the greater part of the history of the world, Satan deceived the nations in a way we would rarely think about. That is, until some unbeliever says to you, 'So God didn't save anyone during all the centuries of history while only the Israelites were believers in God'? And we fumble around trying to give some sort of answer about possible individual non-Israelites who were saved, but it's actually a bit flimsy. Was Nineveh really joining the God of Israel? But even if they were, that was just a city, not a nation. We could cite rare people who acknowledged the living God as most high, but even among them, how many did that to the exclusion of all other gods? Did the Queen of Sheba repent and follow Israel's covenant? What about Naaman? Maybe? How many were really converted outside Israel? Did they repent and enter God's covenant, get circumcised and follow Yahweh's covenantal law, mediated through the holy priesthood? That was the only way to God! Sure, there were some individuals, but how many **nations** turned to the covenant of Israel? Well, actually, not one. What happened to the promise of God to Abraham? *All nations* on earth will be blessed through you! It didn't happen in OT times. We just take for granted those thousands of years of history, people living and dying, hurtling into eternity without the knowledge of God. We are so wrapped in our own importance we scarcely consider them! Didn't those people count? Wasn't the Lord saving people from every nation all along?

Well, no, they were deceived. From Pharaoh and the Egyptians through to the Philistines, the nations all *fought* Israel and tried to exterminate God's people. No nation, *not one,* was saved except

Israel. The same deceiver who deceived humanity in the first place deceived them all. You can take that lightly because you are so far removed from these nations and their inhabitants in time, but you better believe that for all those people of all those nations that it means a lot to them that Satan deceived them. From the time the deceiver was not bound (the Garden of Eden) and then throughout history, century after century he deceived the nations. Have you ever contemplated that? Satan wins?

How we have grossly underestimated the power of the gospel, the power of God for salvation that broke the back of Satan's stranglehold on the nations and the gravity of these words. 'All authority has been given to me, go and make disciples ...' Of what? *All Nations!* We have taken so lightly the fact that if you are not Jewish, that it has been granted to you to believe in the God of Israel. Can you see in a new way how precious are these words ...?

> ... because you were slain, and with your blood you purchased for God persons from every tribe and language and people and nation (5:9).

There have been many nations over the past 2000 years (or 1000 symbolically) where the gospel has gone, and in the broad sense some have called themselves *Christian* nations! So why are these nations able to believe in the God of Israel, when for all of history throughout the OT salvation was confined to just one tiny nation, Israel? Why? Because Satan has been bound by Jesus to pave the way for the gospel to go to the nations! From when? When did Jesus bind Satan? Jesus described it this way ...

> ... now the prince of this world will be driven out! And I, when I am lifted up from the earth, will draw all people to myself (John 12:31-32).

Which people are drawn to him? Not just Israel! *All people!* All nations! Jesus said the *driving out* of Satan began from the time of the cross! It's another metaphor that explains this binding of Satan. But you will always struggle with 20:3 and the binding of Satan if you haven't come to grips with God's primary agenda. It's the *saving agenda* of the Bible. If you have a different agenda for interpreting this text of the binding of Satan—other than the saving of nations— you will never get Rev. 20. How are the nations *saved*? Because Satan has been bound from deceiving them any longer.

From the time of binding Satan comes this radical new era. The gospel spread like wildfire across the nations like nothing in history before it. We take this salvation from the Jews for granted and we forget it *comes from* the Jews. The Jews are God's people, not you—if you are a Gentile. Why should you be included? It's extraordinary to think that if you were there 2000 years ago, salvation meant you had to become a Jew.

But then something radical happened. It started with 12 Jewish disciples (and 120 others). Could you possibly picture this tiny Jewish sect claiming it would go to all nations on earth? Yet here we are 2000 years later and it's now the biggest religion in the world. One in three people who walk the face of the earth claim to be Christian. Many nations now claim to be Christian. From 2000 BC, Abraham and his people had failed to reach a single nation with their faith! But now, so radically did the nations come to the Jewish Messiah that you have forgotten this is actually a Jewish religion you have been grafted into. How could such a thing happen when previously, century after century, this little Israel could barely survive itself, let alone be a light to the nations? How could this explosion happen, which turned the world upside down? Salvation to the nations. How?

The answer is that Satan has been bound and prevented from deceiving the nations. We have missed the magnitude of some of Jesus' words in the gospels and the magnitude of the cross. You live in this '1000-years', this long indefinite period when the devil is bound and prevented from stopping Jesus marching his gospel across the earth ... 'Go to all nations ... and I will be with you.' But Jesus knew it was coming.

You might have missed this in John's gospel, but when the Gentiles came seeking Jesus, it all seemed so strange. The disciples tell Jesus some Gentiles want to see him. And what was his response? 'The *hour has come* for the Son of Man to be glorified' (John 12:23). How is that a response? 'Some people want to see you'—'well then it must be time.' What time? When the Gentiles (the nations) begin to seek Jesus, Jesus says it's time to go to the cross. That is the context in which he goes on to say *now* the prince of this world is driven out and I will draw *all* people to myself. All people? Every human being? We know that not every human being will be saved.

So what did he mean he said he would draw *all* people to himself? All nations (not just Jews, but Gentiles), because 'the hour has come.'

It's the same thing using different metaphors described in Rev. 12. It covers the same timeframe explaining this same event. Jesus is snatched up to heaven. Satan is *cast out* of heaven. He is restricted now. Up until Jesus' work on the cross, Satan had access to accuse in heaven. Why? Satan could rightfully accuse the OT Israelite saints and accuse God! 'How can you allow sinners into heaven? Their sin has not been paid for. They have no right to be in heaven!' But God sent his Son to the cross. Their sin was paid for. For both OT and NT saints. So Satan was cast out of heaven. He was emptied of power to accuse. And he was bound from deceiving the nations.

Does this mean Satan is bound in every other way? No. He still wreaks havoc. He still deceives in any way he can and blinds the minds of individual unbelievers. But think big picture. Satan can no longer deceive the nations out of salvation. Our text concerns a particular topic! Satan is not bound from deceiving people, but he can no longer **deceive the nations** from receiving the gospel. He is unable to stop the ingathering of people from every tribe and nation, the plan of the gospel. *He threw him into the Abyss, and locked and sealed it over him, to keep him from <u>deceiving the nations</u> anymore ...*

So Jesus has Satan shut in to restrict him for the specific purpose of deceiving the nations. Jesus bound him from doing that. It's symbolic. Very few commentators believe a literal chain is holding Satan. Satan is a spiritual being. The best parallel is Job 1:10 when Satan said God had put a hedge around Job so that he can't get to him. Was that a literal hedge that was too high for Satan to jump over? No. It's a metaphor! Satan was bound! A limit was placed on Satan's attack on Job. Did this mean Satan couldn't do anything to Job? Of course not! He still wreaked havoc! Terrible havoc! Likewise, while Satan is bound from deceiving the nations and stopping the spread of the gospel to the nations, he continues to attack in every other way.

I admit there is this tension. Satan is bound and yet is continuing, but it's not really a problem if you think *gospel*. The only way to understand this text is to think *gospel*. All Christians believe the gospel carries this same tension! We say, 'Satan is a completely defeated foe!' Really? We admit he continues to wreak havoc and bother us as the god of this age. We *live* this tension. Satan is both cast out as Christ draws all people to himself, yet the whole world is under Satan's control. The tension is real for all of us in the gospel. Satan rages, but Jesus reigns!

Rev. 20 is the history of the gospel. So yes, there is a tension, but it should be noted that the tension exists in the premillennial view as well. In that view, Jesus reigns for 1000-years in the future from Jerusalem while Satan is bound, but the work of Satan still remains as sin and death continues. So during that 1000-years Satan's work is not bound in the absolute sense. There is a tension in this text no matter what your view.

But there is a difference between the amillennial and premillennial view, in that the latter says Satan is not bound until a *future* time. The amillennial view says he is bound now. So is there any other NT evidence which shows that Satan has been bound since Jesus' earthly work, rather than in the future? Jesus said himself in …

> '… how can anyone enter a strong man's house and carry off his possessions unless he first ties up the strong man? Then he can plunder his house' (Matt. 12:29).

The context there is referring to Satan (Beelzebub). Jesus ties up (binds) Satan, the strong man, and only then can he take his goods. In the original Greek language when Jesus said 'ties up' Satan, Matthew just happens to use the same Greek word used in our text in 20:2 where he 'bound' Satan. Jesus bound, 'tied up' the strongman way back then!

What about the nations Satan formerly owned. Do you remember that? Satan even offered Jesus the nations, the kingdoms of the world! How could Satan do that? He had them in his keeping. But from the time of Jesus' death and resurrection, Jesus can take them back. It's also interesting the way Luke's parallel passage puts it …

> 'But when someone stronger attacks and overpowers him, he takes away the armor in which the man trusted and divides up his plunder' (Luke 11:22).

Here is a different symbol of the same thing. The binding is taking away his armor. It's NT teaching on what Jesus did to Satan …

> And having <u>disarmed the powers</u> and authorities, he made a public

> spectacle of them, triumphing over them <u>by the cross</u> (Col. 2:15).

Wait a minute. How did Jesus' cross disarm the powers if they are still raging against us? Think *gospel to the nations* and you get the answer to the disarming or binding of Satan. The cross wins over the power of Satan's attempts to stop salvation to the nations. And also ...

> Since the children have flesh and blood, he too shared in their humanity so that by his death he might break the power of him who holds the power of death—that is, the devil, ... (Heb. 2:14).

This is what Jesus did! But wait! Did Jesus break the power of Satan? Satan is still around causing havoc. Only if you think *gospel* does this make sense.

If we think *gospel to the nations*, then Satan is bound, but not bound in any other way. He still continues in every other way to try and steal, kill, destroy *and deceive*. He still attacks but cannot penetrate, cannot reach, and cannot deceive who? As Revelation keeps repeating, he cannot touch those who are sealed, those whose names are written in the book of life. He can't stop Jesus' saving work to the ends of the earth, to every tribe, language, people, and *nation*. And that makes Satan even more angry. Satan is in a rage! Satan is in a rage *because* he is bound. This also makes sense as to why it's written like this in Revelation and why the book was written. It's written to encourage believers through the tribulation. It looks like the devil is winning but he is actually bound! Jesus *is* winning! He will save those who are his! From all the nations!

This calls for patient endurance on the part of the saints. Remain faithful. Satan cannot stop Jesus' work to the ends of the earth. He is bound ... but watch out. Did you notice this? **After that, he must be set free for a short time.** When could this happen? This fits with the binding of Satan's Antichrist Beast as described ...

> And now you know what <u>is holding him back</u> [bound], so that he may be revealed at the proper time. For the secret power of lawlessness is already at work; but the one who now holds it back will continue to do so till he is taken out of the way. And then the lawless one will be revealed, whom the Lord Jesus will overthrow with the breath of his mouth and destroy by the splendor of his coming. The coming of the lawless one will be in accordance with how Satan works. He will use all

sorts of displays of power, through signs and wonders that serve the lie, and all the ways that wickedness deceives those who are perishing. (2 Thess. 2:6-10a).

The revealing of the Antichrist could be as late as the moment before Jesus returns and is destroyed by the breath of Jesus' mouth. But before that, Satan is released for a short time. For that to happen you would have to imagine a time in the future with unprecedented false miracles like never before. It could be a time when there are millions of sightings of UFOs in the sky and millions are deceived from NDEs and OBEs by the ruler of the kingdom of the air, who is able to transform himself into an angel of light and deceive millions into believing these things are bigger than the Bible. It could be a time when the Bible would be considered irrelevant and that heaven is for everyone. When Satan is let loose, 20:8 says there will be an intensifying of the nations against God's people, so we could imagine a time when not only nations that were against the gospel, but also nations that formerly claimed to be Christian would join Satan's attacks. It could be a time when there would be more martyrs for the faith than ever before. Beheadings, as we see later in this text, would occur (but people actually getting their heads cut off, when would that ever happen?) like Islamic State has popularized. If Satan is let loose, you would expect radical things like that. You could expect strange things not just in non-Christian countries, but in so-called Christian countries, like the banning of prayers in schools or opposition to religious education in schools. If Satan was let loose, instead of worshiping the name of Jesus, you would hear his name used as a swear word, and this change would happen literally within a generation. In so-called Christian countries! Instead of the ethics of the Ten Commandments being the foundation of society, even a simple thing like taking another human life would actually become legal, to kill the unborn and to kill our elderly. Even a basic God given institution like marriage between a man and a woman would be attacked. Things like that which have never happened before in history. Even our God given biology of male and female could be denied. Even the churches would forsake the gospel and take up with Satan's values of self-indulgent entertainment, or a prosperity gospel so that the world would influence the church rather than the other way around. It would be a time when not just the cults or the RCs

(Pope Francis has already preached you don't need to believe in Jesus to get to heaven), but the so-called evangelical church would operate while hardly opening the Bible. The preachers would give sermons on topical ideas or felt needs rather than Scripture, feel good messages rather than the gospel of repentance and the cross not preached. That is what we could expect in the intensifying of deceit after the 1000-years are up and Satan is released for a short time before Jesus returns. But that is for some time in the future. We can't imagine what that would be like.

He threw him into the Abyss, and locked and sealed it over him, to keep him from deceiving the nations anymore until the thousand years were ended. <u>After that, he must be set free for a short time</u> (20:3).

Study Questions

1. What is the difficulty of Rev. 19 and Rev. 20 being chronological?

2. What way other than chronological could we understand Rev. 20?

3. How does history show that Satan deceived the nations?

4. In what other ways in the NT, outside of Revelation, has Jesus taught that Satan has been bound?

5. How can we say Satan is bound from deceiving nations now when he continues as father of all lies?

6. How can we explain the tension between Satan being bound yet still wreaking havoc?

7. What are two ways Revelation assures believers (of all nations) that Satan cannot bring them down?

8. What might society look like at a time when Satan is set free for that short time?

20
Jews in the 1000-Years?
(Revelation 20:4-6 Part 1)

We have looked at the way the number 1000 is used throughout Scripture as a long, indefinite period, and I argued that the 1000-year reign of Jesus describes the gospel church age and the ingathering of the nations while Satan is bound from stopping the march of the gospel to the ends of the earth. The premillennial view says the 1000-years is literal, and in the future after Jesus returns there are *two* resurrections. You can understand how you might conclude that on a first read of this text …

> I saw thrones on which were seated those who had been given authority to judge. And I saw the souls of those who had been beheaded because of their testimony about Jesus and because of the word of God. They had not worshiped the beast or its image and had not received its mark on their foreheads or their hands. They came to life and reigned with Christ a thousand years. (The rest of the dead did not come to life until the thousand years were ended.) This is the first resurrection. Blessed and holy are those who share in the first resurrection. The second death has no power over them, but they will be priests of God and of Christ and will reign with him for a thousand years (20:4-6).

So, is there more than one resurrection? The premillennial position says that there are two different days of judgment. The day of resurrection of the righteous, when they receive their heavenly rewards, followed by a 1000-year reign of Jesus on earth *after which* there is the resurrection and judgment of the unrighteous. Two great days of resurrection. And surely looking at this text that has to be possible?

But the word of caution is that this is the *only* text in the Bible that speaks of two resurrections in the middle of what is a very difficult book. What is the rule of interpretation when we have a difficult

Scripture? Let God be his own interpreter. So, when we are faced with a difficult text, we go to other parts of the Bible that are clearer on the same topic and let the clear texts interpret the difficult one, not the other way around.

So first we ask, what does the rest of the Bible say? Are there two resurrections, one for the righteous, followed by a 1000-year gap before the resurrection of the wicked? Or is there one resurrection? We looked at this back at Rev. 11 ...

> The nations were angry, and your wrath has come. The <u>time</u> has come for <u>judging the dead, and for rewarding</u> your servants ... (11:18).

The premillennial view says you need to insert 1000 years in between the words 'judging of the dead' and 'rewarding your servants' *and* reverse that order because in the premillennial view, the servants of God are rewarded first when Jesus comes back, but you must wait another 1000 years before the dead are judged. The premillennial view requires the silent insertion of 1000 years in great number of texts. Even later in Rev. 20 ...

> And I saw the dead, great and small, standing before the throne, and books were opened. Another book was opened, which is the book of life. The dead were judged according to what they had done as recorded in the books.... Anyone whose name was <u>not</u> found written in the book of life was thrown into the lake of fire (20:12, 15).

Somewhere between those getting thrown into the lake of fire and those who *have* their names in that book, we need to insert 1000 years before those books were opened. It's the same theme in other parts of the Bible. The resurrection of both the good and evil seem to be clearly one Day of Judgment and resurrection not separated by 1000 years or even minutes! This is a crucial question that needs to be answered to see if our view of Rev. 20 is consistent with the rest of the Bible. Are there two physical resurrections with 1000 years in between? Or is there one resurrection of both good and evil? Even the OT can help us ...

> Multitudes who sleep in the dust of the earth will awake: some to everlasting life, others to shame and everlasting contempt (Dan. 12:2).

Once again, the premillennial view must insert 1000 years, so it reads, *'some to everlasting life* [insert 1000 years] *others to shame and everlasting contempt.'* Or again where Jesus spoke of the resurrection of both believers and unbelievers together, this literal 1000 years must be inserted in between …

> 'Do not be amazed at this, for a time is coming when all who are in their graves will hear his voice and come out—those who have done what is good will rise to live, [insert 1000 years], and those who have done what is evil will rise to be condemned' (John 5:28-29).

It's the same problem all through the teaching of Jesus' parables. Remember the wheat and the weeds?

> The owner's servants came to him and said, 'Sir, didn't you sow good seed in your field? Where then did the weeds come from?' 'An enemy did this,' he replied. The servants asked him, 'Do you want us to go and pull them up?' 'No,' he answered, 'because while you are pulling the weeds, you may root up the wheat with them. Let both grow <u>together until the harvest</u>. <u>At that time</u> I will tell the harvesters: First collect the weeds and tie them in bundles to be burned; [insert 1000 years] then gather the wheat and bring it into my barn' (Matt. 13:27-30).

There is a need to insert 1000 years into 'at that time'. And even if you could insert 1000 years there, again the order is wrong. The premillennial position needs first the wheat, then the weeds.

Here is just one more clear teaching from Jesus on the Day of the sheep and the goats.

> 'When the Son of Man comes in his glory, and all the angels with him, he will sit on his glorious throne. <u>All the nations</u> will be gathered before him, and he will separate the people one from another as a shepherd separates the sheep from the goats. He will put the sheep on <u>his right</u> and the goats on <u>his left</u>.' Then the King will say to those on his right, 'Come, you who are blessed by my Father; take your inheritance, the kingdom prepared for you since the creation of the world.' … [And it takes 1000 years for Jesus to get to those on his left.] Then he will say to those on his left, 'Depart from me, you who are cursed, into the eternal fire prepared for the devil and his angels.' … Then they will go away to eternal punishment, but the righteous to eternal life [Which happened 1000 years earlier.] (Matt. 25:31-46).

How can we get 1000 years in between the sheep and the goats? They are all there together on the single Day of Judgment and again the order is incorrect, it should be first the righteous then the unrighteous. We could go on to a careful study of the parables of the ten virgins, the fish and the net and the talents and find the same issue. It's the same with the apostle Paul who preached 'a resurrection [singular] of the just and the unjust' in Acts 24:15.

Why am I laboring this point? Because the futurists make the charge that if you don't take the 1000-years as future and literal with two separate resurrections, then you are not taking Scripture as it is plainly written. But it needs to be admitted that Rev. 20 is not easy for any of us. I still have to explain why there seems to be two resurrections in Rev. 20, while the rest of the Bible teaches only one. It's difficult! But if you insist Rev. 20 is teaching two physical resurrections, you must *symbolically* force the 1000 years back into the rest of the Bible where it plainly doesn't fit, in all kinds of places including the teaching of Jesus, Paul and Daniel. So both sides have difficulty.

But God interprets God, not us. We should let the rest of the Bible interpret the single difficult text of Rev. 20 rather than try to insert one understanding of Rev. 20 into the rest of the Bible. For example, should people be baptized in the place of the dead? Your Mormon friends will tell you 'yes', and give you 'irrefutable proof' ...

> Now if there is no resurrection, what will those do who are baptized for the dead? If the dead are not raised at all, why are people baptized for them (1 Cor. 15:29)?

Now what are you going to say to your Mormon friends who say, 'This is why we baptize for the dead'? You might say Paul is using an example of a practice, while not condoning it, to make his main point, affirming the resurrection. And the Mormons will laugh at you. That's not the plainest meaning! They've got you! Or have they?

If you study the entire Bible as to what it says about baptism of the dead or second chances for salvation after people have died, it's a no-brainer. Our explanation of 1 Corinthians 15:29 might not immediately seem the easiest, but we don't read this verse, then bend other Scripture by inserting and twisting words, so the verse fits into other parts of the Bible. Rather, the Bible is clear elsewhere that we don't baptize the dead. We admit to our Mormon friends our explanation of 1 Corinthians 15:29 may not be the most plain at first sight, but the Mormons are still wrong because they are out of line with the rest of the Bible. The Bible must interpret itself!

That's my appeal with Rev. 20. What does the rest of the Bible teach on the resurrection? Is it possible people have built a whole theology around a single difficult verse, in the difficult book of Revelation, in perhaps its most difficult chapter, and then sought to try and force that interpretation back into the rest of Scripture where it doesn't fit? If Jesus really taught that when he comes back there would be a resurrection of the righteous, and then 1000 years of him living alongside sinners, before another resurrection and judgment of the wicked, wouldn't he have at least mentioned this 1000 years once in all his discourses on the end times? Just once? Or wouldn't the apostle Paul have mentioned it once? Or the gospel writers, or Peter, James or Jude? Just once? It's not even mentioned again in the whole book of Revelation, let alone the rest of the whole Bible!

As we get further into this text of 20:4-6 in the next chapter, we will find there are difficulties in interpretation no matter what your viewpoint. However, if we adopt the method of using clearer teaching of the Bible to drive the understanding of the difficult text, then this difficult text may become clearer than you think.

But before we get into that, I want to ask, why would credible Bible preachers that we hold in high regard want to break all the normal rules of sound Biblical interpretation in the first place, to even *try* to insert a literal 1000 years back through the Bible where it doesn't seem to fit? Well, there is a reason driving their thinking and is far worthier of consideration and biblical in concept than inserting things back into the text. What is the main motivation for the premillennial view? I believe it is because they are trying to be faithful to the promises of the OT, that Israel will be delivered by their God and restored to their land. That is a worthier point. Does God keep his promises? And of course, the answer is—yes! So starting with those promises, the premillennial Bible student then looks for a literal fulfillment of those prophecies and arrives at Rev. 20-22 and finds the mention of Jesus' 1000-year reign, a new temple and says this must be it!

The Lord did promise Israel they would one day return to Canaan to live in peace. Although we do have to say upfront many of those

OT promises were fulfilled literally under Zerubbabel and Joshua in 536 BC and Ezra in 458 BC, when the temple was rebuilt and the Jews returned to their homeland! But several of God's promises regarding Israel being returned to their land and worship being conducted from Jerusalem in the presence of the Lord seem more far reaching than those earlier fulfillments, especially the promise of peace and prosperity. The premillennial view sees Rev. 20 as the answer to that, and (for many of that view) God's promises mean there must be a separate future for the Jews and their conversion in that 1000-year reign.

Firstly, let's look at the *original* promise to the father of the Jews ...

> 'I will make you into a great nation, and I will bless you; I will make your name great, and you will be a blessing. I will bless those who bless you, and whoever curses you I will curse; and <u>all peoples on earth</u> will be blessed through you' (Gen. 12:2-3).

All peoples on earth blessed through the Abraham, the forefather of the Jews. And indeed, the Gentiles would join Israel ...

> ... Foreigners will join them and unite with the descendants of Jacob. <u>Nations</u> will take them and bring them to their own place. And Israel will take <u>possession of the nations</u> ... (Isa. 14:1b-2b).

Israel is to possess the *nations*, not be separate from them. Or...

> 'Shout and be glad, Daughter Zion. For I am coming, and I will live among you,' declares the LORD. '<u>Many nations</u> will be <u>joined</u> with the LORD in that day and will <u>become my people</u>. I will live among you and you will know that the LORD Almighty has sent me to you. The LORD will inherit Judah as his portion <u>in the holy land</u> and will again choose <u>Jerusalem</u>' (Zech. 2:10-12).

So, Jerusalem is again favored but this time, with the *nations* joined to them! Doesn't this fit with the gospel? It joins Jews and Gentiles together under the one Jewish Messiah. Isn't this what we have seen with the New Jerusalem and Holy City? What does it say at the end of Revelation? ...

> I saw the Holy City, the new <u>Jerusalem</u>, coming down out of heaven from God, prepared as a <u>bride</u> beautifully dressed for her husband (21:2).

The New Jerusalem is the bride of Christ. The church! But what happened to the promise to Abraham's seed?

> <u>If you belong to Christ, then you are Abraham's seed</u>, and heirs according to the promise (Gal. 3:29).

You are Abraham's seed! Jew and Gentile who belong to Christ are all true descendants of Israel through the same faith as Abraham. So did God reject his ethnic people? Did his promises to Israel fail? By no means! It was always there in the OT and into the NT. A remnant of ethnic Israel would be saved. Of course, I am just using the apostle Paul's arguments on the same subject (Rom. 9-11). The fact that it's only a remnant is perfectly in line with Israel in the OT. There was never a majority who were faithful. The apostle Paul says in Romans 11 that Gentiles are being grafted, though they are *not* natural branches. The promises to Israel are fulfilled in the most profound way ... in the gospel of Jesus Christ! It's not for me to say whether there will be a much greater number of Jews converted from here on. I hope and pray that is the case. But I've already noted the number of Jews having come to faith is really quite significant when you consider that out of the whole population of Israel, most Jews are not interested in looking for any Messiah. But don't forget—Gentiles do not *replace* Israel, they join Israel! We should have memorized this text by now, because it is a profound mystery revealed ...

> Therefore, remember that formerly you who are <u>Gentiles</u> by birth and called 'uncircumcised' by those who call themselves 'the circumcision' (that done in the body by human hands)—remember that at that time you were separate from Christ, <u>excluded from citizenship in Israel</u> and foreigners to the covenants of <u>the promise</u>, without hope and without God in the world. But <u>now in Christ Jesus</u> you who once were far away have been brought <u>near</u> by the blood of Christ. For he himself is our peace, who has <u>made the two groups one</u> and has destroyed the barrier, the dividing wall of hostility, ... (Eph. 2:11-14).

They are no longer two, but one. Formerly, you were excluded from citizenship in Israel. What does that mean? Now in Christ, the Jewish messiah, you are *included* in what? Citizenship in Israel! That is the mystery of the gospel! Gentiles joined to Israel. Paul drives his view of end times and the promises of God by the *gospel*. *All* the promises of God are 'Yes' and 'Amen' in CHRIST JESUS! The Jewish Messiah. Gentiles joined to Israel. What does he mean when he says that in the gospel the *wall of hostility* has been broken down? Or *formerly* you were separate, now you are one. The gospel *joins*. A millennial reign that has a separate future for the Jews does the opposite. The wall was broken down permanently by Jesus —'don't put it back up again', says Paul! Later he says …

> This mystery is that through the gospel the Gentiles are heirs together with Israel, members together of one body, and sharers together in the promise in Christ Jesus (Eph. 3:6).

What promise? Heirs *together* with Israel! *One body!* How? *In Christ Jesus!* That's why Paul actually called the Galatian Christians—Jews and Gentiles—the *Israel of God*. This is Paul speaking …

> Neither circumcision nor uncircumcision means anything; what counts is the new creation. Peace and mercy to all who follow this rule, to the Israel of God (Gal. 6:15-16).

Paul calls the believers the *Israel of God!* That is why I keep saying the term 'replacement theology' is misleading, when people think of it as Gentiles *replacing* Israel. If the Gentiles replaced Israel, then the promises to Israel would *not* be fulfilled at all. Gentiles don't *replace* Israel. They are grafted in and joined *to* the true Israel. Not all who are called Israel are Israel, but Jewish believers in Christ are true Israelites and they are not replaced. Our Jewish believing brothers and sisters in Christ should be given that respect and that was Paul's argument to the church at Rome. Gentiles don't be arrogant, don't be conceited, you are not replacing them, but you are grafted *into them!* Jewish believers in Christ are God's true chosen people and in grace we are being joined to them, not replacing them.

If anything, I would suggest it would be more appropriate to say the dispensational premillennial view is replacement theology! Why? The classic dispensational view is that Jesus first came to begin his kingdom and reign over the Jews in fulfillment of OT promises, but the Jews rejected him. But God was not outsmarted and went to a plan B, the church, even though that was not what God wanted firstly for Israel. So the church becomes an interim plan B until this future 1000 years, when God will finally fulfill the promises to Israel at a separate time of salvation for the Jews.

But this means that what we have now (at least the last 2000 years) is a *replacement* of Israel. That is, for the largest chunk of Israel's history they have been replaced! It's a temporary plan B until God reintroduces his Messiah to Israel, and they accept their Messiah. But what about all those Jews of the last 2000 years, are they irrelevant? That is why with the dispensational view you have to decipher which bits in the gospels are relevant to you and which are only relevant to the Jews in some future 1000 years.

But I don't think the gospel is a plan B or a replacement. If we think that the salvation of the Jews is for some future time, we fail to see the urgency of evangelizing the Jews now! We fail to see the preciousness of what God has done through his ethnic believing people who have turned to Christ now and over the last 2000 years! The faithful remnant. Dispensationalism takes a lower view of ethnic Israel in who they are now! It's all very well to talk about Jews coming to faith in great number in some distant future, but what about all the Jews in the world now? Don't they count? Every Jew today who does not receive their Messiah will hurtle into a Christ-less eternity! Today is the day to evangelize the Jews! We fail to see the wonder of the mystery of the gospel that Gentiles are given to be fellow heirs to Israel (Eph. 3:6), not replacing them. Salvation is *of* the Jews, but not separate to the Jews. The Jews *are a blessing* to the nations. The gospel was always the OT plan for the Jews' restoration. Look at the OT promise.

> 'In that day I will restore David's fallen shelter—I will repair its broken walls and restore its ruins—and will rebuild it as it used to be ... (Amos 9:11).

Some premillennialists look at a text like this one and say, there it is, David's fallen shelter (tent, in other translations) restored in the temple in the future 1000-years of Israel. But the apostles interpreted this very text (along with others) as fulfilled in the gospel, not a separate future 1000-years. James at the council of Jerusalem refers to Amos ...

> Simon has described to us how God first intervened to choose a people for his name from the Gentiles. The words of the prophets are in agreement with this, as it is written: 'After this I will return and rebuild

> David's fallen tent. Its ruins I will rebuild, and I will restore it, that the rest of mankind may seek the Lord, even all the Gentiles who bear my name, says the Lord, who does these things,' ... (Acts 15:14-17).

James quotes Amos to describe the gospel, the incoming of the Gentiles with the Jews to rebuild David's fallen tent! The apostles interpret OT promises to Israel as fulfilled in the gospel, not Jews returning to land in Palestine. What a great backward step that would be, that after the gospel of reconciliation there would be a return to separation. The gospel joins and fulfills the promises!

And what of the promises of David's throne? Indeed, Jesus fulfills this, but does he do it only over 1000-years? Almost every OT text you look at that affirms the promise of David's greater son to be on David's throne shows it will *not last a mere 1000-years,* but forever!

> The LORD swore an oath to David, a sure oath he will not revoke: 'One of your own descendants I will place on your throne. If your sons keep my covenant and the statutes I teach them, then their sons will sit on your throne for ever and ever (Ps. 132:11-12).

The greater David does not reign for a mere 1000-years but forever! But what of the promises of Israel's land? Well, the promise of the land of Canaan is not watered down. It is increased! Revelation climaxes with the consummation of all things in the New Jerusalem, as well as the new heaven and new earth. It was something that deep-down Abraham must have known when he was promised the land of Canaan. He knew he was being promised something much bigger than just Canaan ...

> It was not through law that Abraham and his offspring received the promise that he would be heir of the world ... (Rom. 4:13).

Abraham knew the promise of the land of Canaan went beyond to the *whole world*. What world? Isn't that where Revelation is headed with the new heaven and earth? Does that mean Jesus will not rule in his kingdom on earth? Of course he will reign on this earth (Job 19:25-26)! Isn't this where Revelation is heading? A new heaven and new earth! Abraham will see and inherit Canaan, yes, but more! The promise expands to the whole world. As the apostle Paul said, Abraham knew the promise was for the whole *world!*

Jesus also interpreted it that way! Psalm 37:11 says the meek shall inherit the land (meaning Canaan). Jesus quotes that verse, but expands the promise of the land of Canaan and says the meek shall inherit what? You know it well. *The meek shall inherit the earth!* The promises of God are not less than literal, they are *more than you ask or imagine!*

Canaan was part of the plan. Canaan fits that promise in the OT of the restoration and return to Eden. (Isa. 51.3, Ezek. 36.35). It starts in Eden, widens to Canaan, but then Romans 4:13 tells us the promise to Abraham was the whole world. This is the new heaven and earth in Revelation. Not less than literal. More!

Many things fulfilled in prophecy are greater than a limited literal fulfillment. The Messiah himself is an example. When he first came people were looking for Jesus to come as a literal earthly king with military might. They were looking to him to free his people from oppression and come in all the pomp and glory like King Agrippa. And it wasn't just the Pharisees who missed it. The disciples and even John the Baptist were expecting something more literal. When Jesus didn't literally rout the enemies, John the Baptist asked, 'Should we be looking for another?'

So do we then say, 'Jesus didn't literally fulfill the OT promises of the Messiah?' He wasn't the literal military king like David defeating Israel's enemy, the Roman Empire. He didn't literally release Israel from captivity and oppression, bringing literal military peace to Israel. In fact, many rejected him because he didn't literally set himself up as the King in Jerusalem. Does that mean we say prophecy was not fulfilled? No. He fulfilled the promises in a far more profound way. He did give military peace to Israel. It was the greater need of peace between man and God. He did release captives … from their sin, death and hell! He was a far mightier king than a literal military Messiah. So too with the OT promises for the Jews. The new heaven and earth are a far greater and more profound fulfillment. Abraham gets Canaan all right. Canaan is on that new renovated earth, but it's far greater than just that small portion. He gets the whole lot!

Now I seem to have gotten away from the text itself of 20:4-6. Surely it's not good exposition to have talked about the role of the Jews in this 1000-years without finally referring back to the text? But that is the actual point. Rev. 20:4-6 is the foundation text of the premillennial view to explain the 1000-years as the restoration of the Jews in their own land on earth, and astounding as it is, Israel is not even mentioned at all in Rev. 20. Nor is the land of Canaan mentioned. Jews are not mentioned separately in relation to the 1000-years at all in this text! You would need to insert Canaan from the outside.

The reason we must still have respect for the different views is because this text is genuinely difficult whichever view you take. I still need to try and explain how this text can have two resurrections when the rest of the Bible says there is only one. And we need to concede we all carry our presuppositions and I admit I have one. So what presupposition will I carry to understand the hope for the future for Israel? Answer. The gospel! All the promises of God are 'Yes' and 'Amen' in Jesus! He is the one and only way to be saved. Believing in the one Jewish Messiah. That includes the remnant of ethnic Israel who have believed and will believe. And so all Israel will be saved—along with Gentile believers in the Jewish Messiah grafted in to become one people of God.

If this is true and the 1000-years are what we are living now, then what are the implications? The great and urgent implication is this—today is the day to evangelize the Jews! And the Gentiles! Jesus is coming back and there are no future second chances for Jews or anyone else! Today is the day of salvation.

Study Questions

1. On plain reading, does this text appear to teach two resurrections?

2. What might make us cautious about concluding that it teaches two resurrections?

3. What is a rule of interpretation for a difficult text?

4. If these 1000-years do not easily fit in between two resurrections in the rest of Scripture, what might be the overriding factor that makes this the most popular view amongst Christians?

5. How can the promises of God to Israel being restored to the land be fulfilled if these 1000-years are not future and literal?

6. Jesus did not literally fulfill Jewish hopes the first time he came. Explain how his fulfillment was even greater.

7. If Israel is not found in the text of Rev. 20:4-6, what is the implication for our attitude to the Jews today?

21
The Two Resurrections
(Revelation 20:4-6 Part 2)

'There is more than one way to skin a cat.' I never did find that the most inviting proverb (not particularly wanting to skin a cat even once), but it serves its purpose to say there is more than one way to look at Rev. 20. We've looked at the reasons why the view that it teaches two resurrections is at odds with the rest of Scripture. There is only one Day of Judgment. But what *do* we do with these two resurrections in this text? Is there soul sleep for the 'rest of the dead' because they don't come to life for 1000 years? The text opens with what seems to be a heavenly scene. But even that is in dispute. Those of the premillennial view generally say this is not heaven. Jesus has come again, and this is the beginning of his *future* 1000-year millennial reign from Jerusalem on earth. So these 'thrones' are on earth. But I think this scene is heaven *because* of the *thrones* ...

> I saw thrones on which were seated those who had been given authority to judge. And I saw the souls of those who had been beheaded because of their testimony about Jesus and because of the word of God. They had not worshiped the beast or its image and had not received its mark on their foreheads or their hands. They came to life and reigned with Christ a thousand years (20:4).

The book of Revelation mentions **thrones** 47 times and they are always in heaven, apart from Satan's and the Beast's throne of course. And **the souls of those who had been beheaded because of their testimony for Jesus** seems to indicate these people exist in heaven *before* the final resurrection of their bodies. It would be a strange use of the term soul if they were reigning on earth, but not in their bodies. It would be even stranger to have bodies on earth that have no heads.

I think it helps our understanding if we stand in the shoes of the first readers and ask what this text meant to them. Think again of the theme that John opened with at the beginning of this book which is trying to encourage fellow Christians going through suffering,

> I, John, your brother and companion in the suffering (or tribulation) and kingdom and patient endurance that are ours in Jesus, ... (1:9).

We see this same theme in 13:10 and 14:12. *This calls for patient endurance and faithfulness on the part of the saints.* What did the first readers think when they received these exhortations from the starting letters to the churches? 'The one who is victorious will sit on <u>thrones</u>!' They would have understood the message as this: 'Despite much pain, hold fast, you will get there too, because Jesus wins. You will sit on thrones!' Then they come to Rev. 20 and see those who went on before them. There they are on thrones! Just as you were assured in the church at Laodicea *To the one who is victorious, I will give the right to <u>sit with me on my throne</u>, just as I was victorious and sat down with my Father on his throne* (3:21). Now you see it happening! We mourned losing them, but there they are! They are reigning! On thrones!

It's the same message of perseverance the NT taught elsewhere ...

> Here is a trustworthy saying: If we died with him, we will also live with him; if we endure, we will also <u>reign</u> with him (2 Tim. 2:11-12a).

You will *reign* with him! Hold fast, you will be vindicated. Here it is. **I saw thrones on which were seated those who had been given authority to judge ...** How will Christians judge? Paul mentioned in 1 Corinthians 6:2 *Do you not know that the saints will judge the world?* What exactly does that mean? It could simply be the saints sit with Jesus and give their 'Amen' to the judgment of Christ. Or is it more? It seems strange to us. Jesus is the judge. But whichever way it works, the overcoming victory is so great that in some sense the believers *are* reigning with Jesus. Most scholars from the different views agree these believers likely include more than just martyrs who lost their heads, but rather all Christians who are victorious. Some were killed in other ways, not just beheading. But also many more who, as the last line says, were simply faithful: **they had not worshiped the beast or his image and had not received his mark on their foreheads or their hands.** But the text does highlight the extremes of martyrdom—God's holy people are beheaded. Also, the mark on the forehead indicates what you think or believe, and the mark on the hand indicates your actions—what you put your hands to. In other words, these are the faithful believers who persevered in the faith without compromise and they made it!

> (The rest of the dead did not come to life until the thousand years were ended.) This is the first resurrection (20:5).

This is where the Futurist premillennial view says, 'Aha! Two different days of judgment with two resurrections separated by 1000 years.' When Jesus returns the resurrection of the righteous occurs, followed by the 1000-year reign of Jesus on earth. After this *then* comes the resurrection and judgment of the unrighteous. Most agree **the rest of the dead** are unbelievers. What is controversial is that unbelievers don't **come to life** until the *end* of the 1000-year reign of Jesus on earth ... **this is the first resurrection**. So the believers receive the first resurrection, unbelievers don't. Two resurrections—one for believers and another for unbelievers. Two days of judgment separated by 1000 years.

But previously we surveyed the OT and NT and both uniformly confirmed there is only one Day of Judgment, and the resurrection of the righteous and wicked occur at the same time. And inserting 1000 years in between was totally unnatural. So what do we do with the two resurrections? We don't want to insert two resurrections back into the rest of the Bible, but what *does* this text teach? One premillennial scholar (Alford) says, you can't have 'coming to life' meaning spiritual in one sentence (20:4) and physical in another (20:5) in the same text, so it must mean two physical resurrections![22]

However, elsewhere the NT does exactly that and we think nothing of it. The words for *life* and *resurrection* can mean a spiritual or physical resurrection even within the *same* sentence!

> ... The one who believes in me will live, even though they die; and whoever lives by believing in me will never die (John 11:25-26a).

Jesus is speaking about *spiritual life* and a *physical resurrection* in the same sentence.

---

[22] Henry Alford, cited in *Revelation, Four Views,* Ed. Steve Gregg (Nashville: Thomas Nelson Publishers, 1997) pp. 466, 468

> ... just as Christ was raised from the dead through the glory of the Father, we too may live a new life ... we will certainly also be united with him in a resurrection like his ... but rather offer yourselves to God as those who have been brought from death to life ... (Rom. 6:4, 5, 13).

One is physical 'coming to life', the other is our spiritual 'newness'. Or John 5:24-29, *the one who believes has crossed over from death to life ... a time is coming and has now come when the dead will hear the voice of the Son of God and those who hear his voice will live.*

Other texts also speak of *spiritual life* and being *raised up* in the spiritual sense (Eph. 2:5-6). So too, the words *come to life* and *resurrection* in Rev. 20 could mean a *spiritual* come to life and *physical* within the same text. This would explain this text *without* compromising the rest of the Bible's teaching that there is only *one physical resurrection* of believers and unbelievers, one Day of Judgment. The **first** resurrection here simply refers to the believers going to heaven! It's not that complicated. What happens when believers die? Even though you die, you *come to life* in your soul in heaven. Though the body dies and rots in the grave, the soul comes to life in the presence of the Lord! Even those who had heads cut off *come to life*.

But they still await their final *second* resurrection. That is the final day—the only Day of Judgment—the one *and only* day of *physical* resurrection when their bodies are raised to life. Both believers and unbelievers experience this together at the Day of Judgment and resurrection. Bodies raised into the presence of the Lord.

But for unbelievers, that resurrection day is the first and only time they *come to life* into the presence of the Lord. They have no part in the first resurrection. That is, when they die their souls *don't* go into the presence of the Lord (in other words they don't *come to life*) until the 1000 years (the church age) is completed and Jesus returns. They *don't* experience that first resurrection. Indeed, we know from other parts of Scripture that when unbelievers first die they go into hell, as in a remand or holding cell awaiting final judgment and condemnation. They wait through the 1000-years, that long, indefinite period of the church age, and they don't *come to life* into the presence of the Lord until the Lord returns for that Day. For the unrighteous, that's their first and only resurrection, *coming to life* to eternal condemnation.

So while two *physical* resurrections don't fit with the rest of the

Bible, a twofold rising for believers *does*. Christians of all persuasions believe in this twofold rising. First to heaven in your soul and second in your body at the last day. Unbelievers rise only once. When they die they descend, but on the last day they are raised up in their body for the Day of Judgment. This solves the problem. And this is why you are so blessed if you take part in the first resurrection. Your soul rises to life to be with the Lord when you die. That is what it says in the next verse …

> <u>Blessed</u> and holy are those who have part in the first resurrection. The second death has no power over them … (20:6).

They are blessed because they go straight to heaven. Even though they die, they come to life in the presence of the Lord. Then, as if to confirm this is not just a clever idea of a twofold rising for believers, this very text does the same thing with 'death' for unbelievers. How many times do you die? Well, again go to the Bible elsewhere and it is clear. *It is appointed for man to die <u>once</u> and after that to face judgment* (Heb. 9:27). So why is this text saying there is a **second death** if you can only die once? Well, just as Rev. 20 uses *coming to life* as a twofold rising for believers—first the soul lives (resurrected to heaven), then the body is resurrected on the Day of Judgment, so too there is a twofold death for *un*believers—physical death (first death), followed by the second death. What is the second death? We learn later …

> Then death and Hades were thrown into the lake of fire. The lake of fire is the second death (20:14).

The second death is *eternal* hell! Does that mean the Bible contradicts saying *we only die once*? No. But the full consummation of death is not just when unbelievers physically die (though they might wish it was). That's not the end. They are held in hell until Judgment Day, then the full consequences of death and eternal hell come with the physical resurrection—when the body is joined to the soul in the *second death*.

This way of looking at the text enables us to make sense of Rev. 20 without having to rewrite the rest of the Bible, or to insert 1000 years and an extra resurrection. It allows God to be his own interpreter, letting the clearer passages interpret this difficult one. We can admit this understanding might not be obvious at first, but the crucial point is to let God interpret himself. Our interpretation must fit with the rest of the Bible.

To recap, 20:1-3 describes the gospel going forth to the nations *on earth*. Satan is bound from stopping the gospel going to the nations in the 1000-year long, indefinite church age.

Then, Rev. 20:4 gives us the heavenly perspective of the timeframe—*I saw <u>thrones</u> on which were seated those who had been given authority to judge.* [Believers who have died are in heaven including those martyred for the faith. Victory!] *And I saw the <u>souls</u> of those who had been beheaded because of their testimony for Jesus and because of the word of God.* [Where else could you have headless bodies except in their souls in heaven? This is before the return of Jesus and the resurrection of our bodies.] *They had not worshiped the beast or his image and had not received his mark on their foreheads or their hands. They <u>came to life</u> and reigned with Christ a thousand years.* [During the church age 1000-years, these souls are waiting for the Day of Judgment. They are the believers who have died and are in heaven. They 'came to life' in Jesus' presence, reigning in victory. Then the unbelievers ... 20:5.] *(The rest of the dead did not come to life until the thousand years were ended.)* [They don't come to life in the presence of the Lord until the Day of Judgment, at the end of the 1000-years church age. Then their bodies are raised 'come to life' together with believers who also receive bodily resurrection.] *This is the first resurrection* [relating back to before the brackets what happens to the believers when they first died and came to life. So naturally ... 20:6] *Blessed and holy are those who have part in the first resurrection.* [The souls of believers who die, go to be with the Lord and are blessed.] *The second death has no power over them* [hell cannot touch you if your soul has gone to be with the Lord after death], *but they will be priests of God and of Christ and will <u>reign with him</u> for a thousand years.*

They reign with Jesus! Doesn't this fit with the way Jesus spoke at the beginning of Revelation, when he told the first readers he was writing to them ...?

> ... and from Jesus Christ, who is the faithful witness, the firstborn from the dead, <u>and the ruler of the kings of the earth</u> (1:5).

He does not say he *will* rule. He reigns over the kings of the earth *now*. Jesus is ruling now in the church age. This is what we have seen in the seals, trumpets and bowls. He is in control. No one else can open the seals. He is the ruler and King of kings. Isn't this what the wider teaching of the NT teaches? *For he must reign until he has put all his enemies under his feet* (1 Cor. 15:25). And … *not only in this present age but also in the one to come* (Eph. 1:19-21).

So what is the point of this text? John says he is the fellow sufferer in the tribulation. And this book of Revelation is a word to the churches to remain faithful because Jesus wins. But what about when your Christian brothers and sisters are persecuted, even martyred for the faith? What of them? This vision answers that. Triumph! Victory. Being with Christ. *Reigning* with Christ. Isn't this what this book has been doing? Look at those seven letters again. Jesus tells them to keep going! Why? To the one who is victorious … you will sit on thrones! You will reign with me.

This is the text I turned to when I had to try and strengthen one of our elderly saints who had become so distressed on learning about children being beheaded by ISIS to the point she was being paralyzed by it. 'What can the Lord be doing?' The thought of this being done to children literally cast her into depression. The point of this text is to answer that very question! What is the Lord doing? The film shot of heaven says God did not simply provide a consolation prize for the suffering of his children. It's not, 'Well they went through a bad time and now they are relieved.' No! They are *reigning!* The victory and blessedness cannot be watered down to mere sense of relief. No. It's *triumph!* It simply will not do to posit the heaven of our imaginations where we say, 'At least the bad stuff is over and they are at peace now.' No! This film shot of heaven gives an almost unfathomable victory, and Christians can't seem to scale it's heights (or we take it for granted), because he uses the word REIGNING! Christians actually reigning? Isn't that something only the Lord does? It's not something we really think about. It's not just 'finish the race'. It's not just relief or 'well done', but so profound is this victory and blessedness that it can only be described as *reigning!* Children of God who were beheaded do not just 'make it home', they are *soaring* in such a way that the only appropriate term is *reigning!*

This text speaks into the 1000-years when we are confronted by evil with Christians beheaded and persecuted to death, and times we think surely the enemy is winning? What good is your Christianity to you now? Look at all those killed. This is the answer! They are NOT DEAD! They *came to life!* They not only live, but are *reigning* in triumph! Enemies thought they were defeating Christians when they killed them, but all they were doing was transporting them to glorious thrones of power and victory! This is written for Christians. Even Christians fall into the trap of looking for 'justice in this life'. If God is there, why does this one suffer? Why does God allow this one to die? Well, what does this text tell us? They didn't die! Even those who had such a horrible death as having their head cut off live. But not just live—they live in a victory! They are reigning! Reigning!

We are meant to read this going through tribulation and realign ourselves with the perspective we are supposed to have all along. This little short life is not the end, but an infinitesimal part of the whole picture. Believers who have passed on from this life are not complaining about what they went through. **Blessed and holy are those who have part in the first resurrection. The second death has no power over them, but they will be <u>priests of God and of Christ</u> and will <u>reign</u> with him for a thousand years** (20:6). This was applied to all believers back in 1:5 and 5:10. You will be for me a kingdom and priests. There are your loved ones who went on. Serving the Lord and reigning with him now.

All through this book we have said the big picture of Revelation is 'Jesus wins'. Now we are introduced to something new. Jesus not only wins—Jesus is winning! Now! Jesus wins the series! He reigns on high during this age as well as the age to come. This is radical thinking according to the popular view that says Jesus reigns only in a future 1000-years after his second coming. I invite you to look at the texts again that say Jesus reigns now (1:5, Eph. 1:19-21, 1 Cor. 15:25). These texts support the idea that 20:4-6 is saying in these 1000-years Jesus is reigning now!

The implications of this are astounding. Look at Ephesians 4:7-11, where Jesus is supplying gifts into his church—now! Look at Hebrews 1:3, he is sustaining all things in this whole universe—now! Re-read Revelation and look at the only one who could open the scroll. It's Jesus who is bringing about his judgments on the earth, but at the same time his saving work to the ends of the earth. What did Jesus mean when he told his disciples, 'All authority in heaven and earth has been given to me' (Matt. 28:18). Or 'It's to your advantage that I go away' (John 16:7). Why? Because before, his ministry was confined to wherever he walked around Palestine, but when he went away, he began his reign on high at the right hand of the Father, sending out his Spirit to the ends of the earth. This is big. What do you really think of when you think of Jesus in heaven? Slain lamb? Yes. You thought life was out of control *until* Jesus wins. But he is winning now! What does this mean for you right now? Are you stressed because of things that are happening, or does life seem out of control? You shouldn't be! Jesus reigns over all things *now!* The same one who gave himself up for you at the cross in humility is reigning for his kingdom and his people now!

Here is another one of those tantalizing speculations. This is a picture of what is happening now in heaven during the 1000-year church age. We see the souls in heaven are reigning with Jesus now. What can that mean? It brings up a fascinating thought when it says … **but they will be <u>priests of God and of Christ</u> and will <u>reign with him</u> for a thousand years.** So they are priests serving him. But they also *reign* with him now. At the very least it might mean the believers in heaven have a knowledge and interest in the workings of Jesus' reign on earth below throughout history, as he reigns on high (they reign with him). He sends gifts into his church, brings judgments on earth and sends his message through his Spirit to the ends of the earth. So if they are reigning with him in this work, does that mean they are watching and are involved in his work as they reign with him? We saw back in 6:9-11 that the saints were inquiring how long the state of affairs below would continue, and they were told there was still more to come in yet. And we asked the question: Do texts like Rev. 6 and Luke 15 (which speak of joy in the presence of angels over one sinner who repents) mean there is an awareness in heaven over the state of peoples' souls? Who do you think would be rejoicing and cheering the loudest in the presence of angels when you repent? Could it be your loved ones who have gone on in the Lord? Could they be watching us with interest right now? Do you know anyone who has gone on in the Lord? What a thought? They could be aware of you.

Now do you know why this is written? It's written for you and all who are going through tribulation. It's written that you might look at the heavenly perspective. You are not forgotten. Those who have died in the Lord are definitely not forgotten. They are with Jesus and are involved in his reign, as he is working out great things through your pain. Look at what happens. *Jesus wins* from beginning to end!

Blessed and holy are those who have part in the first resurrection. The second death has no power over them, but they will be <u>priests of God and of Christ</u> and will <u>reign</u> with him for a thousand years (20:6).

Study Questions

1. Is this text a scene of heaven or earth? Give reasons.

2. How can unbelievers only come to life after the 1000-years? Is that soul sleep?

3. Could spiritual and physical resurrection 'coming to life' occur in the same text? Give examples.

4. What is the first resurrection for believers?

5. What is the second resurrection or 'coming to life' for believers?

6. What is the first death for unbelievers?

7. What is the second death for unbelievers?

8. What happens to believers and unbelievers respectively who have died during the 1000-years?

9. What do you say to those who find it difficult to accept the cruel death of God's people?

10. What might it mean for believers to be reigning with Jesus now?

22
Tormented Forever
(Revelation 20:7-10)

We have looked at the 1000-years, symbolic of a long, indefinite period, just as the number 1000 is used symbolically consistently throughout Scripture. We've looked at Christ's reign in heaven during this time of the church age. We've looked at Satan bound from deceiving the nations, which makes sense as long as we think 'gospel to all nations'. But that is not the end of the story. After the 1000-years, there is a burst of greater opposition than ever before. Why? ...

> When the thousand years are over, Satan will be released from his prison and will go out to deceive the nations in the four corners of the earth—Gog and Magog—to gather them for battle. In number they are like the sand on the seashore (20:7-8).

As usual, Revelation draws on OT history to explain a more profound fulfillment. Gog and Magog represent nations opposing God. One thing I have reflected on, as I have studied the different views in Revelation, is how often those who say they interpret the text literally still interpret many or even most things symbolically. For example, John MacArthur says Gog and Magog are symbolic of all nations.[23] I agree with him 100%! Most agree that Satan is not literally a Dragon. From Beasts coming up out of the sea to promiscuously dressed prostitutes riding the Beast, these are taken symbolically by one and all. But then we must ask the question, 'Who decides when things are *not* symbolic?' On what basis do we suddenly demand that this text with Gog and Magog is symbolic of all nations, but then switch to a literal gathering around the Holy City? Or that the 1000-

---

[23] John MacArthur, *Because the time is Near*, (Chicago: Moody Publishers, 2007) p. 302

years has to be literal? Why would people be literally marching to have a literal physical war with a *symbolic* Gog and Magog, fighting a literal city?

I have been saying all along the only way to remain consistent is to take Revelation as it has been written, which is to take the visions and images symbolically. The people marching together doesn't necessarily mean they form an army platoon, 'left, right, left, let's go up and fight Jesus.' It means they are united, or joined and advancing together, in some way at Satan's beckoning, which should at least make us think of a possible Satanic or spiritual gathering. What about the rest of the text?

> They marched across the breadth of the earth and surrounded the camp of God's people, the city he loves. But fire came down from heaven and devoured them (20:9).

What is the **city he loves** that these enemies surround? The literal city of Jerusalem? All those unbelieving people march to Palestine to trap Jesus and his people, surrounding him in his Jerusalem temple? If we let these visions speak for themselves, only a few verses later there is another vision of the same *city God loves*, described in Rev. 21 as the Holy City, the New Jerusalem, the bride of Christ, which means *the people of God*, not a literal city!

So Revelation itself says the city is symbolic of the people. It is not a literal city. If we let the book of Revelation interpret itself, Jerusalem symbolizing God's people was first mentioned early in Revelation in the letters to the churches. At Philadelphia, the Christians were told if they were victorious they would become temple pillars in the city, the New Jerusalem (3:12). This theme ends with Rev. 21 saying the city is the bride of Christ.

Now the people, the *city*, is also called **the camp of God's people**. What would John the apostle think when he saw a vision of a *camp of God's people?* Israel in the wilderness! This is what Rev. 12 already told us. God's people during the tribulation are said to be going through the *wilderness* (desert) from the time of the ascension of Jesus (12:5-6). 'Camp' is also an OT concept of a military camp of Israel defending themselves against their enemies. Here God's people are defending themselves against their enemies. As ... **they marched across the breadth of the earth and surrounded the camp of**

God's people, the city he loves. They are attacking God's people and the cause of Christ. But God intervenes in final judgment. **But fire came down from heaven and devoured them** ...

> And the devil, who deceived them, was thrown into the lake of burning sulfur, where the beast and the false prophet had been thrown. They will be tormented day and night for ever and ever (20:10).

The Beast and False Prophet were thrown into the fiery lake of burning sulfur in Rev. 19, and now it's the Devil's turn in Rev. 20. You can understand at first glance why the premillennialist takes this chronologically. In Rev. 19 the Beast and False Prophet are thrown into the burning lake, then Rev. 20, the devil is thrown in 1000 years later, **where the beast and false prophet had been thrown**. But it's also grammatically possible in the original Greek language to mean all three at once. The devil was thrown in, *as were* the Beast and False prophet, meaning they were thrown in at the same time.

The demise is from the least to the greatest—like dominoes. The crash of Rev. 18 revealed Babylon, the great city, is destroyed—burned with fire (Rev.17). Then the Beast and False Prophet crash—into the lake of fire (Rev. 19). Then Satan himself, the ringleader, is thrown into the lake of fire (Rev. 20). If you read straight through from Rev. 17, it's been crash, crash, crash! They are all thrown into the lake of burning sulfur one after another. It's all one story! But it's close-up camera angles of each individual's demise. No matter how powerful these enemies appeared, they all end up in the same place. Even the most powerful, Satan. Revelation is doing what it has been doing all along. It's giving different camera angles and lead up to one Day of Judgment. Not several days of judgment, just one, described in these details.

The reason we know the demise of Babylon, the Beast, the False Prophet, and Satan are different camera angles of the same event, is because the same key elements of the last day are in all of them. All the nations gather, and all the nations are decimated in each crash, of Babylon, the Beast, the False Prophet and Satan. It was called the Battle of Armageddon back in Rev. 16 and *the* war. What happened there? Just as in our text in 20:7-8, all the nations advance together against Christ's people. Satan is behind this gathering together, back in Rev. 16. Satan's minions gathering!

> They are <u>demonic spirits</u> that perform signs, and they go out to the kings of the whole world, <u>to gather them for the battle on the great day of God Almighty</u> (16:14).

Don't miss it. Who is gathering together? The whole world! It's the same as Rev. 20. How many times can there be a 'great day of God Almighty'? This is it!

It's the same completeness of judgment in 16:19 for Babylon, with the cup *filled with the wine of the fury of his wrath.* Filled! Babylon is also burned with fire (17:16)! So Babylon ends up in the fire. What about the senior enemies? Sure enough, if we go back over Rev. 19, we see that the Beast and the False Prophet end up in the fire.

Remember there is an article before the word *battle* or *war* in the original Greek language. The article 'the' emphasizes *the war*, meaning there can only be *the one war* in all three stories. It's not just any war or three separate wars, but THE one and only final war. It's called THE war in Rev. 16, when Babylon ends up in the fire. In THE war in Rev. 19, the Beast and False prophet end up in the fire. And so too, in our text (20:8), the original wording for 'battle' is literally THE war, and Satan ends up in the fire.

In Rev. 19 this war also draws on Ezekiel's war with Gog and Magog. What are Gog and Magog doing back in Rev. 19? It's because it's the same symbol of Gog and Magog, in the same war in Rev. 20, describing the same event. And what happened in that final war back in Rev. 19? The nations gathered!

The Premillennial view says Rev. 19 was a lesser separate battle than the one in Rev. 20, and that after the war of Rev. 19, Jesus reigns over the nations on earth for 1000 years. But there was nothing left of the nations! Remember this was that ugly text where the judgment birds ...

> ... eat the flesh of kings, generals, and the mighty, of horses and their riders, and the flesh of <u>all people</u>, free and slave, great and small (19:18).

There are no nations left to rule over! Why? They were eaten up. It's all describing the last day—the great day of God almighty. That is why it ends with the same devastation in the fiery lake for the enemies of God. It gives the same details because it is the same event. Rev. 19 said the nations gathered against Christ and his people. How do they gather?

> When the thousand years are over, Satan will be released from his prison and will go out to deceive the nations in the four corners of the earth—Gog and Magog—to gather them for battle. In number they are like the sand on the seashore. They marched across the breadth of the earth and surrounded the camp of God's people, the city he loves. But fire came down from heaven and devoured them (20:7-9).

The people of this whole earth who don't know Christ will take part in a new intensity of animosity *gathered* against the people of God (the city) towards the end, before the fire comes down. How will they be gathered? It doesn't have to be one of those apocalyptic Hollywood movie style scenes, but something far more relevant to what either is happening now or will intensify in the future. The vision teaches a time when Satan is released from a previous restriction of the gospel to the nations. There comes a time of a new intensity of deceit towards the end. It's the joining together of the nations against Jesus and his people. They don't have to be physically marching, but they all march to the same drum. This is a vision. They will march even from inside the church. Satan's greatest attacks on the church will come from people marching inside, in the name of Jesus! Not only hypocrites, but false and weak teaching watering down the gospel with messages that people want to hear. They are gathering together with the world against Christ and his people.

This text is actually repeating (from 20:3) that Satan is let loose for a short time after the 1000-years. And just as we said of 20:3, this will be a time when the message of Satan (i.e. rule yourself, save yourself), will be heightened. We asked if there has ever been a time with the church under attack from deceit that even the leadership would promote self-saving? Well, in some measure, the RC church since the Middle Ages has promoted a works-based salvation plus Jesus. But could older devout RCs imagine a time when a Pope openly says you don't even need to believe in Jesus at all? Just in case you thought I was exaggerating when I referred to Pope Francis' sermon, here is an excerpt.

> 'The Lord has redeemed all of us, all of us, with the Blood of Christ: all of us, not just Catholics. Everyone! 'Father, the atheists?' Even the atheists. Everyone! ... 'But I don't believe, Father, I am an atheist!' But do good: we will meet one another there.'[24]

---

[24] Pope Francis, Vatican Mass sermon May 22nd 2013

The RC church used to teach works plus Jesus for salvation, but now the Pope openly 'gathers' with the world saying you don't even need to believe in Jesus at all. Popes have never been popular with unbelievers of the world, but the world loves today's Pope like no other because he 'gathers' the unbelieving world together with attack on the gospel.

> ... and will go out to deceive the nations in the four corners of the earth—Gog and Magog—to gather them for battle (20:8).

Gather them for battle. How do we understand this battle? Think 'gospel'. Think, 'for or against Jesus'. Every religion and every ideology says, 'You don't need to believe in the Savior, just be a good person.' Look at the way the world is gathering against Jesus' people. The created order of marriage that the Bible begins with is one man and one woman. It finishes in Revelation as the great metaphor for Jesus' wedding banquet union with the church. Look at the momentum of the nations, gathering on same-sex marriage. Nothing like this has been seen in history, let alone in Christian countries. The man and woman in marriage were supposed to be Christians reflecting Jesus and his church. No wonder Satan wants to attack marriage! Its true definition points to Jesus! This has become heightened in our time where even those who were once for the biblical definition of marriage are now against it.

We also have the Beast telling us we can defy our God-given biology and 'decide' to change our gender. The name of Jesus is the only name you can publicly blaspheme. They all gather and march together. How can we resist this juggernaut and make our stand? Times are a changing from what was unthinkable only a few years ago.

Before, unbelievers would brush you off with, 'Believe what you like as long as you don't bother me.' Not anymore. Now the atheist push is to *gather* people together to stamp out faith. Newspapers are happy to publish calls for bans on organized religion. Outlaw faith in public! Christian schools' rights are being threatened simply to be able teach biblical concepts and hire only Christian staff.

Christians have always been persecuted. The unusual thing now is the aggressive joining together against Christianity in so-called Christian countries. A *marching* against the city (the people of God), to squeeze them out of places that formerly accepted them in schools, in laws, and in public.

We don't know when the end will come, but be careful if you are getting comfortable thinking, 'Well, the predictions of Revelation would be fulfilled in a more obvious way. Things have always been bad, so it could get dramatically worse.' That could be true. But remember the book of Revelation is the same one in which Jesus tells us he comes like a thief. Unexpectedly. The end can't be that obvious. I often reflect on some of the fulfillment of Jesus' first coming. 'Out of Egypt I called my son' (Matt. 2:15). The OT forerunner to this was the great Exodus where the nation of Israel dramatically and miraculously escaped Egypt through the sea. And the fulfillment? Joseph and Mary having sneaked their baby out of Bethlehem, traveling to Egypt to live for a while on their way to Galilee. That's it? Too subtle for our expectations? But it was true nevertheless. Just as the Lord's fulfillment of prophecy will be absolutely true, it will be his way in his time, always with this one overriding factor ...

Jesus will come upon us like a thief! It will not be obvious. And yet, there will be a time when the opposition to the church must clearly increase. Our text says this time happens *after* the 1000-years of the church age, and it won't last too long. There have been shifts in society in the last generation that were unthinkable only a few years ago. We can't say whether we are in that last short time, but whenever that last *short time* begins, it does not just keep going on and on. It doesn't last long. It will only be short! And then?

Jesus comes back and **fire came down from heaven and devoured them. And the devil, who deceived them, was thrown into the lake of burning sulfur, where the beast and the false prophet had been thrown. They will be tormented day and night for ever and ever.**

The old translations say *fire and brimstone* rather than *burning sulfur*. You've heard of the 'fire and brimstone' preachers. This is where that saying comes from. Personally, I'm not a fire and brimstone preacher. Before I actually knew what brimstone was, for some reason I pictured it like those large stone boulders they would use in ancient Roman baths. Something nice and cool you lie on in your toga after you have had a steam bath. Relaxing on the brimstone.

Because of that I thought, 'I don't want to be a wimpy brimstone preacher. I'm a *lake of burning sulfur* preacher!' But brimstone means sulfur anyway.

But *they will be tormented day and night forever and ever.* We shudder at this. Is this fair? Do we have a proper perspective on sin, as sinners ourselves? It's like asking an alcoholic whether another drink would be a good idea! Do we ask a sinner if eternal punishment is fair? What does sin really deserve? Just how bad is your sin, really? Only someone who has never sinned can know. Only God can know. And this is God's verdict. Sin is so evil that it can never be purged. It must be punished eternally. Satan deserves it! We are okay with Satan copping that eternally, but people? Well, we entered into Satan's sin in our own way. Self-rule. 'I am Lord of my life. I will determine right and wrong.' That was Satan's rule from the beginning. So you get to live with … yourself and all the consequences of what you did in your 'self'.

Our sin really does deserve punishment forever and ever. Do you believe it? If you haven't fully committed yourself to Jesus yet, or you are lukewarm, picture your future. Imagine yourself in that lake of burning sulfur. I had a quick thought of it once. Imagine being stuck there, there is no coming back from it. No way out. Here I am. I got what I really deserved. Of course, none of us are anywhere near as bad as Satan, not even in the same league. So you will just be up the shallow end of that lake with floaties. He's up the deep end. But you are there. Just like jails have different levels of confinement—solitary, high security, then low security (less harsh), etc. Each one receiving their justice according to the things they have done. Have you ever really contemplated how you really deserve to be there? That's where the majority of humanity will end. Living with themselves forever. But wait …

Now picture Jesus in that lake of fire going in your place! He didn't literally go in there. But he *literally* took the full *penalty* of it. What did Jesus do on the cross? Do the math. The eternal Son of God had to go through the burning of the eternal wrath of God until … it is finished! He had to pay an *eternal* redemption (Heb. 9:12). Picture the eternal one from the creation hurtling through the lake of fire with the names of those who are written in the book of life from before the creation of the world!

Only when you have seen yourself in that lake of fire and seen that grace in what *he* did to free you, will you really be free to serve him, even fight for him. If you *believe!* But what if you are caught up in a secret sin, or you know you are not walking with Jesus, or you live with what people call the RC guilt, because you are trying to do enough to make God happy. You can't! Eventually you will either develop some delusional self-righteousness, or you'll just chuck in the towel, hoping he has lowered the standard. But he doesn't, and he won't. The standard is the lake of fire. But what if all your sin was washed clean? What if the record was erased and you were pure and clean? Through faith in Jesus it happens. None of us can see how bad our sin is compared to God's perspective, but by *faith* we *believe* what he says is true! Sin really does deserve eternal punishment. And by faith we can believe the magnitude of what Jesus went through to take it away. You can't be sent into the lake of fire if your sin has already been punished. He has done it! It's by grace you are saved, through faith. Just faith. So now you can go and *live* that faith!

And the devil, who deceived them, was thrown into the lake of burning sulfur, where the beast and the false prophet had been thrown. They will be tormented day and night for ever and ever (20:10).

Study Questions

1. Is the battle at Gog and Magog literal? Give reasons for your answer.

2. How do the nations gather and march together if Jesus comes back like a thief?

3. What is the *city that God loves,* and how does that help explain this text?

4. Rev. 19 has the Beast and False Prophet thrown into the fiery lake, then Rev. 20 has the devil thrown into the fiery lake after the 1000-years. Is this chronological?

5. What kind of things would we expect to see if Satan was released from his prison near the end?

6. Is it possible for that to happen before our eyes without us noticing?

7. Give examples of how Jesus' first coming was seen as too subtle for those who were there at that time.

8. Does the 'torment forever' give you food for thought about what sin really deserves?

23
The Great White Throne
(Revelation 20:11-15)

John the apostle has seen some amazing visions, but this is as big as it gets. John gets to see the Great White throne, the Lord in all his glory. He sees the Creator of the universe on his judgment seat. How cosmic, how terrifying is the end of the world? The *earth and sky flee!*

> Then I saw a great white throne and him who was seated on it. The earth and the heavens fled from his presence, and there was no place for them (20:11).

We hear terms like 'naked before the throne on Judgment Day', but how naked is this? Even the *earth* and the *heavens* (some translations have *sky*) have fled! All that is left is the people ...

> And I saw the dead, great and small, standing before the throne ... (20:12).

This is a vision. Visions are allowed a certain license. After all, if the earth and sky have fled, then what are all these people standing on? But these visions always convey literal truth in this book of symbols, and we should not miss it. When Judgment Day arrives, everything is laid bare before him to whom we must give account.

The earth and sky are part of the creation. They existed by the power of God's word. And here are Jesus' words coming to fulfillment. 'Heaven and earth will pass away but my words will not pass away' (Matt. 24:35). God is not dependent on the creation for you to exist or be able to stand before him. You will stand! He created the world and gravity!

This reminds us of the way Genesis is written in the creation account. Modern scholars think they find a contradiction in the way the creation account is written. 'Let there be light' occurs *before* there is a sun and moon or stars created. 'Ah ha, it's a contradiction!' they say. No. In fact, it is making a crucial point. Moses' first readers were even more startled by the account that God created light before the sun. Why? Because the world of Moses' day worshiped the sun! The sun is the god who provides the light. What is the living God saying in the creation account? The same thing he says at the end of Revelation. Light does not come ultimately from the sun (though practically that may be what God uses), but ultimately light and indeed all things in creation, earth and sky, come from God himself! At the end of all things, Revelation says there will be no sun in the new heaven and earth. The Lord himself and the Lamb are its light.

God is not pantheistic, a part of the creation. People have tried to give the creation the credit for creating itself. Some have said that the creation is eternal. People realize you can't get something out of nothing, so they say the creation, or some kind of matter, or hydrogen has always been there. So this non-living matter had in itself the power, the intelligence, and foresight to bring about a finely tuned universe and produce a living, intelligent precision designed creation. All from non-living matter. Really? Truly the creation is worshiped today as much as ever.

Save the planet they say! But the planet will not be saved. Take a look at this text. The planet is gone! As Christians, we should be environmentalists because we believe God created this world for us and we were given a mandate to take care of it. But we keep it in perspective in that we don't hold the creation's importance above God, or even man, because one day it will flee!

So appropriately, this vision shows the day of the Lord, when he appears on his throne, and there is no security for us in the world itself, no other gods, not the creation, no worship of the planet. It will be whisked out of the way. Just you and this ... **Then I saw a great white throne and him who was seated on it. The earth and the heavens fled from his presence, and there was no place for them.** This scene reminds us of Daniel 7:9-10, where the Ancient of Days takes his seat on the throne. The multitudes assemble and books are opened. In Daniel, it is the Father who is the judge, and we saw God seated on the throne in 4:2 and 5:7. But other NT teaching clearly speaks of Jesus having been given the authority to judge (Matt. 22:1-3, 25:31-46, John 5:22, Acts 17:31, 2 Cor. 5:10, 2

Tim. 4:1). Jesus is the Lord and judge. So who is on that judgment throne? The Father or the Son? The apostle Paul helps us here ...

> This will take place on the day when God will judge people's secrets through Jesus Christ, as my gospel declares (Rom. 2:16).

So the Father judges, but through the Son!

> In the presence of God and of Christ Jesus, who will judge the living and the dead, and in view of his appearing and his kingdom ... (2 Tim. 4:1).

When Jesus comes back, he will judge *with* the Father. So coming back to our text ...

> And I saw the dead, great and small, standing before the throne, and books were opened. Another book was opened, which is the book of life. The dead were judged according to what they had done as recorded in the books (20:12).

A Christian can never be judged for their sin, and yet they too have to give an account. Some say Christians are in both the *book of life* and the *record of deeds*, as a testimony of a life lived to their faith. Christians are promised individual rewards depending on what they did with what the Lord gave them. That would suggest a recorded assessment. As the apostle Paul includes Christians when he says ...

> For <u>we must all appear</u> before the judgment seat of Christ, that each of us may receive what is due us for the things done while in the body, whether good or bad (2 Cor. 5:10).

He said **we must all appear** to Christians. So even though as Christians we can never be condemned for our sin (John 5:24), God cares about the life you live as a Christian. The things we do count. The Lord has promised to reward you according to what you have done. As some have put it, everyone's cup will be full in heaven, but some will be given larger cups. Some say the desire for heavenly rewards would be a wrong motive for doing good. But rather, we should look at it as meaning that the Lord notices and cares what his people go through and cares about faithful service. There are those who stand for Jesus in lands right now who are being tortured for Jesus. Does he care? Yes, and he promises to reward them according to their particular faithfulness (God's compensation matches their trials). He watches and records your love for your enemies ...

> But love your enemies, do good to them, and lend to them without expecting to get anything back. Then your <u>reward</u> will be great, ... (Luke 6:35).

When you love your enemies, the Lord notices and *rewards*. He notices the way you react to criticism.

> Blessed are you when people hate you, when they exclude you and insult you and reject your name as evil, because of the Son of Man. 'Rejoice in that day and leap for joy, because great is your <u>reward in heaven</u>' (Luke 6:22-23a).

How many rewards have you lost because you fought back when people insulted you instead of rejoicing?

The Lord also notices your giving.

> But when you give to the needy, do not let your left hand know what your right hand is doing, so that your giving may be in secret. Then your Father, who sees what is done in secret, <u>will reward you</u> (Matt. 6:3-4).

In that same passage, Jesus talks about storing up treasures in heaven! So the Lord is not indifferent to our trials, efforts, and sacrificial love. Even our commitment to the fellowship of God's people. When did we not meet with you? When you did not do it for the least of these, you did not do it for me. We must repeat that a Christian's sin has already been judged and punished at the cross. Jude 24 says he will present you faultless in the presence of his glory with exceeding joy! But for the unbeliever it's different. It's been recorded, everything they have ever done ...

> And I saw the dead, great and small, standing before the throne, and books were opened. Another book was opened, which is the book of life. The dead were judged according to what they had done as recorded in the books (20:12).

Notice there is only one book with the names, the *book of life*, but we need lots of books (plural) to record all **according to what they have done as recorded in the books!** Numerous volumes. But one thing is for sure—everyone is there on that day. The implication from our text is that everyone is there, but some are thrown into the lake of fire. *Anyone whose name was not found written in the book of life was thrown into the lake of fire* (20:15). There are not two judgments separated by 1000 years. Everyone is together ... **And I saw the dead, <u>great and small</u>, standing before the throne, and books were opened**.

So people you have read about and thought of as just ancient stories will all be there. You will see them. Look at this vision John is having. *And I saw them.* Adam and Eve are there. Cain is also there, standing next to his brother he killed, Abel. That must be embarrassing. All are there. You can see all the sheep and the goats. The righteous and the unrighteous, *great and small.* Noah is there. But also are those who ridiculed him for building the ark. Ham is also there, Noah's son who made it on the ark but whose heart was not right. You can also see Moses and the faithful Israelites. But what about all the unfaithful Israelites who worshiped the Baals? Now they face the living God. All the nations were deceived through those generations until Jesus came. They are all there. And hey, there is Judas. Suicide didn't help him escape because there he is. And Pilate. Pilate once judged Jesus—now he faces Jesus as Judge. His face is whiter than the great white throne. The hypocrites are all there. Not just those of Jesus' day, but those who used the name of Christ and the church as a means for power and corruption. There are those from the Middle Ages who withheld the gospel. False teachers. Fast forward a few centuries into our day, and there are those who preached a false gospel, who went around saying, 'Thus saith the Lord', when the Lord had not spoken. There are also the pedophile priests. They didn't get away with it! They are all there! Oh, but look, so are the people who used those hypocrites as their excuse to reject Jesus' church. They said, 'The church is full of hypocrites, so I reject Jesus' church.' Now it's exposed that it was Jesus they rejected. Now they also take their place on the left *among* those very hypocrites. And there are those who spent their lives lukewarm, never committing their life fully to Jesus. And then there are those who press forward confidently thinking they will be okay, though their inner life was not right. They are crying out in confidence. 'Lord, Lord, didn't we do good in your name?' Only to hear soon those frightening words, 'I never knew you. Away from me you evil doers.'

Also those who had never heard the gospel were there. They were judged according to the things they had done. But look at this! The greater punishment is going to those who *did hear* the gospel and rejected it. They get the hottest part of the lake of fire. They said, 'I reject God, he can't be fair because of all those people who never heard.' But now it turns out they are in much greater trouble than those who never heard. The Lord had it all worked out so fairly and justly. He had said that in advance ...

> 'The servant who knows his master's will and does not get ready or does not do what his master wants will be beaten with many blows. But the one who does not know and does things deserving punishment will be beaten with few blows. From everyone who has been given much, much will be demanded; and from the one who has been entrusted with much, much more will be asked' (Luke 12:47-48).

It's all so fair now. Now everyone can see that no one had any excuses, because each one is judged fairly, according to what they had done with the knowledge they had. So the mentally disabled, children, people who never heard the gospel, people who were abused or had an environment that shaped their opportunity, on this day there is no confusion because the Lord knows exactly how to take all that into account. And it turns out there was not a single one who would have responded that missed out. Not one of his sheep was lost. The Lord reached every single one of those who were his. Jesus lost none of the names the Father gave him (John 6:39). And all those who had judged God, thinking it wouldn't be fair, are dumbstruck because he judges even motives. They shouldn't have judged before this appointed time ...

> Therefore judge nothing before the appointed time; wait till the Lord comes. He will bring to light what is hidden in darkness and will expose the <u>motives</u> of the heart (1 Cor. 4:5).

Even the motives are recorded in the books. The computer history is all recorded. The CCTV was in every dark corner, and now it's all in sharp focus! The camera was on you all along and it's recorded in detail in the books because you are there too!

People who thought they were getting away with things were being filmed for this record, and now it's all coming out as the books are opened. All those who thought God grades on a scale are in shock. They thought sin is only as bad as it looks compared to others. 'I'm not as bad as some.' But now on this day it's exposed. Sin was sin. It doesn't get better just because others do worse than you.

If you think people will be horrified if they knew everything you think of them now, or all your dark secrets—you're right! On this day they are horrified, but nowhere near as horrified as you are if those books are opened with your sins recorded there. There are no comparison scales compared to anyone else. 'Hey, I slashed your tires.' 'That's okay, I slashed yours too.' 'Oh, that's okay then.' No! It's not okay. It's terrible!

And yes, *you* are there on that day. And if your sin is recorded in those books, you will be judged, exposed—to everyone! Everyone is there to see it. It is the ultimate public humiliation … **The dead were judged according to what they had done as <u>recorded in the books</u>.** All your friends and family, the people you worked with and knew are all there. Nothing is hidden from them now. Some of the people you knew are cursing you for not telling them the gospel. Those who did you wrong finally get justice—those who insulted Jesus and proudly did whatever they wanted. But also, those who just couldn't care less. There are also those who outwardly appeared good, even members of the church, but had secrets they thought were secret. Well, the secrets were never secret. God knew all along. Now the record is being opened! It's all there!

There are also those who said on that day they would ask for forgiveness. But the day for repentance has passed. And all those boasters who said they would have a few things to say to God have their mouths stopped up at the revealing of this record against them. The terror in the hearts for those waiting for their name and their record, even down to their motives and thoughts, is put up for public display.

And at this point, everyone's eyes are on those books. You thought you got stressed over that interview or exam? This is like no other exam you ever faced. And you have to wait. Because as each one appears, more of the dead arrive …

> The sea gave up the dead that were in it, and death and Hades gave up the dead that were in them, and each person was judged according to what they had done (20:13).

No one escaped by being buried in the grave or in the sea. Those who died and had gone on to Hades, the holding cell of punishment for their soul, even they are called up in the resurrection of their bodies, **and each person was judged according to what he had done**. Whatever was done in the body (2 Cor. 5:10), now the bodies are given back to each one to receive what they did in that body. It all comes back to what you did in that body and you can't hide from your own body on this day …

> Then death and Hades were thrown into the lake of fire. The lake of fire is the second death (20:14).

Death as we know it is destroyed. The last enemy is death. **Hades,** the holding cell of pain for the unsaved—even that is gone. What is left is the permanent eternal state. The **second death**. The second death is not dying twice. It is the second stage of the fullness of death. Death is separation. The first stage is physical death, which we all go through. The second is receiving the full consequence of sin—with separation. That takes place in the body with which you committed the sins. The second death is also called the lake of burning sulfur. An unending conscious punishment (14:10-11). It's outside the city of God, separate from God and his blessing. You rejected God and his salvation and now you get what you wanted. Separation.

What happens in this lake of fire? Well, this is a vision of course. It's symbolic, but as with all symbols, its symbolic *of* something. It's not annihilation. It fits with other NT teaching that it is a place of burning with conscious existence. In Luke 16:19-30, the rich man was in conscious torment in the heat. Jesus said it's a place where there is weeping and gnashing of teeth. The crying of regret and gnashing teeth in anger over the foolishness of lost opportunity. Where their worm does not die. But who goes there?

> Anyone whose name was not found written in the book of life was thrown into the lake of fire (20:15).

Anyone whose name was not in the book of life! This is the final exam as each one is checked to see if their name is in the book of life or if they are *thrown* into the lake of fire. At this moment, everything you thought you needed to worry about is irrelevant. In fact, when this moment comes, you are saying to yourself, 'What was I thinking!' At this point you won't be thinking, 'Man, I really had a hard life financially,' or, 'Why couldn't I have had a happy marriage, or an easier life?' Now all you are thinking is—am I in that book! Everything else is irrelevant. The only thing that matters now is this: Is your name written in that book of life? Are the names of your loved ones in that book? Your life flashes before your eyes. All the things you thought you needed. Where did you spend your time and money? Where did you find your portion? What other gods, idols crept in? How did you use the gifts God gave you? For his kingdom? Jesus' words echo in your mind, *Don't rejoice about your gifts. Rejoice that your names are written in heaven* (Luke 10:20).

But is your name written there? It's either there or it's not, because it was written from the creation. How can you know if your name is in that book? Well, you don't have to wait until then to find out. Have you thrown yourself on his mercy? I mean your whole self. Or have you been holding back a little 'something for me'. Is Jesus enough? By faith have you got up and followed him? Look back over Revelation. It's a wake-up call. Are you lukewarm? He will spit you out of his mouth! Come out of her Babylon! Did you come out? Have you repented? This is a peek into the future. There you are at the judgment seat of Christ. If you haven't repented, then do it now! Even now you can make sure your name is there. Because if you believe in him truly as Lord and Savior, then even as a sinner your name is there. You see, the full title of the book of life is the *'Lamb's book of life'* (13:8). The Lamb who was slain. That's why as a sinner your name can be there. The Lamb has been slain from the creation of the world, hurtling through eternity through that lake of fire. But when he did that, he took those names with him. He carried the names of all those in that book of life. He took all of what would have been recorded against you with him to the cross. He did it for all who would truly repent and believe in him.

Anyone whose name was not found written in the book of life was thrown into the lake of fire (20:15).

Study Questions

1. What is the point of the vision of the earth and sky fleeing?

2. Who is the Judge? Jesus or the Father?

3. Can a Christian have any sin brought before them at judgment?

4. How can a Christian be 'judged'?

5. What is there in this text that helps us understand judgment as appropriate to the individual?

6. What do you say to the skeptic who questions how judgment can be fair for a mentally disabled person?

7. How is the second death different from those who had experienced Hades up to this point?

8. Is your name written in the book of life?

9. How do you know?

24
The New Heaven and Earth
(Revelation 21:1)

We have finally reached heaven. The new heaven and the new earth. This is it! Many, especially those of the Premillennial view, see this new heaven and new earth as a totally new creation out of nothing. That is one possibility. There is a good argument for this being a new planet with a new heaven. After all, it is a *new* heaven and *new* earth.

> Then I saw 'a <u>new</u> heaven and a <u>new</u> earth,' for the first heaven and the first earth had passed away, and there was no longer any sea (21:1).

There are two common words usually translated as **new** in the original Greek language. One is *neos*, which is more commonly used to indicate newness of time. The other is *kainos*, which is more commonly used for newness in quality (as in a renovation). It's that second word *kainos* which is used here in 21:1. This at least presents the possibility that rather than a new heaven and new earth being a newly created planet, that this is a judged, purged and totally renovated heaven and earth. So radical is its renewal that it is appropriately called *new*.

But why is it new in quality rather than a new planet altogether? The answer to this question goes back to the meaning of Revelation. Jesus wins! Through the fall our bodies experienced death and corruption. Why did that happen? Satan's work in tempting man was to bring in sin and death. Thus, man's body dies and decays. Satan destroys God's creation. Now if God simply gives us new bodies, then Satan wins. Satan has destroyed the old and God cannot win it back, so he has to start something new (as in totally different). But the Son of God became a man, went through death, and was resurrected *in his same body* so that we too will be resurrected in our bodies. New yes, in the sense of radically restored and glorified, but a renovation and continuity with the old body. Jesus wins. Satan does not.

It's the same with the creation. Satan and sin cause the corruption of the creation (*All of creation groans ...*). If God has to throw it away completely and start with something entirely different, then Satan has outdone God and Satan wins. But the new heaven and new earth are the final defeat of Satan. The old version is destroyed and purged by fire, but it is redeemed, restored and re-created from the old. Jesus wins!

The Bible teaches a literal destruction of the earth as we know it, just as our bodies literally die and decay. That is why Christians generally prefer burial to cremation. Pagans burn bodies because they see no continuity with the body (Greek philosophy even saw the body as evil). But burial is the usual Christian option. That is, not deliberately destroying the body because we have the hope of the resurrection of our bodies. Of course, God is able to raise us again from the dust as he did in the beginning for those who have been cremated or burned in fires etc. But this new heaven and new earth will be like the glorified body. It will have continuity with the old, but will be so radically renewed that it's new!

There is an unshakeable permanency about the *new* heaven and earth. We looked at John's vision of the earth and sky which fled on the Day of Judgment, but other parts of Scripture tell us that this symbol points to everything being laid bare before him to whom we must give account, not necessarily its literal disappearance. Even though the earth is destroyed by fire, the bare bones are still there after the fire purges it ...

> But the day of the Lord will come like a thief. The heavens will disappear with a roar; the elements will be destroyed by fire, and the earth and everything in it will be <u>laid bare</u> (2 Peter 3:10).

It's still there, but it's *laid bare*. It's the same thought the apostle Paul has ...

> ... that the creation itself will be liberated from its bondage to decay and brought into the freedom and glory of the children of God. We know that the whole creation has been groaning as in the pains of childbirth right up to the present time (Rom. 8:21-22).

So the creation is in bondage to decay, but like a new birth, it will be freed from its old corruption like our resurrected bodies. Notice it's not to be eliminated altogether, but renovated and *brought into freedom*. This makes the cross of Christ and his resurrection something far greater than you thought. The cross and resurrection bought redemption and the re-creation of our bodies as well as the whole creation itself! Satan does not win. He didn't defeat God by destroying God's creation permanently. Jesus redeems and wins it back. Jesus wins.

It's returning us to the Garden of Eden. God restores and gives us back the original venue without the corruption. What Satan and sin ruined is overcome! Jesus wins. Rev. 21:5 seems to be underlining this. *'I am making everything new!'* This sort of language suggests that everything which existed in its old state is now made new! It's the anticipation of newness that began at Jesus' resurrection. Jesus is the firstborn in resurrection. And through Jesus' work and the Holy Spirit this brings us new life spiritually as a deposit of what is to come.

> Therefore, if anyone is in Christ, the new creation has come: The old has gone, the new is here (2 Cor. 5:17).

The reason it is good to spend time on this is because it helps us understand more of the deeper things of the cross. You thought Jesus was just saving your soul. But there is more to the cross than that. He was also reconciling the world!

> The Son is the image of the invisible God, the firstborn over <u>all creation</u>. For in <u>him all things were created</u>: things in heaven and on earth, visible and invisible, whether thrones or powers or rulers or authorities; <u>all things have been created through him and for him</u>. He is before all things, and in him all things hold together. And he is the head of the body, the church; he is the beginning and the <u>firstborn from among the dead</u>, so that in everything he might have the supremacy. For God was pleased to have all his fullness dwell in him, and through him to <u>reconcile to himself all things</u>, whether things on <u>earth</u> or things in <u>heaven</u>, by making peace through his blood, shed on the <u>cross</u> (Col. 1:15-20).

It's the cross that reconciles all things, even the creation (the earth) is redeemed. Satan and sin brought corruption to man and the creation. But Jesus' work on the cross restores man and creation.

Isaiah 65 foretells this new heaven and earth. The Premillennial view sees Isaiah speaking about the future reign of Christ for 1000-years on earth, so Isaiah is *not* referring to *this* new heaven and earth in Rev. 21. It's the same with the Postmillennial view, which sees Isaiah 65 as a picture of the 1000-years of extraordinary peace on earth *before* Jesus comes back. Proponents of both these views rightly point out that Isaiah 65 presents problems for the Amillennial position. For example, Isaiah is prophesying a rich time of blessing in the future (which I am saying is describing this new heaven and earth in Rev. 21), and yet Isaiah speaks of people living at least 100 years, and are accursed if they don't. It also speaks of no child dying in infancy (Isa. 65:20). Based on this, we can understand why many say it has to be more likely that Isaiah is talking about Jesus' 1000-year reign on earth, because death still exists. Therefore, it can't be the final new heaven and earth.

But if we are being fair, Isaiah presents real difficulty no matter which view you take. The first reason I think Isaiah is not talking about a 1000-year future, but rather about this new heaven and the new earth, is because that is exactly what Isaiah *says* he is talking about. Revelation seems to be alluding directly to Isaiah …

> 'See, I will create new heavens and new earth …' (Isaiah 65:17).

Isn't this what is being quoted in Rev. 21? It would be strange indeed to have two 'new heavens and new earths'. And yes, Isaiah gives us some curly temporal and 'this worldly' sounding blessings, but the OT almost always talks of its blessings in temporal terms. OT blessing meant Abraham was rich, with physical health and full of years. Cursing meant poverty or physical illness or physical death. It's only when you come to the NT that Jesus fully develops the greater eternal life and eternal blessings and rewards they were pointing to.

In fact, Isaiah's description is typical of OT prophecy. He describes a coming deathless world in figurative and rhetorical language: long, earthly life. *No baby will die in infancy; to die at 100 years of age would be accounted mere childhood* (how can dying at 100 be mere childhood? It's saying it's beyond your earthly imagination). Or *all the inhabitants will fill their days*. In other words, he is saying rhetorically *endless life!* Revelation even alludes to this when it says there will be *no more mourning or crying* (21:4), which is taken from that same passage in Isaiah 65:19, *no more weeping or crying*. It's the same thing. Why? It's the same new heaven and new earth.

In fact, Isaiah not only says he is prophesying of the new heaven and new earth, but he also says some things that can only be the eternal state and can't fit with a temporary 1000-year reign of Jesus on earth. As Isaiah continues this topic talking about the new heavens and earth …

> 'As the <u>new heavens and the new earth</u> that I make will <u>endure before me</u>,' declares the LORD, 'so will your name and descendants <u>endure</u>. From one New Moon to another and from one Sabbath to another, all mankind will come and bow down before me,' says the LORD. [It sounds like the Day of Judgment.] 'And they will go out and look on the dead bodies of those who rebelled against me; the worms that eat them will not die, the fire that burns them will not be quenched, and they will be loathsome to all mankind' (Isaiah 66:22-24).

This sounds like the final judgment and eternal state described in Revelation, albeit with figurative language, but way beyond living on this earth. In other words, this is the same new heaven and new earth of Rev. 21 that looks back to the lake of fire (Rev. 20), and then forwards—behold the new heaven and new earth! Isaiah also says in this new heavens and new earth that the former things will be remembered no more (Isa. 65:17). How does this fit with the promise of the new heaven and earth in the NT, that we will recognize one another and even know people we never met? You will sit down with Abraham, Isaac and Jacob. How can you recognize people you have never met? Well, Isaiah explains it himself. In the very verse before, he explains why the former things will not be remembered.

> … For the past troubles will be forgotten and hidden from my eyes (Isa. 65:16c).

It's the *past troubles* that will not come to mind. Everything that caused you pain will no longer be remembered or come to mind. But the resurrection will be a great continuity and remembrance of all that was good. Only sin and its pain and consequences will be forgotten. We will see and recognize Jesus' wounds which he showed his disciples, but in joy for what he did for us. Everything that is good will continue, such as relationships with other Christians and even good deeds (their deeds will follow them, 14:13). The nations will bring their splendor into it (21:24). Anything that is good and worth remembering will remain, but without the taint of sin or death or pain. There is a hint in our text …

> Then I saw 'a <u>new</u> heaven and a <u>new</u> earth,' for the first heaven and the first earth had passed away, and there was <u>no longer any sea</u> (21:1).

We have seen before in Revelation, the idea that the sea represents chaos (as in the OT) and the threat of rebellion against God's good world. In Revelation the Beast comes up out of the sea (13:1). There were those standing over the sea in victory to sing the song of Moses and of the Lamb, just as the Israelites did in Moses' deliverance through the sea. So the removal of the sea in this vision speaks of the removal of the threat of the old world. This is the new heaven and new earth. No raging sea. So no more surfing! They only have surfing in the lake of burning fire! Well not exactly. Remember there is the element of symbol and vision. It could be simply referring to the removal of the old sea and all that was threatening, so it's not impossible that there will be a non-threatening sea like we have already seen in that vision of heaven in Rev. 4, where there was a sea but it appeared like glass (still not good for surfing). But we won't try and get too clever with symbols and rule in or out a calm sea.

But this new heaven and new earth in our text is the ultimate consummation. Even when we die now we don't experience what is being described here. When believers die now they go to heaven. They reign with Christ for the 1000-years (church era), but not in their physical bodies, only in their souls. It's not until this time of the new heaven and new earth and the resurrection of the dead that our bodies are joined to our souls—on the Day of Judgment. So this is bigger than anything before. This is the fullness to which even the current heaven can't be compared.

When people die now, they go to what we call the intermediate state. They are in heaven or hell, as in the story in Luke 16 with the rich man and Lazarus, where one goes to heaven, the other to hell. They were in joy and pain respectively, but not in their final bodily state. Their souls had gone on to that intermediate state of either heaven or hell (see for example 2 Peter 2:9). But that is not the final state either. The final state of the unrighteous is the lake of fire that we read about at the end of Rev. 20. The final state of believers follows here in Rev. 21, in the new heaven and the new earth. So we believe that we will indeed live on the earth again. Albeit, a totally renewed one. And Jesus will reign on that earth.

> I know that my Redeemer lives, and that in the end he will stand on the earth. And after my skin has been destroyed, yet in my flesh I will see God; ... (Job 19:25-26).

This is where the millennial views finally agree. It took until nearly the end of Revelation, but we got there. Will Jesus reign on the earth? The Premillennial says yes, in a future 1000-years. The Amillennial also says yes, Jesus will reign on earth in the future, but forever, in the new heaven and new earth. And it is the beauty of all this that we want to capture. Jesus is on the earth again. But with the removal of all that caused us pain. It's light. It's bright. Jesus provides its light. Jude says it is exceeding joy. It's far above all we could ask or imagine. It's the deliverance on the promises to Abraham, Isaac and Jacob. They inherit the land. But more than they imagined! *All* the land. All God's promises have come true. You will eat that fruit in the paradise of God, just as he promised (2:7). No more longing and feeling unfulfilled (21:4). The original Garden of Eden was paradise lost. This is paradise regained! Jesus wins! Eden is won back again! Literal earth!

From Eden, man was supposed to have dominion over the whole earth. Now that is restored. But everything that could harm you on the old earth has been removed. The promise after the fall was the one to come who would crush Satan. Now Satan and his cohorts are cast into the lake of fire.

And forget the idea that in the new heaven and earth you get bored just singing in a choir or trying to learn to play the harp forever. This new life is activity, serving the Lord...

> 'You have made them to be a kingdom and priests to <u>serve our God</u>, and they will reign on the earth' (5:10).

It's filled with vibrant joyful activity because it's in the presence of the Lord as a kingdom and priests and reigning on the earth! It's real and it's rich. It's earth! The new earth! Even our environment will have all negative elements removed. No more toil! It was at the fall where work became toil (Gen. 3:17). Now you can still do gardening but there will be no weeds, thorns, or thistles. It's reversing the fall (Gen. 3:18), returning to the original garden.

This is where we can draw on Isaiah's new heavens and earth and all that language of living in houses, planting and eating *to be a delight and its people a joy* (Isa. 65:18). It speaks in down to earth language that we can understand of a rich life of delight, free from all the intrusion of sin. All that was beautiful in that original garden, and indeed all that is beautiful on earth now. The beauty of the mountains, trees, rivers, flora and fauna, the cities of beauty, people, real people, all restored. But no longer any sinners. People ask if animals are there? Isaiah says ...

> The wolf and the lamb will feed together, and the lion will eat straw like the ox, ... (Isa. 65:25).

Is that figurative for peace on earth? Or are animals included in the new creation? Certainly everything that is good about the original creation will be restored and reconciled. There will be a continuity of everything that is good. Jesus was a man on earth and resurrected as Jesus. So too, you will still be you. John sees heaven and identifies people from every tribe, language and nation. So ethnic appearance must still be there. Husbands and wives are not married in the new age, but their fellowship will be stronger than it was on the old earth, as it will be with all the saints. Earthly marriage will fade into insignificance as we see the richness of what it was pointing to in our ultimate marriage to Christ! Relationships will be more, not less! They will be heightened, and yet the central focus is on the Lord, not each other.

This brings us to the main thing about this new earth—Jesus is there. The highest earthly highs, even God-given love, sex, and intimacy, will seem boring compared to the fullness of face-to-face with our heavenly spouse. Then I will know fully as I am fully known.

Good memories will still be there. The rich man and Lazarus recognized each other and remembered the past, but Lazarus is in joy, he is no longer a beggar who lay at the rich man's gate. He is 'comforted'. There will also be lots of laughter in heaven. Jesus said that …

> … Blessed are you who weep now, for you will laugh (Luke 6:21b).

Hebrews 4 speaks of Canaan, where Joshua gave Israel rest that was to be fulfilled in the true rest in the new heaven and new earth. In Hebrews 11, the patriarchs were not looking back to the old Jerusalem but looked to a city to come whose builder was God. Abraham saw the fulfillment beyond explaining. All the promises to Israel are fulfilled, not spiritualized away so that they have no grasp in those earthly promises. And the fulfillment is not less, but far greater. The "real" land promise is delivered. Canaan—plus! Plus the whole world! Remember the apostle said *that Abraham and his offspring received the promise that he would be heir of the world* … (Rom. 4:13).

Abraham and all the Jewish believers will rejoice that God kept his promises, far above what they imagined. Many OT promises to Israel look to an expectation of God giving them real land, and we say 'Amen' to that. This is it, the new heaven and the new earth! Just as we mentioned how Jesus interpreted it that way. Psalm 37:11 told the Jews the meek would inherit the land of Canaan. Jesus went further when he said *blessed are the meek, for they will inherit the earth!* (Matt. 5:5)

Abraham not only gets Canaan, but also is heir of the whole world! If you believe in Christ, you are also heirs of the promises of Abraham (Gal. 3:29). This is how the land promise is for all who have the faith of Abraham. This is how we all fit in the land! The overflow of Canaan goes over the whole earth. This is why it's important that this new heaven and new earth is a renewal (not a replacement) of the old, and has continuity with the old, because Canaan was part of the old earth and the promise is delivered in this renewed earth.

The message of 21:1 is that, exhilarating as this is—you are not there yet. The point of this is 'take a look at where you are headed and don't give up'. Jesus wins. This calls for patient endurance on the part of God's people going through tribulation. You were told to endure and be faithful. You felt like giving up. You were told Jesus won. Well, here it is! He not only wins saving your body and soul, but Jesus wins over the fallen creation with the new heaven and new earth. This is what awaits his faithful ones.

Do you long for this? All the pain of this life will be removed. Contemplate on a deeper level what the cross of Christ has done in reconciling all things. Marvel at the cross and resurrection. It is far more cosmic and far-reaching than you thought. Contemplate it and ... be faithful. Stop putting your hopes in this earth. Jesus died to give you all this—more than we could ask or imagine. But if all the action and blessedness is going on this new earth, where does the new heaven fit in? Stay tuned ...

Study Questions

1. What is the best argument for the new heaven and earth being a totally new creation?

2. Why might the victory of Jesus over Satan be an argument against this?

3. Does Isaiah 65 speak into this text?

4. Why would there be no more sea? Is that literal?

5. What is the intermediate state?

6. Give reasons why the new heaven and earth is different from heaven now.

7. Will heaven be boring? Explain.

8. Will animals be part of the new heaven and earth?

9. If heaven has no married couples or earthly intimacy, how will it be better?

10. How will the promises to Israel be fulfilled in the new heaven and new earth?

25
The New Jerusalem
(Revelation 21:2-4)

We have arrived at the celestial city. The Holy City. The heavenly city. The New Jerusalem. Warren Wiersbe says this city is so amazing that even with the description given, it's hard to imagine.[25] It's the capital city of heaven says John MacArthur.[26] Surely they are right. This is big! The point of debate is this: Is this a literal city? The most popular view is that this *Holy City* is the literal city of heaven. Our text seems to be saying it is more complex than meets the eye. It is definitely a city.

> I saw the Holy City, the new Jerusalem, coming down out of heaven from God, prepared as a bride beautifully dressed for her husband (21:2).

A city, yes. But described as a bride. How do we put these two together? If we remember that John the apostle is seeing visions, and this book has been filled with symbols since we are told to expect symbols from the first verse, therefore it may have *more* to teach us than just a literal city.

So far we have been careful readers of Revelation, and the idea of a woman who is both dressed as a bride and yet is a city is not new. We have already been introduced to a woman dressed in splendor, which symbolized the people of God in Rev. 12. Then we met another woman, in fact *the* 'other woman' in Rev. 17 (v.18). She was also a city! Babylon. Two cities—two women. Babylon offered the alternative salvation to the pure woman, the church. And now we

---

[25] Warren Wiersbe, *The Wiersbe Bible Commentary*, https://asucru.files.wordpress.com/2008/01/wiersbe-commentary-new-testament.pdf p. 1080

[26] John MacArthur, *Because the Time is Near*, Moody Publishers, Chicago, 2007, p. 315

meet this pure woman. We know from Ephesians 5:25-32 that the bride of Christ is the church. And this city is that bride. Later in Rev. 21 an angel says it even more clearly that she is both a bride *and* a Holy City ...

> One of the seven angels who had the seven bowls full of the seven last plagues came and said to me, 'Come, I will show you the bride, the wife of the Lamb.' [We know this is the church. But what does she look like?] And he carried me away in the Spirit to a mountain great and high, and showed me the Holy City, Jerusalem, coming down out of heaven from God (21:9-10).

The angel confirms what John saw coming down from heaven. The bride *is* the Holy City. Not the bride is *in* the Holy City, but she *is* the New Jerusalem. This confirms what John saw of this city. **I saw the Holy City, the new Jerusalem, coming down out of heaven from God, prepared as a bride beautifully dressed for her husband.** The church is finally *prepared!* This was what 19:7 was all about. The bride had to be prepared. She had to 'make herself ready'. This is what history was all about. How long O Lord before I am ready? Prepared. The whole city! *All* those who make up the bride have to be prepared. Her preparation stretched to the ends of the earth through every tribe and nation, but it also stretched throughout every pocket of history. The Lord has been gathering his people until this moment. The church, this bride, had to be fully prepared. But also, each individual Christian who makes up that bride needed to be prepared in their lives. The world and the trials won't be over until the last one is prepared. You might want to complain to your brothers and sisters who are holding us up because they are taking so long to get prepared. Or maybe it's you who is holding us up? Or more importantly, others who still need to be saved to complete the bride and her preparation. We won't get to this point of Rev. 21 until the bride is fully prepared.

The idea of a holy bride being *prepared* is not new to the NT ...

> Husbands, love your wives, just as Christ loved the church and gave himself up for her to make her holy, cleansing her by the washing with water through the word, and to present her to himself as a radiant church, without stain or wrinkle or any other blemish, but holy and blameless (Eph. 5:25-27).

She is being cleansed through the word. Preparation.

It also turns out the idea of the heavenly *city* Jerusalem, the New Jerusalem, being the actual *church* was also there all along in the NT.

> But you have come to Mount Zion, to the city of the living God, the heavenly Jerusalem. You have come to thousands upon thousands of angels in joyful assembly, to the church of the firstborn, whose names are written in heaven ... (Heb. 12:22-23).

When you have come to the heavenly Jerusalem, you have come to the church says the Hebrews writer! Why does the NT describe the bride (the church) as the Holy City? The New Jerusalem? Why not say the bride is 'in' the New Jerusalem, the Holy City? The OT access to the Holy God was through the high priest entering the holy of holies (in the temple in Jerusalem). When Jesus died on the cross the temple curtain, the access to the holy God, was torn open. For whom? All who trust in the mediator, the Christ, the head of the church! What was previously only mediated through the priesthood and temple in the old Jerusalem, is now open to all, if you are part of the new city, the church. Here is something significant. The Holy Spirit on the day of Pentecost did not fill the temple, but the people! This new covenant is amazing. God's people are the new temple says Paul (1 Cor. 3:16-17). So this New Jerusalem, the Holy City, is the place where God himself dwells with his people, as we will see in 21:3.

We have already seen the church introduced as the New Jerusalem in the letters to the churches. In the letter to Philadelphia both Jew and Gentile are the New Jerusalem (3:12). And this is where Rev. 21 is headed. The temple (21:10-14) has as its very foundations the names not only of the 12 tribes of Israel, but also the 12 apostles.

So the New Jerusalem, the bride of Christ, the church, comes down out of heaven. To where is she coming down? Well, we have been told in 21:1 it's a new heaven and new earth. We know the Lord dwells in his special presence in heaven, 'Our Father in heaven', but I'll bet you didn't learn this in Sunday school. Heaven actually comes down to earth! The people of God, the New Jerusalem, come down *with the Lord,* and he dwells with his bride. This Holy City actually comes down to earth! The new earth! God comes down with heaven and dwells with his people on earth.

> Then I saw '<u>a new heaven and a new earth</u>,' for the first heaven and the first earth had passed away, and there was no longer any sea. I saw the Holy City, the new Jerusalem, <u>coming down out of heaven from God</u>, prepared as a bride beautifully dressed for her husband. And I heard a loud voice from the throne saying, 'Look! God's dwelling place is now among the people, and he will dwell with them. They will be his people, and God himself will be with them and be their God' (21:1-3).

This might be new to you if you have always thought that our final destination was to be in heaven on its own. Perhaps you imagined a kind of surreal, floaty existence without much grounding in reality as we know it. But in the last chapter we established that the Lord is providing a new earth, totally renovated and liberated from the old fallen one. This time we learn that heaven comes down and meets earth! It is real and 'down to earth'. But joined by heaven.

This emphasizes the wonder of our God who promised he would be with his people. Jesus already broke into this world as 'God with us' (Immanuel), and that is who God is to his people—God with us. It's a wonder. The God who comes down. Unbelievers can't comprehend it. You ask them what heaven is like and for them it is all to do with themselves or worldly pleasures—their favorite things of this world. The Quran has Muslim men supposedly provided with multiple virgins with full breasts for their sensual pleasure (Surah 78:32-33). But the unbeliever's understanding of heaven misses one thing, and that is God! God comes to live with his people.

If you don't know God, then heaven on earth seems weird and strange. This is why we say if you have never known the God who sent his Son, slain from the creation of the world, then you would hate heaven. It's clearly not meant for you because the Lord is the center of heaven. If you don't want to be with the Lord now, you would hate this. If you find worship or spending time with him in prayer a chore, then you would hate heaven. Heaven is relational with God.

We who do know the Lord can scarcely comprehend the thought, let alone imagine what it would be like having the God who loved us *coming down* to live right with us. **<u>God's dwelling</u> place is now among the people, and he <u>will dwell</u> with them.** Eden is finally restored, where man *walked with God on the earth*. This is the full circle. This is the bride of Christ. It's the gospel that enabled people from every tribe, nation, and tongue to become the people of God. God will be their God and will dwell with them. He had promised it all along to Israel ...

> My dwelling place will be with them; I will be their God, and they will be my people (Ezek. 37:27).

In fact, this is one of the oft repeated OT phrases. You can find it in Leviticus 26:12, Jeremiah 7:23, 32:38, Hosea 1:9 and Zechariah 8:8. *I will be their God, and they will be my people.* The apostle Paul quotes this in the NT and says it is fulfilled in the church.

> ... For <u>we are the temple</u> of the living God. As God has said: '<u>I will live with them and walk among them, and I will be their God, and they will be my people</u>' (2 Cor. 6:16).

Here is the new temple in the New Jerusalem. It's the Lord in the midst of his people. It's the same thing here in Revelation. **God himself will be with them and be their God.**

There are a couple of common words in the original Greek language that could be used to translate *dwelling*. One has been used many times in Revelation already for those *dwelling* on the earth. But that is not the word used here. The one used here is usually translated in the NT as 'tabernacle'. It's that same strange way the word is used in John 1:14 where it says that the word became flesh and dwelt, literally tabernacled, among us. It's a strange way to put it, but it's deliberate in that it alludes to the tabernacle.

The OT tabernacle was the forerunner for the temple in Jerusalem that signified God dwelling with his people. But Rev. 21:3 is the *new* Jerusalem. Now the tabernacling of God is with men. The consummation of all things and the promises of God to Israel are fulfilled literally in the promise of the land on this new earth (Canaan included!). And the promises to us of heaven are fulfilled. But who would have thought of putting the two together! Heaven comes down and meets earth! God dwells with man on earth. The promises to Israel and the church are both in this new heaven and earth. This is fulfillment and then some! *God's dwelling place is now among the people, and he will dwell with them. They will be his people, and God himself will be with them and be their God.* This is the full return to the Garden of Eden. Face to face, walking with the Lord in the cool of the day.

With this is the removal of everything that caused pain and regret. How? *He will wipe every tear from their eyes* ... There is no crying in heaven. Every tear is wiped away. Only joy on this day. What an amazing picture God's word uses to describe the hope for all of us travailing through this life through pain and tears. Surely this is one of the most moving scenes in the whole Bible. A time we can scarcely imagine and yet captured in this heartfelt way. God himself with his people, but this ...

> He will wipe every tear from their eyes. There will be no more death or mourning or crying or pain, for the old order of things has passed away (21:4).

Have you had any tears? Loss of loved ones? Physical or emotional pain? Breakdown of relationships? Living with difficult people or abuse? Overwhelming stress? Missed opportunity? Life passed by and you feel you missed out? What a picture of how all things end when it's the Lord himself who wipes away the tears. He makes all things new! Praise God for this vision (and it is a vision), because this means it is teaching something greater than simply God with lots of tissues. It's even more than God comforting the sorrowful. It's a consummate eternal wiping away of tears and pain. It speaks of restoration! The removing (of crying itself) and reversing of all that ever *caused* you tears. **He will wipe every tear from their eyes. There will be no more death or mourning or crying or pain, for the old order of things has passed away.**

The *new order* will bring about the restoration in full for every one of his. No matter what you have gone through, this day you will say, 'Now it's all worth it. The preparation for the wedding banquet of this life was worth it.' Picture this like a mum or dad wiping away the tears of the child who is crying and the child finds that warm and cozy security. Everything is all right when mum or dad wipes away the tears. How much more this picture is meant to convey the wiping away of old pain, and the fullness of restoration and comfort.

It also depicts a heavenly Father. Some of us have had fathers who have not lived up to what they should. Even the most caring, loving father on earth can never live up to this. This is the father we never had. Our heavenly Father. Some think of the Father as the stern judge of the OT. Yes, Jesus died for us, but it's the Father who loved us and sent his Son to take away our sin. God the Father so loved the world that he gave his One and only Son. The Father is like the picture in the prodigal son where the Father runs out to meet the son. Here we read that God comes *down* to earth to dwell with us. And we almost picture the Father kneeling down to us, wiping away every tear.

Unbelievers complain that God is unjust to let evil happen. 'What about those who have been abused? God can't reverse the hurt!' But this language is saying that is exactly what God will do.

Whose tears does he wipe away? There are plenty of people who never have tears. People who don't need a thing. They have plenty stored up for themselves. They have everything they want (or so it seems). They do what they want. No tears there. And so often they are not the ones who seek God. They don't have the tears of repentance with a broken and contrite heart. Often, it's the broken, the lonely, the afflicted, the ones who are weak, and the ones who are abused who have tears. So often it's those who the Lord brings in this great reversal that ends in exceeding joy. When they have cried tears of repentance ...

> Blessed are those who mourn, for they will be comforted (Matt. 5:4).

> But God chose the foolish things of the world to shame the wise; God chose the <u>weak</u> things of the world to shame the strong. God chose the <u>lowly things</u> of this world and the <u>despised</u> things—the things that are not—to nullify the things that are, ... (1 Cor. 1:27-28).

On this day, those who said, 'Why me O Lord, why so much pain in my preparation?' will not be crying then. You will be rejoicing that he set his love on you and you will rejoice at the rich reward and the great reversal when he will wipe every tear from your eyes.

The wiping away of all tears also suggests the opposite will happen. Laughter. Just as Jesus said, *Blessed are you who weep now, for you will laugh* (Luke 6:21b). No more tears, no more pain, no struggle. Those who were disabled are restored, and the mentally and physically weak are now rejoicing. **The old order of things has passed away.**

The great contrast is this. For those who are not in this new heaven and earth, now they have tears! Tears flowing forever. *Weeping* and gnashing their teeth. Those who never cried tears of repentance will cry in the next life. You didn't need a Savior. You will be Lord of your own life. You will get what you want. But later you have tears. Later you have regret with many tears.

Those who still think of heaven as boring, endless singing, or floating around like a piece of cloud need to read this book. This is not only down to earth literally, but look at this personal intimacy of the Lord himself being with his people and wiping away every tear. This is relationship on the deepest level. This will be our personal experience, albeit glorified and sinless and perfect in body and mind, but we will be ourselves in rich fellowship. In Jesus' resurrected body, he was not a piece of floating cloud. He maintained his appearance, his gender. He was able to sit down and talk and eat with his disciples. And one day, we will sit down with him at the wedding banquet. Real fellowship. God with us.

And no, it can't be boring living forever. That's impossible. We long for relationships to be perfect. This is always the excited anticipation of a new couple in love. The initial excitement controls every moment in joyful anticipation. A new love fills people. Oh, but that love often fades. But this love will never diminish! This is the height of heaven meeting earth. The bride and her spouse together, overflowing with excited anticipation and a love that never ends. Everything that causes tears in relationships wiped away forever.

This is the completion of the wedding supper of the Lamb in Rev. 19. This reminds us that the only marks of the old order remaining on anyone will be the marks Jesus bore for us at the cross as the *Lamb* of God. This reminds us how much we are loved by this bridegroom. Now the bride is fully ready. Imagine being seated at the table. 'You prepare a table for me …' Well, now it's here. It's time to rest. No more pain or toil. You know those good times at a wedding banquet when you enjoy that rich time of company in celebration? Well this is the ultimate. Seated with all your loved ones and friends who went on in the Lord. But the main thing our current text is teaching is that the center of heaven is the rich intimate fellowship with God himself.

> *… God himself will be with them and be their God. He will wipe every tear from their eyes. There will be <u>no more death or mourning or crying or pain</u>, for the old order of things has passed away* (21:3-4).

Study Questions

1. Is this a literal city?

2. What other NT teaching confirms your answer?

3. Why would heaven be coming down to earth?

4. Give at least a couple of reasons why unbelievers would not like heaven even if they could get there.

5. How does the NT relate the idea of 'temple' in the new covenant?

6. How does Genesis 3:8 relate to this text?

7. What might the wiping away of tears be teaching beyond the literal?

8. What is the great contrast of that of tears for believer vs. unbelievers?

9. How is the bride prepared?

10. Why will heaven not be boring?

26
The Fiery Lake
(Revelation 21:5-8)

Throughout the book of Revelation we have had heavenly scenes, and there have been great announcements from great and mighty angels. But this must be some kind of climax, because this is one of the few times, and the last time, that the voice actually comes directly from the throne. It is God himself. What is so important?

> He who was <u>seated on the throne</u> said, 'I am making everything new!' Then he said, 'Write this down, for these words are trustworthy and true' (21:5).

It must be something special for us that it's preserved and passed down, because John is told to **write this down**! This is what John did, otherwise we wouldn't be reading it now. And this statement **I am making everything new** is drawing on Isaiah (43:18-19), just as we have seen Rev. 21 drawing on Isaiah (65) for the new heaven and new earth. We looked at this in the last chapter, that is, the mind-blowing plan God has for us with no more crying, mourning, or pain. The old order of things has passed away, and the promises to Israel and the Gentiles are fulfilled in this new order! Heaven comes down to earth and the two combine to fulfill all things. This is bigger than we can imagine. Write it down John! These words are trustworthy and true.

> He said to me: '<u>It is done</u>. I am the Alpha and the Omega, the Beginning and the End. To the thirsty I will give water without cost from the spring of the water of life' (21:6).

The cry **it is done** reminds us of Jesus at the cross! 'It is finished' or 'it is accomplished'. What Jesus did on the cross saved our souls. But we have learned the cross is bigger. Jesus was reconciling the whole world for the new heaven and new earth. He was **making everything new.** *It is done!*

Then he says, **I am the Alpha and the Omega, the Beginning and the End.** Alpha and Omega are simply the first and last letters of the Greek alphabet. It is like saying he is from A to Z. God was already there in the beginning, at creation, but God will also be there at the end, when he brings about the final consummation. But as the beginning and the end, he is also Lord *in between!* That means he was there all along from Alpha to Omega, through all the pain of history, through all your personal trials. He was not just waiting at the end to bring judgment. He is the God who was directing all history to this very point. It's like that *Footprints* story. You know that story with the two sets of footprints in the sand indicating your walk through this life and you say to the Lord, 'But why were there times when there was only one set of footprints? Where were you then Lord?' And the Lord's response is 'That is when I was carrying you.' I love the footprints story, but it turns out it's wrong. He wasn't just carrying you in the difficult times, but *all* the time! From beginning to end, Alpha and Omega. He is God of every moment. *Write this down, for these words are trustworthy and true!*

For those who did struggle but held fast to the Lord, he promises that he will fully satisfy his faithful ones. He will by no means cast out any who sought him. **To the thirsty I will give water without cost from the spring of the water of life.** Isaiah 49:10 and Jeremiah 2:13 show this is talking about the living waters of eternal life. Remember the woman Jesus met at the well who thirsted? She had been married five times and was living with a man who was just using her, because to live together unmarried in the ancient world meant she was an outcast. That's why she is drawing water at the well on her own. She had basically given up. So she thirsted. She longed for an answer to life. Jesus gave her more than she imagined.

> Jesus answered her, 'If you knew the gift of God and who it is that asks you for a drink, you would have asked him and he would have given you living water' (John 4:10).

This living water, as Jesus said, wells up to eternal life (John 4:14)! And it's *without cost*. It's a gift God gave. Better *write this down, for these words are trustworthy and true!* Better take hold of this offer. *To the thirsty*

I will give water <u>without cost</u> from the spring of the water of life. If you try to quench that thirst with the world's temptations, you just end up thirsty again. Have you noticed that? Your favorite pleasures, coveting, you need to keep going back to them. They never fully quench your thirst. You just get thirsty again. If you are thirsty, if you are longing, if you know something is missing—there is only one fountain with the water of life.

But there is this tension here. On one hand God speaks of this living water as free, *without cost*, but then he directs it back to our lives and responses ...

> Those who are victorious will inherit all this, and I will be their God and they will be my children (21:7).

Those who are victorious? Is it free or not? Oh, it's free all right. But if you are really one of his you will hear the call of Revelation and respond. There is a terrifying comparison with those who didn't respond before we get to the end of 21:8. Those who *aren't* victorious end up in the lake of burning sulfur. So, who is victorious? Those who never sin? We know it can't be that. It is by grace you have been saved, a gift of God. Isn't that what this text just said? The living water is offered to drink *without cost*. But all of Revelation has been addressing the spiritual warfare and attacks and troubles that go on in this world and the need for Christians to have *patient endurance*. The one who is victorious through the tribulation described throughout Revelation is the one who doesn't give up.

Being victorious is down to earth, practical, everyday fighting the good fight. We know this because the seven letters (Rev. 2-3) had the same refrain—*The one who is victorious*. Victorious over what? If we went back over those letters, the call for Christians was to be victorious over everything from resisting sexual immorality, resisting false teaching, and avoiding idolatry in its various forms. And the promise in those letters was that the one who is victorious receives the new paradise, eating from the tree of life, manna, status, being part of the new temple, new clothes, and most of all, the one who is victorious will enjoy the intimate presence of the Lord. Well, this is what the climax of this text reveals. The one who is victorious **will inherit all this, and I will be their God and they will be my children.**

This is an extraordinary thought. It's an unusual 'Christian' idea to be *child of God*. We presume it in our Western culture, but the concept to have God as a parent is actually offensive to many (especially in Islam). But it's all so personal. Have you seen the intimate way this verse describes what being saved really means? You *will inherit all this* (new heaven and earth) but get this last bit! *I will be their God and they will be my children*. Rev. 21:3 had the promise to all the people, but now it's applied individually. I'll be with you as a personal Father is to his child. We take the wonder of that for granted. God has only one natural Son, Jesus. But we creatures of God, enemies of God (Rom. 5:10), are not only reconciled, but adopted as God's own children. Better ... *Write this down, for these words are trustworthy and true!*

Then, in complete contrast to those victorious, we come to those outside. Cast out and into the lake of burning sulfur.

> 'But the cowardly, the unbelieving, the vile, the murderers, the sexually immoral, those who practice magic arts, the idolaters and all liars—they will be consigned to the fiery lake of burning sulfur. This is the second death' (21:8).

Remember, the first death is when you physically die. The second death is eternal hell, the fiery lake. Who goes there? Top of the list are cowards! Of all the things to begin a list of evils, which includes murderers and the sexually immoral, the very first ones are cowards. Why cowards at the top? The hint comes from our context. Cowards are in contrast to those who are victorious. How often does the Christian faith call on us to stand? To stand for Jesus. To be victorious despite ridicule. There are tough 'macho' guys I've met in the neighborhood who have said the reason they couldn't come to church is because they couldn't take it if their mates found out. Too cowardly. Have you ever noticed how much pressure there is on the church to make Christianity 'cool' and not different from the world? It appeals to cowards.

The cowardly give in to the world's pressure. Why do churches take on beliefs that are in conflict with the Bible? The world says we discriminate. We are sexist. 'You are against equality in marriage. Other churches are fine with these things.' So the pressure even comes from churches (weren't some of those seven churches willing to be more 'tolerant'?). It takes courage to believe in Jesus and just trust him that he knows more than we do on difficult issues. But the cowards won't stand.

Some of *the cowardly* said they 'believed', but wouldn't let that interfere with their life. They caved to pressure from family. 'If you are a real Christian you would not be so judgmental and go along with us to that event.' Young people feel it when their friends say, 'Don't be a wimp, come with us! Try this.' What happens is some will be victorious, and some will be cowards. They wouldn't stand for Jesus, so—lake of burning sulfur.

The next sin that characterized people who ended up in the lake of fire was the unbelieving.

But the cowardly, **the unbelieving**. Again, this seems surprising to make second on the list. The murderers and the sexually immoral still have to stand in line. All this time people used unbelief as an excuse, 'I don't believe, so God can't blame me. I wish I could believe like you.' No, you don't. Now it's exposed. Unbelief is a grievous sin. Deep down you knew. You just didn't want Christ's rule over your life. Contemporary society tries to portray unbelief as the neutral ground. People of faith are the biased ones. But what is exposed here is that unbelief is one of the chief *willful* sins against God. In fact, we are told elsewhere in the NT that people are not on neutral ground in unbelief.

> ... [They] suppress the truth by their wickedness, since what may be known about God is plain to them, because God has made it plain to them. For since the creation of the world God's invisible qualities—his eternal power and divine nature—have been clearly seen, being understood from what has been made, so that people are without excuse (Rom. 1:18-20).

They *suppress the truth* and are *without excuse*. There is no neutral ground. They just wanted self-rule! Look at the bias of unbelief.

In recent years, the scientific world has presented new theories challenging the truth of the big bang. Now wait a minute. Haven't we been told all this time that the big bang is scientific, as in like proven in a science lab or something? Don't they have experiments to prove it? Now they are telling us they were wrong. Do we rip all those pages out of the science books? So, what do they do with that? If there was no big bang to drive the universe into existence, then should we consider the God hypothesis? No way! Unbelief says I can even admit

I am totally wrong in my theories, but no matter what, I will never submit to a simple thing like 'there is a God who made this universe.' We need someone unbiased like Charles Darwin. Darwin said in his autobiography that he couldn't understand why people would want the Bible to be true, because if it were, then his unbelieving family and friends along with himself would then be confined to eternal punishment. To Darwin, this Christian belief was repugnant. Does that sound like a dispassionate unbiased scientist in search of a scientific explanation for the origins? No. He was biased against the God of the Bible and went in search of many schemes to justify himself.

After the cowardly and the unbelieving comes **the vile, the murderers, the sexually immoral.** The letters to the seven churches showed that these things were creeping into the church. The *vile* reminds us of abominations of idolatry in both OT and NT. It included murder. There was the common pagan practice of child sacrifice. Today there is a push by many within the South Pacific islands to return to their ancient cultural roots before the missionaries introduced Christianity, and many in the islands embraced it. I wonder if that means they want to go back to the practices like cannibalism and the common practice of sacrificing their children in the footings of their buildings? Now the West is into child sacrifice more than other cultures. But they are more sophisticated, they kill the children *before* they are even born. When Tanya Plibersek was acting opposition leader of Australia, she proposed a unified vote on same-sex marriage rather than a conscience vote as with abortion, because she said the abortion issue was a matter of life and death. At least we have clarity on the abortion issue. She said it was a matter of *life and death!* But she still personally insists we should be allowed to kill babies. Murderers are on this list.

The *sexually immoral* are also on the list. The word in the original Greek is pornea, so we know where we get the word pornography from. In the older translations it's called 'fornication'. It simply means any sex outside of heterosexual marriage. I remember when I was an unbeliever thinking if the Bible is true, then God must have changed his standards to meet today's society, otherwise that lake is going to be overflowing because 'everybody's doing it'. But God hasn't changed his standards and Jesus said sexual immorality includes looking lustfully (pornography is rampant today). So what happens to the sexually immoral? Better *write this down*, because the lake of burning sulfur is filling up.

The next group of sinners listed is **those who practice magic arts.** The original Greek word is *pharmakea*, meaning sorcery. It's those pharmacists again! Magic arts are not referring to slight-of-hand magic, but to spiritual practices, séances, fortune tellers, Ouija boards, spiritualists, and magic spells. Today we have the whole fascination with wizards and witches who have become culturally cool. Kids films celebrate it. Grown-ups love to play with it. But it's on God's list of people who end up in the lake. The same word in Greek (that we get pharmacy from) can also be associated with drug-induced spells etc. So there go all the illicit drug users too. That lake of fire is filling up!

Next on the list come **the idolaters**. Idols! The things that we covet! Okay, we can understand those murderers and sorcerers, but leave my idols alone. These are the things of the crash of Rev. 18. Many were good ordinary things turned into idols. Had to have more and better stuff. Addictions. Had to have.

Who are the last ones to fill that lake? **Liars**! That's those who don't tell the truth. But this particular Greek word for liars is rare in the NT. It is the same word used at Acts 6:13 to speak against false witnesses and church members whose faith is in contradiction to their actions (1 John 2:4, 22, 4:20). Those who 'call themselves God's people but really are not' (see churches at Ephesus 2:2 and Philadelphia 3:9). So 21:8 has book-ends on that list of those for that lake of fire. It begins and ends with what? Hypocrites! It starts with cowards who wouldn't stand for the faith and ends with liars in the faith.

So what if you have been caught up in any of these things in 21:8? What if you have been a coward or have grumbled against God in unbelief? What if you have been caught up in pornography or some other sexual immorality? What if you are still clinging to idols or have secret addictions? Or what if you have been involved in murder or sorcery, or are living a lie? Then what? Better, *write this down, for these words are trustworthy and true!* You are headed for the lake of burning sulfur. The second death from which there is no escape.

But there is an escape. See the man upon the cross. Like when

Nebuchadnezzar saw the son of God in the fire, Jesus went into that lake of fire in your place if you believe. This is why this message is written. It's not too late. Seek forgiveness and turn from that sin with all your heart. And the one who went to the cross will take that punishment away. Jesus became the murderer and the sexually immoral. He became sin for us (2 Cor. 5:21). Repent and believe in what he did. And look!

To the thirsty I will give to drink without cost from the spring of the water of life. Forgiveness is without cost to you because it *cost* him everything at the cross.

And finally, when he says *Write this down, for these words are trustworthy and true,* aren't all things in Revelation true? Why is he saying this here? Because this is so unfathomable to our current senses. We can't see it. We can't see the Lord making everything new, removing all the past hurts and richly rewarding those who are victorious. It's mind blowing. But we also can't see the lake of burning sulfur and people screaming as they are tossed in. It's a forever we can't comprehend. Even we, who believe it, can't imagine it and quickly get back into the 'reality' of this life.

But this message is written for you to take hold of this emphasis. In fact, *write it down!* This is really going to happen—whether you feel it or not, whether you *think* about it or not. You are headed for one of these two alternatives, for eternity. And so are the people around you! God came into this world in person and told John to write this down! We've got it in writing from God! Your world is not a long-term reality. It will pass. *This* is reality! It's revealed by God. The call of Revelation is to live life *now* in light of this truth. There are two options. Victorious, or lake of fire!

Write this down. It's trustworthy and true. It's the word of the God who came down.

Study Questions

1. Why might this message be so important John is told to write it?

2. How does meditating on God as the Alpha and Omega help us in times of trial?

3. In what way is the water free of cost?

4. Why do you have to be 'victorious' if it is free?

5. What is unique about God being a Father to us, and we his children?

6. Why would 'cowards' be first on the list of sinners cast into the lake of fire?

7. Why is unbelief considered such a great sin?

8. In what way does this list have a book-end pattern?

9. How can this list in 21:8 be used to help us and others?

27
The Heavenly City
(Revelation 21:9-21)

There are many books available about people who have allegedly visited heaven and come back. They give us an inside look and preview of what heaven is really like, not by faith but by sight! Quite a few of these visitors to heaven have been children, so you know it's real because children never lie or exaggerate. Apparently one of those children who visited heaven has grown up now and said he made the whole thing up. I don't quite know how all these heaven reports reconcile with what the apostle Paul said, speaking of himself in the 3rd person …

> And I know that this man—whether in the body or apart from the body I do not know, but God knows—was caught up to paradise and heard inexpressible things, things that no one is permitted to tell (2 Cor. 12:3-4).

Paul says you are not allowed to tell even if you really did go to heaven. So how come these people who saw heaven are disobeying God? The Bible is the only reliable source of revelation.

What the apostle John is seeing now is a picture of heaven and its dimensions and decorations. And depending on your interpretation of Revelation, what we are about to see is either a literal description of heaven, or symbolic of something beyond description, and these brilliant precious jewels and ginormous architecture are descriptions seeking to convey the unconveyable.

The primary reason I don't agree with the popular view that this city is meant to be literal, is because we are told up front in our text that this is a vision which symbolizes *not* a literal city, but the bride of Christ. The church …

> One of the seven angels who had the seven bowls full of the seven last plagues came and said to me, 'Come, I will <u>show you the bride, the wife of the Lamb</u>.' And he carried me away in the Spirit to a mountain great and high, <u>and showed me the Holy City, Jerusalem</u>, coming down out of heaven from God (21:9-10).

After the angel says he is going to show John the bride, *then* he **showed me the Holy City, Jerusalem.** So he actually tells us that this great city we are about to explore is actually *the bride, the wife of the Lamb.* The church! But how can the church be a city? Well, we are not surprised. We have already been introduced to a tale of two cities and both are women. But now the pure woman, the church is called a city. She is the bride of Christ with God ...

> It shone <u>with</u> the glory of God, and its brilliance was like that of a very precious jewel, like a jasper, clear as crystal (21:11).

It shines *with* the glory of God. So unlike Moses having to see God's back, or Isaiah trembling as a man of unclean lips in the presence of the Lord's glory, the people are all united *with* the Lord in the presence of his glory with exceeding joy. **It shone with the glory of God**. Rev. 21 began with God 'tabernacling' with his people (21:3). And *God himself will be with them and be their God.* This is being developed further here. The real point is the presence of God *with* his people. This is why the security of this fellowship with the Lord is so beautifully described by these walls.

> It had a great, high wall with twelve gates, and with twelve angels at the gates. On the gates were written the names of the twelve tribes of Israel. There were three gates on the east, three on the north, three on the south and three on the west (21:12-13).

What is all this? Put yourself in John's shoes. If you knew your OT like John, this is not so strange. It's straight out of Ezekiel. The Premillennial view generally says this temple can't be connected to the temple complex in Ezekiel 40-48 because Ezekiel's temple plan is a blueprint for the temple to be built during the future 1000-year reign. Christians disagree over this, and does it really matter? After all, Jesus still wins no matter what your view. But I hope to show you that if *this* text is a fulfillment of Ezekiel's temple, it unfolds a bigger picture of the whole Bible story. So first let's take note of some similarities to Ezekiel's temple.

If both this temple and Ezekiel's are symbolic visions, they don't have to be identical, but first notice there are striking parallels between Ezekiel's commissioning to bring the message and John here in Revelation.

> In visions of God he took me to the land of Israel and set me on a <u>very high mountain</u>, on whose south side were some buildings that looked like <u>a city</u> (Ezek. 40:2).

Compare this with John's commissioning ... **And he carried me away <u>in the Spirit</u> to <u>a mountain great and high</u>, and showed me the <u>Holy City</u>, Jerusalem, coming down out of heaven from God.** Both are visions of the city of Jerusalem. Both are taken up to a very high mountain and both shown a city. And also in Ezekiel's temple.

> Then <u>the Spirit lifted me up</u> and brought me into the inner court, and <u>the glory</u> of the LORD filled the temple (Ezek. 43:5).

This is what we have seen in the temple that John sees! *It shone with the glory of God...* (21:11). But this is just the introduction. Look again at what John sees. **It had a great, high wall with twelve gates, and with twelve angels at the gates. On the gates were written the names of the twelve tribes of Israel. There were three gates on the east, three on the north, three on the south and three on the west.** Ezekiel 48 *also* has twelve gates in the city that are *also* divided into *north, south, east and west!* Three gates each. Ezekiel's twelve gates *also* have the names of the twelve tribes of Israel just like this city John saw! But John's vision introduces something new.

> The wall of the city had twelve foundations, and on them were the names of the <u>twelve apostles</u> of the Lamb (21:14).

Twelve tribes *now* combined with the twelve apostles. All of God's people, Jew and Gentile making up what? Let's not forget 21:9-10 told us we are seeing a vision of the bride of Christ depicted as this building. This is familiar to us as NT readers. Jew and Gentile believers in Christ depicted as a building. We remember again those at Ephesus being told they are a building and a holy temple made up of Jew and Gentile believers all one in Christ Jesus (Eph. 2:20-22).

Most people with the Premillennial view see separate futures for Jew and Gentile because Ezekiel's temple is meant to be where that future 1000-year reign of Jesus is, and it is made up of mostly Jews. But I hope to show there is a connection in the entire Bible of one salvation, one people of God, one future for both Jew and Gentile, and one building of precious stones John has just described here in 21:11. Where have we heard this before?

> ... you also, like <u>living stones</u>, are being built into a <u>spiritual house</u> to be a holy priesthood, ... (1 Peter 2:5).

The metaphor of God's people as a building made of precious stones is not new to us. Let's not forget the church of Philadelphia where both Jew and Gentile were told they would become pillars in the new temple and receive the name of the New Jerusalem (3:12).

John also sees another similarity to Ezekiel ...

> The angel who talked with me had a <u>measuring</u> rod of gold to measure the city, its gates and its walls (21:15).

Ezekiel also had to measure the walls (Ezek. 40:3-5). So Revelation is doing what it has been doing all the way through. Using OT places, events and people to teach an even greater fulfillment. The OT temple and city of Jerusalem had its walls broken and entered by Babylon. Many Bible interpreters of different persuasions see **measuring** as symbolizing God's protection and security. It's the same as in the sanctuary in Rev. 11 as well. The difference in the temple of Rev. 11 is that it was measured only inside. The security during the church age back in Rev. 11 was limited. But this heavenly city is measured both inside *and out*. Before we were secure as believers, but there was still opposition from the outside and the enemy could still kill the body. Now believers are protected even from that. Here there is no more death or mourning, crying, or pain, for the old order of things has passed away. Now in a new order of protection there is the *eternal* security. Measured.

> The city was laid out like <u>a square</u>, as long as it was wide. He measured

> the city with the rod and found it to be 12,000 stadia in length, and as wide and high as it is long (21:16).

It's the same concept in Ezekiel. He was to measure **a square** by length and width (Ezek. 45:2-3). But 12,000 stadia? Nearly 1,500 miles (over 2300 km). These figures make little sense if you are taking them literally, converting them to contemporary measurements and trying to imagine a cube city that big. It's half the size of Australia! My wife has always liked those old buildings with the high ceilings, but this ceiling is literally over the top. The ceilings are the height of the distance from Melbourne to Alice Springs? And Melbourne to Alice Springs wide and deep? But the walls surrounding it are only 70 yards/meters high? How do you make sense of such a thing?

It's easy to get caught up trying to picture this architecture as a literal city and forget what the angel told John in 21:9-10, that this is a picture of the bride! Jesus' people. If we remember that, then we can ask what might these numbers be trying to teach us symbolically? Firstly, we note the recurring of the number of the people of God— 12, only here it's in the 1000s. Remember the number 1000 is the Bible's common symbolic number for a large, indefinite number. So, 12,000 stadia x 12, and we get 144,000. It's the same figure we had back in Rev. 7 and Rev. 14. It's 12 apostles x 12 tribes of Israel, Jews and Gentile believers in great number, in the 1000s.

So why does 21:16 say it's a perfect square when that would otherwise be nonsensical for a city? But it's not strange if we think *The Lord with his people*, instead of bricks and mortar buildings! If we use the Bible to interpret rather than our imagination—where did the Lord meet with his people in the OT? The high priest entered into the holy of holies on behalf of the people. The holy of holies was a *square!* Now *this square* is much larger and what else? It's open to all of God's people. The complete number, 12 x 12, old and new in the 1000s. A great indefinite number—144,000. So this square is one giant holy of holies, 12,000 stadia each side. It's enormous. There is no limit to its accommodating all of God's people.

> The angel measured the wall using human measurement, and it was 144 cubits thick (21:17).

Again, if we take it literally, 144 cubits is not much of wall for a city that is nearly 1500 miles (2300kms) high! Translations that convert these numbers to our modern western measurements miss the point. It's those specific numbers that are teaching us again. 144 cubits thick represents multiplying the people of God, 12 x 12, Jew and Gentile together, tribes and apostles, Israel and church all one.

We also read in 21:17 that the angel measured the wall using **human measurement**, reminding us that this dwelling place of God is with men. Remember Rev. 11 *measures* the worshipers, the actual people!

> The wall was made of jasper, and the city of pure gold, as pure as glass (21:18).

Why **pure gold**? The holy of holies was covered in gold! Then in the following verses we get this list of jewels similar to the 12 precious stones on Aaron's breast-piece. Again, what was only for the high priest is now for *all the people*. You are a kingdom and priests (1:6, 5:10). It's the priesthood of all believers. So the high priest, Aaron's 12 precious stones ...

> ... The foundations of the city walls were decorated with every kind of precious stone. The first foundation was jasper, the second sapphire, the third agate, the fourth emerald, the fifth onyx, the sixth ruby, the seventh chrysolite, the eighth beryl, the ninth topaz, the tenth turquoise, the eleventh jacinth, and the twelfth amethyst. The twelve gates were twelve pearls, each gate made of a single pearl. The great street of the city was of pure gold, as pure as transparent glass (21:19-21).

Twelve pearly gates, not one! And St. Peter is not in sight of any of them! In fact, 21:12 already told us angels attend the gates, not Peter. So we reject the RC myth that Peter alone received the keys and stands at the pearly gates. And 70-yard gates (if literal), must have been mighty big oysters to produce 70-yard pearls! But remember we are not locked into literal pearls. We take the *symbol* and think Bible! A *pearl* of great price! Open to all of God's people.

Notice **the great street of the city was <u>of pure gold</u>, as pure as transparent glass.** As we noted, just like the holy of holies, it's lined with gold except with one difference. 1 Kings 6:30 says only the priests are allowed to walk on the gold covered floor. Here it is in the actual street for everyone to walk on!

Yes, this building appears to be strange. And yet we are told quite explicitly (21:9-10) that this city is actually the bride of Jesus, Jew and Gentile believers in Christ who will dwell in the new heaven and new earth depicted as a city dwelling with God. What is going on?

What was the OT temple all about? The presence of God in the holy of holies, unapproachable for the rank and file people of God, but the new square, the new holy of holies, the New Jerusalem is the bride (the people of God), with the glory of the Lord in her midst. So what is this all saying? Everything OT (including the OT temples) was *all* pointing to Jesus in the presence of his people. All the promises of God are 'Yes' and 'Amen' in Christ.

Ezekiel's temple was never built. The Premillennialist says therefore it must be the one to be built in the future 1000-year reign. It's the ideal temple. But is it meant to be built or to look forward to the ultimate temple? In Ezekiel's vision of the temple he was taken up on a mountain overlooking Jerusalem (Ezek. 40:1-2). But *there is* no mountain overlooking Jerusalem. There's more than a hint that it's symbolic when Ezekiel says it's 'something that *looks like* a city' (Ezek. 40:2).

So what does Ezekiel's temple point to? Ezekiel 47:1 has a river flowing out of the temple, but so does 22:1-2! Where else was there a river flowing out? The Garden of Eden! Ezekiel's temple concludes that 'the Lord is there'. Ezekiel is looking forward to a return to the Garden. God with his people. This is where Ezekiel was headed. This is where Revelation has been headed. This is where the history of salvation is headed. This is where the Holy City and all temples in the Bible are headed! The river of life is flowing from God's presence to nourish the whole new heaven and new earth. So all those details of the OT temples are pointing to Jesus and his people together.

Have you ever read through Ezekiel 40-48? How can such a complex, detailed building instruction of the ancient city of Jerusalem and its temple be pointing to a people with their God? We looked at this in Rev. 11, but it bears repeating because there is more detail here. We said back then it's understandable that on the first read of Ezekiel 40-48, with all that detail of the temple and city, you could wonder if this is not meant to be literally built, otherwise why all the detail? Mind you, all attempts to reconstruct it fail because it's so incomplete as a piece of architecture. But why would God take up nine chapters in Ezekiel of specifications on a city and temple that is just meant to signify Jesus together with his people? Good question.

But it's the same answer we had back in Rev. 11. This is what the Lord did with many things in the OT. Have you ever read through Leviticus? 'I'm trying to be pious Lord, but I'm falling asleep reading all this repetitive detail of guilt offerings, sin offerings, sacrifices for this sin, sacrifices for the priest, page after page of grim details. Cut up this bit, don't use that bit, wave this offering and sprinkle that one. Sacrifices for everything. Why all this detail? Are you telling me *all* these multitude of offerings and sacrifices all simply point to Jesus?'

Absolutely, that's exactly what they did. It was all pointing the ancient Israelites by shadows to Jesus, the complete sacrifice. They learned that God provides from every possible angle, every possible sin, every possible way you need cleansing. All those promises are all 'Yes' and 'Amen' in the perfect sacrifice of Jesus. So what about that temple in Ezekiel? Why would the Lord give such a detailed list to the Israelites for the temple construction if it's never meant to be built, but simply pointed to Christ with his people? For the same reason he gave the detail of the sacrifices, as shadows pointing them to Christ. And all the temples (tabernacles) including the ideal temple in Ezekiel, all the OT, is all about Jesus who came and tabernacled among us. He is the true tabernacle. God with us.

But how could Ezekiel's temple point his first readers to Jesus with his people? What did Ezekiel's temple mean to the first readers in all its detail? The future ideal! Perfect *worship*, perfect *sacrifices* and the perfect *presence* of God. How is that fulfilled? Only in Jesus. In fact, it is fulfilled right here in Rev. 21. The greater holy of holies with the glory of the Lord filling the presence of God's people. Jesus' bride.

A consistent Premillennial view has Ezekiel's temple literally built, with all its instruction on animal sacrifices to be reintroduced during the 1000-years, not as sacrifice for sin but as memorials to what Jesus did. I have always struggled with this view. Jesus did away with sacrifices and we already have the only memorial meal pointing to the cross, the Lord's Supper. But if we see Ezekiel's temple pointing to Jesus with his people — perfect worship, perfect sacrifices, perfect presence of God then …

All of Ezekiel's detail was teaching the Israelites what everything else in the OT teaches. Jesus! The history of the kings was pointing to the one great king. The detailed instructions for the priesthood were all pointing to the great high priest. The prophets were all pointing to the ultimate Prophet. And the temple they served in? Pointing to Christ dwelling with his bride. All the promises of God are 'Yes' and 'Amen' in Christ. Now the dwelling of God is with men. And how does Ezekiel's construction conclude? The last words of Ezekiel ...

> ... 'And the name of the city from that time on will be: THE LORD IS THERE' (Ezek. 48:35).

It's a strange name for a city, but not if all the promises of God are 'Yes' and 'Amen' in Christ.

We need to start reading the OT through that lens. If you want the key to understanding the OT and the promises of God, it's this: God is not on about buildings and architecture or sprinkling the blood of bulls and goats. God is on about Jesus. Those other things served their purpose only as nothing more than shadows of what God was on about—Jesus and his bride. Hebrews tells us straight out that the OT temple buildings are *not* the real thing but only shadows. The real thing is the heavenly temple. Everything else ... just shadows. If you want to build another earthly temple, you are doing what? Going back to shadows! Where is the true temple?

> I did not see a temple in the city, because the Lord God Almighty and the Lamb are its temple (21:22).

It was there all along. Jesus said one greater than the temple is here (Matt. 12:6). Jesus is constantly referred to as the temple's cornerstone (Matt. 21:42, Mark 12:10-12; Luke 20:17-18; Acts 4:11, Rom. 9:32-33, Eph. 2:20, 1 Pet. 2:4-8). Jesus is the cornerstone and the people are also part of that temple. That's what we have been looking at in 21:9-21. Both the 12 apostles and 12 tribes are named in the very foundations and gates of the new city. Didn't John introduce that theme in his gospel? *The Word became flesh and made his dwelling among us* (literally tabernacled, John 1:14). The forerunner for the temple, the tabernacle, is fulfilled in Jesus. Isn't this the temple theology that Jesus gave us himself? *The temple he had spoken of was his body* (John 2:21). Jesus is the true temple. Jesus said a time is coming when you will neither worship in Jerusalem or Mt. Gerizim, but in spirit and in truth (John 4:21-24). That doesn't sound like Jesus is looking forward to worship being in an earthly temple! But in Spirit and in truth, through the temple who is the truth. The true temple! Jesus.

The message of Rev. 21 is one of intimate connection with the Lord. Unbroken, fully pure, fully protected and secure, fully planned, eternal fellowship, with Jew and Gentile believers together.

In the OT in God's city, Jerusalem, the temple of God represented the presence of God. But only the high priest bringing a sacrifice into the holy of holies could enter into God's presence. But when the Messiah comes and is sacrificed on the cross, the 30ft curtain of the temple is torn in two. Access to God made open for all! Jesus is the true temple (the way into God). The same generation of the people who saw Jesus die also saw the old temple demolished, never to be built again. Why? The true temple has come!

And yet strangely Jews are still looking for a temple and city built by human hands. Even more strangely, Gentile Christians are looking for another earthly temple to be built. But God told us plainly the true temple is *not* made with human hands. If you want to evangelize Jewish friends, don't point them to buildings. They don't need a building! They need the true temple—Jesus! There is no other way into God's presence. The city that *is* Jew and Gentile together! One house. One city. One gospel.

I did not see a temple in the city, because the Lord God Almighty and the Lamb are its temple (21:22).

Study Questions

1. Why can we only get reliable information about heaven from the Bible?

2. Why might this temple not be literal?

3. Does Ezekiel's temple point to the Rev. 21 temple or another?

4. What does measuring signify and how does it differ from Rev. 11?

5. What do the dimensions of the building signify?

6. Why would a city be a square?

7. Why would it be paved with pure gold?

8. Why would God give Ezekiel such a detailed description of a temple if it was never to be built?

9. How might our understanding of this text affect the way we read the OT?

10. What must be our focus in evangelizing the Jews?

28
Nothing Impure Can Enter
(Revelation 21:22-27)

The temple is a central theme throughout the Bible. The Jews had a forerunner to the temple in the tabernacle. Then the temple was built by Solomon and destroyed by Nebuchadnezzar, but later it was rebuilt by Zerubbabel and again much later by King Herod. Yet there was still the promise of a future temple as prophesied by Ezekiel and other prophets. And now towards the end of Revelation we see the fulfillment of the temple. Temple theology concerns the way God's people meet with God. We left off last time with the culmination of all the temples. All the promises of God are 'Yes' and 'Amen' — in Jesus ...

> I did not see a temple in the city, because the Lord God Almighty and the Lamb are its temple (21:22).

The need for an earthly building temple is over, because the way to God is open like the gates of the city. In this city, there is no more need for the people to go *to* the temple. There is no one going to church. Why not? The heavenly city existence is continuous church. What is church? The people of God with the Lord. This is why Christians gather together on the Lord's Day, in anticipation of this. (Is this climax at the end of Revelation another reason John had these visions on the Lord's Day? 1:10). As Hebrews 4:9 promised, a Sabbath remains for the people of God and this is fulfillment! God's people gathered at the temple, but not a building this time. They are face to face with Jesus. And for us who long for the presence of the Lord and his people, it will be far above what we asked or imagined.

> The city does not need the sun or the moon to shine on it, for the glory of God gives it light, and the Lamb is its lamp (21:23).

Everything that is a blessing comes from the Father above. God even gives good weather, light and brightness. But that is through agencies, such as the sun, moon and stars. Now it's all directly from the Lord. Jesus is the light of the world! But this is more than just light. This is the glory of the Lord in the midst of his people.

> The nations will walk by its light, and the kings of the earth will bring their splendor into it (21:24).

All this time you thought that in heaven you would be standing around singing or playing a harp forever. But here we see the people **walk** by the light of heaven. This is like the original Garden of Eden, walking in the cool of the day with the Lord. Of course, *walk* can be a metaphor for all of life's activities. Your 'walk with the Lord' could imply even more fulfilling activity in the new heaven and earth.

> On no day will its gates ever be shut, for there will be no night there (21:25).

In the ancient world, city gates were shut at night. But here there is **no night**. Everything that could have been a threat to enter has now been cast into the lake of fire, so the doors can stay open without any fear. This is the sense of freedom and security. No more night. No more darkness. No more death, mourning, crying, or pain.

We also will see in 21:27 that no sin can enter. Before we had restrictions because of our sin. Even as believers in Christ, now we still need boundaries. I would not have known what sin was if the Lord had not told me the commandments (Rom. 7:7). So God sets the boundaries and we have to resist, sometimes under great stress, the pressure and temptation of sin. But this is different. This is free from sin and free from restriction. In this state there is no temptation to sin, we are free from the old man warring against us. Do you look forward to this? This is why Revelation is written! Live now in light of this ... you have a future!

> The glory and honor of the nations will be brought into it (21:26).

Notice it is *nations* specified, not just people in general. Wasn't that the original plan of the gospel? The Lord will gather a people from every nation, tribe and tongue (5:9). This is the answer to the promise to Abraham that all nations on earth will be blessed through him.

This is multiculturalism as it is supposed to be. Nationhood, and it seems ethnic appearance, are maintained because the people are recognized according to their nations. But the great difference is the nations no longer take pride in their culture or patriotism because they all have a new heavenly citizenship together. Most importantly, the center is the Lamb!

Now, **the glory and honor of the nations will be brought into it.** Like much of this text, the future promise of all this light, open gates, and now *glory* of *nations*, is taken from Isaiah. In Isaiah 60:11 it is prophesied that the wealth of the nations is brought into the future Zion. But it is not riches that will be brought in. You can't take that with you! Even if you could, it would pale in insignificance. In the last chapter we saw the streets were paved with gold! This is like the story told of the man who thought when he died he would defy the old saying, 'You can't take it with you'. He was buried with his gold bars so he could take them with him. He arrived at the pearly gates and the angel (not St. Peter) said 'What are these bags?' He says, 'Gold! Gold bars!' The angel says, 'You brought paving?' How pathetic would worldly treasure look in this city! The city is already lined with gold! But this is symbolic. The nations will not bring material wealth into what is already the most glorious city ever!

So what does it mean, that *the glory and honor of the nations will be brought into it?* This could be the nation's bringing glory to the Lord, praising him just as in 4:9, 11; 5:12, 13. But 21:26 says it is the glory and honor *of* the nation's brought into it. So it could be all that they did in preparation (making themselves ready 19:7) for the wedding banquet, that is, all that they did to glorify God on earth is also brought into the heavenly city. This would mean everything achieved in this life for the glory of the Lord counts. It will be brought into this city. As we said of 21:24, there is walking in heaven and activity abounds, but not work that will be toil. The curse has gone. As the glory of the nations is brought into it, we can think of the parable of the talents. You have been faithful with these things, so I will put you in charge of many. Again, this implies a life of activity. Picture that. On earth, if you were faithful with small things, it is replicated into receiving many things. Nothing you did for the Lord's glory was wasted. Now it's brought in and received back a hundredfold.

All that is good in this life has continuity in the next life in the new heaven and new earth. The next life will not be in any way less, or less real, or missing anything good from the old earth, but only infinitely more. So we can picture any and every good gift that we enjoy in this life, but with one big difference. The Lord is there. He is the center. He is the temple! And yes, even an activity of walking will be pure pleasure ... with the Lord. Nothing done for the glory of God will be lost or forgotten.

There will also be no regrets in heaven. The only place where you have regrets is in hell. It was the rich man in hell who had regrets. Hell is filled with regret for lost opportunity to glorify God in this life. There is no meeting up with friends. But on the other hand, the new heaven and earth is a rich reunion with loved ones and will not be less but more. Our names are remembered in the new world. Well, of course they are! They are even written in the book of life (21:27)! There will be no boredom in the new heaven and new earth. Boredom only occurs on earth because we are without the Lord face to face. The heavenly city will always be filled with that heightened sense of excitement and anticipation! And one of the reasons for that is here.

> Nothing impure will ever enter it, nor will anyone who does what is shameful or deceitful, but only those whose names are written in the Lamb's book of life (21:27).

Nothing impure. This city is greater than the original Garden of Eden because Satan was able to enter that garden. Here nothing impure will ever enter it. There is not one single sin that can ever enter it. Nothing! So if you have ever sinned, on what basis could you go to heaven? Some will say, 'forgiveness'. Yes, but forgiveness still can't compromise this fact. No sin can enter! In itself, being forgiven doesn't remove the reality of things you have done wrong, and this text says *nothing* impure can ever enter. Many people say, 'Well, I've lived a good life and I'm not as bad as some.' But that is not the question. The heavenly city is a place where *no* sin can enter.

If you want to cut to the heart of how Jesus' teaching is radically different from everyone else in the world and throughout history, it's right here. God is pure. **Nothing impure** can enter his heaven. God has an answer to evil. He has a judgment to deal with everything anyone has done wrong in thoughts, words or actions. This is radically different from every other religion, philosophy and even non-religious views. In all others, God is not entirely pure. Pursue this question with your Jewish friends, with your Muslim friends, with JWs, with Mormons, with your average non-religious friend. Pursue it with your family. Pursue it with yourself. Why should God let you into a heaven where nothing impure can ever enter? Every answer they give will fall into the category of God overlooking impurity in some measure.

They will have God grade on a scale, where he lets some impurity into heaven. The Quran says scales weigh up your good and bad deeds and whichever outweighs determines whether you go to hell or go to heaven (Surah 23:102-103). This is the same philosophy of the average unbeliever. 'I've tried to be a good person, I'm not as bad as some, so God will see I have done more good deeds and he will overlook anything impure that I've done.' The JWs will answer why God would let them into salvation on the new earth saying, 'We bear the fruit, we do more door-knocking than anyone.' Everyone will generally answer with that same philosophy, that some evil must be overlooked. In other words, heaven is a place where sin *can* enter. It's just a matter of how much. If you do enough good, whatever bad you have done can just slide into heaven unnoticed.

What people don't realize is that this implies God is impure and corrupt in his judgments. Is heaven perfect or not? How can anything impure ever enter it? No one really believes good deeds outweigh bad deeds. We are outraged when a public figure such as a politician is caught out in some minor traffic offence and expects to be let off because they have done good other times.

But worst of all, if God let any sin into heaven, he would be corrupt as a judge, and heaven would be corrupt. The same stuff that ruined this world and sent it off its axis in the first place—sin— would be there again! That's why 21:27 says no sin! Nothing impure can ever enter! And **nor will anyone who does what is shameful or deceitful.** You might say, 'Oh well I haven't done anything shameful.' But the standard won't be what you determine is shameful. It will be anyone who does what is shameful as defined by the pure God! We have seen that those who end up in the lake of fire include idolaters (21:8). An idol is anything that causes you to put God in second place. And 'all liars' is the same thing as in 21:27, when it says anyone who does what is *deceitful*. Have you ever told a single lie? On that basis alone you're out! Can't enter. Nothing impure will ever enter!

Press anyone who is willing to look honestly at this question. If nothing impure can ever enter heaven, then why would God let you into such a place? The answer has to be: There is *no reason!*

So what are you going to do? It won't do you any good to try and clean up your act. It won't do any good to start getting some religion into you, because you still have a record that is blemished. You have lied. You have done shameful things, even had shameful thoughts, things that are impure. What is the answer?

There is only one answer. The light of the world shines out and stands out in a world that has no answer. The temple. The way into God. Evangelism is not complicated. It comes down to this ... You need to have your sins removed. You need to be cleansed of *all* unrighteousness. There is only one Savior who has promised to take *away* all your sin as far as east is from the west. And people miss this, but there is no other religion that even *offers* a way to do that! This is why the cross stands out like no other. It *removes* your record of shameful and deceitful acts. Because *nothing impure will ever enter it, nor will anyone who does what is shameful or deceitful, but only those whose names are written in the Lamb's book of life*. Notice the reminder again? He's called the Lamb! The one who was slain in our place. Here is that reminder again about that *book of life*. It's like this whole section is the reminder to everyone in the tribulation that there are only one of two endings. The beautiful city or the lake of fire. If your name is not in that book, then you won't make it in to the city.

So this text is an encouragement for the saints to persevere, but also a warning to the unsaved. Today is the day of grace while it is called today. That day will be too late. You will see Abraham, Isaac and Jacob, but you yourselves will be thrown out. But also, if you are one whose name is written in the Lamb's book of life but are involved in anything shameful or deceitful, it's written to say to you *'wake up!'* If your name is really there, then you will hear this warning and repent. We will spend eternity in one of the two descriptions of Rev. 21. Outside ... or inside! Which will it be? One day you will walk the golden streets with Jesus—or be cast out. Nothing impure can ever enter it. Have you had your impurity cleansed?

That's why we need to get away from phony evangelism that says becoming a Christian is just a decision you make. Or 'come to Jesus because he loves you' without telling people this bit here. God is a pure judge and can overlook nothing. All people who are impure will miss out if their 'impurity' is not dealt with. We need a Savior, so we need to know what we deserve and what Jesus went through to become sin for us at the cross. We need to know the only right response is belief and repentance, in which case you have really believed in the evil of sin and hate the things that nailed Jesus to that cross. Phony evangelism is deceiving people into hell. Faith in Jesus is not something you just add on to your life. It's not like signing up to a petition ... sign on the line if you believe in saving the whales. This is how some have portrayed the faith. Make a decision. Sign a confession in the back of the Bible and you are in. This is attractive to many.

I had a call from a young couple experiencing demonic attacks right in their home, weird things happening that were terrifying them. They wanted to understand it all, and when they heard the gospel they thought it was a great idea. The power is in Jesus to set us free. He alone is good and this thing in our home is bad. They were all for it. As long as it didn't involve having to change anything in *their* life. Jesus, fix up my life, as long as I can add 'belief in Jesus' to my résumé without it interfering with my life. As long as I don't have to change my walk! I don't mind Jesus walking with me on my path, as long as I don't have to *walk* with him. This brings us back to our text. It's about those who walk by the light of Jesus (21:24). Those whose names are written in the book of life will walk with him in this life and will walk with him in his light in the next. Those who don't walk with him can never enter this city.

In the back of the mind of many unbelievers when first confronted by the gospel (I was one of them) is this, 'Okay, if I believe in Jesus, that's great what he does for me, but what is this going to entail? As long as I don't have to hang around those Christians and church. As long as I can believe in him from my place and not have it affect my life, goals, money or time.' But that is not walking with Christ. There is no such thing as a Christian who tacks Jesus on to the old life. In fact, this picture here of walking with Jesus and bringing all your gifts to his glory is a total package. The reason is bound up in the message of Revelation. Jesus is the true King! In faith we renounce our own kingship and hand over kingship to him. Only unbelief sees that as bad news. Walking with him and he with you. Using your gifts for his glory will be multiplied in this new city. This is the most glorious thing ever. Purpose, meaning, and leading of the Lord. Total security. It's the total assurance that even if you sin and fail, he is the Lamb who took away your sin. You can get back up again and walk with him. And you are united to the bride that is the church. You have life, a plan, and a future!

The temple is God and the Lamb. The center, the focus of life is Jesus. He is the source of all light. The source of every gift you have or ever will have. Walk with him. And this is your future.

I did not see a temple in the city, because the Lord God Almighty and the Lamb are its temple. The city does not need the sun or the moon to shine on it, for the glory of God gives it light, and the Lamb is its lamp. The nations will walk by its light, and the kings of the earth will bring their splendor into it. On no day will its gates ever be shut, for there will be no night there. The glory and honor of the nations will be brought into it. Nothing impure will ever enter it, nor will anyone who does what is shameful or deceitful, but only those whose names are written in the Lamb's book of life (21:22-27).

Study Questions

1. Name all the different temples and their purpose.

2. What might it mean that the nations walk by the light of the city?

3. What could the 'glory and honor of nations' brought into it mean?

4. How does this surpass the purity even of the Garden of Eden?

5. What sets apart the God of the Bible from all other religions?

6. What is the flaw with a god who grades on scales, as in Islam?

7. How can this text be used in evangelism?

8. Explain how faith is more than an intellectual assent.

29
Paradise
(Revelation 22:1-6)

The Bible has saved the best until last. At the end of Revelation John is given this vision which is described symbolically because the reality is too wonderful to explain. This is the picture of the wonderful city, a continuation of 21:9-10 where John is told *come I will show you the holy city, the bride of Christ.* In Rev. 22 he is shown the New Jerusalem.

> Then the angel showed me the river of the water of life, as clear as crystal, flowing from the throne of God and of the Lamb ... (22:1).

This is drawing on both Ezekiel 47:9 ... *where the river flows everything will live,* and even further back in Genesis 2:10 ... *A river watering the garden flowed from Eden.* In the original Garden of Eden there are also references to precious gold, bdellium and onyx, just like the precious stones in 21:18-21 around the river. What's the meaning of Revelation? Jesus wins! But Jesus wins in a far more profound and complete victory than just casting down his enemies. That's what we see here as things have come full circle.

The promise in the beginning of the fall was that one born of the woman would crush the head of the serpent. What was all that? Well, it is the complete defeat of the devil ... Jesus wins, but it is much more. It is the *work* of the devil that is defeated (1 John 3:8), and Jesus is returning us to the Garden of Eden. The work of the devil was to bring death, destruction, and a cursed world. If Jesus died on the cross to save us only from hell, but did not give us back the new heaven and new earth, the garden with that river flowing out of it, and the rich fellowship of strolling with the Lord in the cool of the day, then his winning is not complete. But the beauty of this plan goes way beyond simply winning over enemies.

> ... down the middle of the great street of the city. <u>On each side of the river stood the tree of life</u>, bearing twelve crops of fruit, yielding its fruit every month. And the leaves of the tree are for <u>the healing</u> of the nations (22:2).

Remember that tree of life that we could not eat from in the garden after the fall? Here it is for everyone to eat in abundance. This symbol here of the river and water of life flowing out of this city is rich in its speaking of **healing of the nations**. It's not simply that the Lord has brought everything into judgment. What do we say to the person who has suffered abuse, whether as children, adults or vulnerable people, even over a long period? The answer is Jesus wins in two ways. He brings judgment to the abuser (as we have seen in the lake of fire), but it's much more for the victim. It's healing! It's restoration! It's real compensation. Not in the human sense where money can never really compensate or replace what has been lost in hurt, pain or life. This is the ultimate healing. This is the ultimate reversal. This is the win no one thought possible. When God said the Messiah to come would crush the head of the serpent, he did far more than just punish him in the lake of fire (20:10). The completeness of that reversal starts with this picture of Eden and with this river flowing out that has the *healing of the nations* which flowed from the cross. But this is even beyond the first Eden. We left off last time noting sin can never enter this city (21:27). In the first Eden sin *could* enter. Satan could enter. But here the blessing and richness is even greater.

> ... 'What no eye has seen, what no ear has heard, and what no human mind has conceived'—the things God has prepared for those who love him (1 Cor. 2:9).

So Jesus doesn't just win, he blitzes it! *All* the promises of God are 'Yes' and 'Amen' in Jesus because these waters are living waters just like the woman at the well was promised, welling up to eternal life. But look at the source from where those waters flow ... **the water of life, as clear as crystal, flowing from the throne of God and of the Lamb**. It's all flowing from God the Father and Jesus! It's Holy Spirit filled. Remember what Jesus said ...

> ... 'Let anyone who is thirsty come to me and drink. Whoever believes

> in me, as Scripture has said, rivers of living water will flow from within them.' By this he meant the Spirit, whom those who believed in him were later to receive (John 7:37-39a).

Jesus equates the Holy Spirit with the symbol of the living waters. And look at what else we have in this city ... **twelve crops of fruit, yielding its fruit every month.** Healthy food! From that tree of life! The number 12 again is used as representing the people of God. *Now* those first readers in the church at Ephesus can see what Jesus was saying, *to the one who is victorious I will give the tree of life* (2:7).

One topic of debate concerning the new heaven and new earth is the question of time. Will it be timeless or just never-ending time? We haven't experienced it, so we don't really know. But these symbols just happen to use the concept of time to describe the ongoing abundance. It's *yielding its fruit every month*. It's monthly! At the very least it seems to be time without end—but in abundance. In this life, time is always running out. We want to do all this stuff while we are still young. Then when we have the time, we are too old and decrepit to enjoy it. But there is no shortage of time or youth in this new city! Notice more evidence of this connection with Ezekiel's temple. Compare 22:2 *yielding its fruit every month*. And *the leaves* of the tree are for the *healing of the nations*, with ...

> 'Fruit trees of all kinds will grow on both banks of the river. Their leaves will not wither, nor will their fruit fail. Every month they will bear fruit, because the water from the sanctuary flows to them. Their fruit will serve for food and their leaves for healing' (Ezek. 47:12).

Both Ezekiel and Revelation speak of this healing. The *healing* of the cross is completed by the time of this fulfillment. It is finished. But the benefits of the cross flow on. This is restoration. Here there is no more death, mourning, crying, or pain, for the old order of things has passed away. This new creation is all encompassing. It's the city of Jerusalem in the new heaven and earth. The OT temple pointed to Jesus with his people in the new heaven and earth. G.K. Beale introduces a deeper look at the temple as a microcosm of God's plan for the earth.[27] The sanctuary itself being a tiny replica of the earth.

---

[27] G. K. Beale, *The Book of Revelation NIGTC* (Grand Rapids, Michigan: William B. Eerdmans Publishing Co. 1999) p. 1109

> He built his <u>sanctuary</u> like the heights, <u>like the earth</u> that he established forever (Ps. 78:69).

The OT temple was built *like the earth*. The temple furniture in 1 Kings 7:23-26 describes the gigantic washbasin as the sea! In Ezekiel 43:14 the Hebrew literally says the altar is *from the bosom of the earth*. 2 Chronicles 4:2-5 describes the temple furniture with the sea on top of the bulls facing north, south, east and west on the four corners of the earth. The ark in the temple is said to be the footstool of God. But Isaiah 66:1 says the whole *earth* is the footstool of God! Is the temple a microcosm of creation? Interestingly, even ancient Jews like Josephus and Philo understood the seven lamps in the temple as planets—the seven 'lights', as Genesis 1 calls the sun, moon and five planets visible to the naked eye. In Exodus 26:1 the flying cherubim are woven into the curtain that has colors of the sky. It's as though they are flying through the sky depicted in various hues of blue, purple and scarlet. When Isaiah saw the Lord in his temple, the glory of the Lord filled the temple. But Isaiah 6:3 says the seraphs were singing in that temple and *the whole <u>earth</u> is full of his glory*. The temple is filled with his glory but wait—it's the whole earth!

In Genesis 3:24 two cherubim were stationed outside the garden to guard the way into the tree of life. The temple has the two cherubim either side of the ark in the holy of holies. This makes us think of the lampstand outside the holy of holies, with its flowering branches looking very much like an image of the tree of life. Eden's entrance was from the east, and so too the tabernacle. Later temples were also entered from the east. Adam was to fill the earth and rule and subdue it, extending the glory of Eden over the whole earth, but failed. What the first Adam failed to do, the second Adam, Christ, has done in this fulfillment with Eden covering the whole heaven and earth. Jesus wins! In fact, there is an expanding from Eden to Canaan (Canaan is said to be like Eden, Isaiah 51:3), with its similarities in rivers and boundaries, then expanding to the whole earth! And here it is in Rev. 21-22. No temple—Jesus and his people in the new heaven and earth.

We saw in Rev. 21 the giant square was covered in gold, just like the holy of holies in the OT temple. We were told that was the bride of Christ, and the wider temple sanctuary represented the earth and cosmos. So here in Rev. 21-22 we have the bride of Christ with the

Lord as the temple *in* the new heaven and new earth where God will dwell with his people.

Think of the old temple structure and what it represents. The outer court is the visible earth. The holy place is the visible heavens, the cosmos. And the holy of holies was that invisible, unreachable, heavenly dwelling of God. The square that could not be approached. But the plan was always that *the Lord's presence with his people* would spread throughout the whole earth. The Israelites were to be a light to the Gentiles and spread the presence of his glory to the ends of the earth.

Well, here it is with abundance! It's overflowing, the ever increasing of richness in this new world. Did you notice in 22:2 that the tree of life is on both sides of the street? How can one tree be on both sides? The original Greek words translated *tree of life* have no article, indicating it could be talking about a *type* of tree. So it would be such an abundance of this type of tree that it lines both sides of the street. This also connects this to Ezekiel (47:7), where the street has trees either side.

It's symbolizing the tree that was so out of reach from the fall, with cherubim guarding the way against reaching it. Now the tree of life is within reach for all and is truly at hand and at all times in abundance. It's the same abundance as in Ezekiel 47, where the volume of water flowing from it increases the further the water travels. That's physically impossible in our world (suggesting Ezekiel's temple is pointing to something beyond this world). But if this is the 'living water' of the new heaven and new earth, it makes sense. This is where abundance flows. This is the abundant life that Jesus promised, now consummated. It's a complete contrast to this life because even when you think you have everything you want in this life, there is always something missing. Not in this new place! The abundance continues to overflow. It also has complete security.

> No longer will there be any curse. The throne of God and of the Lamb will be in the city, and his servants will serve him (22:3).

This is the great reversal of what happened in the Garden of Eden at the fall. A curse came upon the earth due to man's sin. Now there is no more curse! Before there was death, mourning, crying, and pain. Now there is no more death, mourning, crying, or pain. Before man was ejected from the presence of God and the beautiful garden. Now all can enter the presence of the Lord and the beautiful garden with its fruit trees and river. Before there was no more access to the tree of life. Now there is abundant access. All is reversed, as is everything that came with the curse. A world with sin meant evil people doing evil things, and the whole creation was affected. Why do we have earthquakes, tsunamis and hurricanes? Why is work such a toil? Why is childbirth painful? Why is there conflict in the world, in nations, in families, and in relationships? Answer: Because this is a cursed world!

No other religion or philosophy can explain this world. How is it that this creation can be so beautiful with intricacy of design which speaks of a designer of beauty, and yet this same creation can cause such grief when 'mother nature' bites back? The creation is not evolving, it is winding down. How is it that we can believe in love and relationships that go beyond anything evolution can explain? There is no survival value in love. It can even be counter to survival of the fittest. Why don't we rejoice when rapes and murders happen and go, 'Yeah, the fittest have survived again'? Instead we grieve and know there are such things as right and wrong, love, compassion, and tenderness. Yet so often these are tainted, even perverted, and instead we have conflict and abuse. How do you explain this world of contradictions?

There is one way. A curse! It's a world given as good but has been cursed. That's a radically different and more logical explanation than a world with no right or wrong which is evolving and getting better. World religions have no explanation for the evil and suffering in this world. But there is an explanation. This is a cursed world. And that is the significance here. Why? Because the curse is removed! How? Jesus became a curse for us! (Gal. 3:13). The whole creation has been groaning (Rom. 8:22), waiting for the completion of the reversal achieved through the work of the cross! **No longer will there be any curse.**

Now there is restoration and then some. Notice 22:3, they **serve** the Lord. Not endless harp playing, but abundance in every way. Serving the Lord means real activity, productive things but without the curse, so instead of it being toil, it's joy in the things we do. Exceeding joy!

The primary reason it's so abundant is that the light of this city is the Lamb. It's Jesus! That makes this more abundant than even the original Garden of Eden. In the original garden Adam and Eve walked with God in the cool of the day. But in this new Eden we will all experience God and walk with God in a way that could never be conceived. God as the Lamb! Before, man knew God as Almighty Creator. Here we know him as both Creator *and* as the Lamb, the savior. This is personal. We will know and see and walk with Jesus, the King of kings and yet as a man!

> They will <u>see his face</u> and his name will be on their foreheads (22:4).

We will actually **see his face**. Face to face! Surely this is the greatest abundance of all. You know when you have been apart from a loved one and then you see their face how it fills you with joy and love! Well, this is the homecoming to end all homecomings. This is the Lord, face to face! You will recognize him and relate. Why? God actually became a man. He will still have the marks where he bore the nails on the cross and the mark of the spear in his side that he showed his disciples. There will be no other blemishes seen in this new city, but these remind us of the love he poured out on us as the Lamb. Before, you couldn't see God's face and live, now the Lord has removed all that stood between us …

> For now we see only a reflection as in a mirror; then we shall <u>see face to face</u>. Now I know in part; then I shall know fully, even as I am fully known. And now these three remain: faith, hope and love. But the greatest of these is love (1 Cor. 13:12).

And also, **his name will be on their foreheads**. What is that? The name of God was on the forehead of the high priest in the OT. Now his name is on everyone, not just the high priest. All come to him and have the security of his name. This is the wildest dream come true. We can scarcely imagine this while we are going through this cursed world, but this is the greatest.

> There will be no more night. They will not need the light of a lamp or the light of the sun, for the Lord God will give them light. And they will reign for ever and ever (22:5).

The Lord provides all the light. How do we even comprehend the victory described as the saints **will reign for ever and ever**? There is a sense that the Lord is sharing his victory with us as we also *reign*. We can't begin to understand that. We'll have to leave that one until we get there to fully comprehend. *Reign forever!*

Remember why this book of Revelation was written? John started by saying he was with his readers as a companion in tribulation and patient endurance required in the kingdom (1:9). What we have seen in these last chapters of Revelation is a contrast between the endings of two women. Two cities.

From Rev. 17-18 it was the end of Babylon. The city that enticed you to compromise came crashing down. In contrast, the city in Rev. 21-22 has foundations where you reign forever. What is the message? Choose this day which city you will be a part of. The city that surrounds you now, or the bride of Christ. What did he say to the churches? To the church at Ephesus, to the one who is *victorious* I give the right to eat from the tree of life that is in the paradise of God. So what is this beautiful picture meant to do for us? It's to tell us *you must be victorious*. Be faithful. This is gonna be so worth it. Don't give up!

This is what we long for. The apostle Paul said to be in the presence of the Lord is better by far! Abundance. We long to be at home with the Lord. This is the true home for the believer. Don't be afraid of meditating on this. Don't believe the nonsense that you can become so heavenly minded you are of no earthly use. The more you have this picture, the more it will give you the strength to keep going and make the most of this life. There is a goal!

Have you ever noticed how in this life even its finest moments are only fleeting? This life was never meant to be home. We struggle. We fight. We are cast down waiting, waiting. Something is always missing. Do you know what that something is? *Home!* Home is missing. When you are there, nothing will be missing! You will never want to leave. This really is paradise. This is what you are patiently enduring for. It's not for your annual leave, nor your retirement, nor the travel you hope to do. Nor is it for the time when you 'make it' in this life. It's this. Being face to face with the Lord. Paradise is just a little further up ahead, but you must be victorious. You say, I am ready now. No, you are not, or you would be there already. You have to be victorious to get to paradise! To be face to face with our Lord who bought all this with his own life and planned it all from before the creation of the world. To eat from the tree of life. And finally ...

> The angel said to me, 'These words are trustworthy and true. The Lord, the God who inspires the prophets, sent his angel to show his servants the things that must soon take place' (22:6).

This is the conclusion of 21:1-22:5 (and effectively of the whole book). So what does it say? This is **trustworthy and true**. It's real and it's gonna happen **soon**. But didn't we already believe it's true? Yes, but while we live through this cursed world we get sidetracked away from looking to the finish line. It will happen to you this week. You'll forget this and need to come back to this reality. These words are real and alive. And it must soon take place. It could be upon us sooner than we think.

Study Questions

1. How does this text relate to 21:9-10?

2. Give more than one reason for the significance of the 'tree of life' appearing here.

3. How could 'healing of the nations' speak to those who have greatly troubled lives?

4. Is there 'time' in the new heaven and new earth?

5. What are some evidences that the ancient sanctuary might be pointing beyond to the whole earth, and what would the significance be in light of this text?

6. How can Ezekiel's temple have water volume increasing as it flows, and how might that relate to this text?

7. What does 'no more curse' mean?

8. Why does the cursed world provide a more logical explanation of life than other beliefs?

9. Give reasons why this text alludes to a very personal relationship with God and richness of activity.

10. What is the overall point of this section of Revelation for the first readers and us?

30
I Am Coming Soon
(Revelation 22:7-11)

We have arrived at the epilogue of Revelation and it takes us full circle, connecting us back to the opening introduction in 1:1-3. Both the introduction and this epilogue identify Revelation as a prophecy. There are all kinds of parallels in these two bookends. Both draw on the language of Daniel but with one difference. The introduction pronounces a 'blessing' on anyone who reads it and takes it to heart, and now the epilogue concludes 'blessed are those who *keep* the words.' It then finishes with a curse on those who don't.

This epilogue sums up the whole message of Revelation, which is that Jesus wins and those who persevere through the tribulation will be blessed. The previous section wound up when he said it's all trustworthy and true. Everything you have read in this book is true, not least of all this last section on the New Jerusalem. And these things will take place soon.

Now, the message of Revelation and the *Jesus wins* theme is summed up by this fact. Jesus is coming back soon! ...

> Look, I am coming soon! Blessed is the one who keeps the words of
> the prophecy written in this scroll (22:7).

This is an amazing interjection because it's actually Jesus himself speaking here. Most of the visions and messages of Revelation have been shown or spoken through angels. So what must it have been like for the apostle John? He has been seeing visions of cosmic proportions. He has seen history unfolding and the great warfare that goes on behind the scenes. One scene after another, one vision after another, messengers, angels telling and showing John this vision and that. Then all of a sudden, it's like John is in the movie theatre and the leading man in the movie suddenly comes down out of the screen and appears in person. It's Jesus himself who interjects! I don't normally see any advantage in Bibles with Jesus' words in red letters because all Scripture is God breathed, not just the bits in red. But if you have one of those Bibles when you are reading Revelation, it's kind of helpful to see it from John's point of view as to when Jesus jumps out of the movie screen in person and speaks. It hardly happens at all in Revelation. Rev. 2-3 sets the scene with Jesus' letters to the churches, so naturally those chapters are filled with Jesus' words (in red letters), but after the letters to the churches and the start of Rev. 4 it's all black text throughout Revelation until we get to the end of the last chapter. That is, except for two interjections. The first is at 16:15 and here at 22:7.

It's like Jesus is letting these visions tell the story, then he steps into his own story in a dramatic live cameo. What we should take note of is *what* is so important that Jesus interjects with on these two occasions? The first one (in red letters) ...

> 'Look, I come like a thief! Blessed is the one who stays awake and remains clothed, so as to not go naked and be shamefully exposed' (16:15).

The other is in our text...

> 'Look, I am coming soon! Blessed is the one who keeps the words of the prophecy written in this scroll' (22:7).

Then we see Jesus say the same sort of thing in 22:12 *Behold, I am coming soon!* ... Then Jesus follows with his warnings of blessing or cursing for those outside. Jesus continues this theme to the end, at 22:20 ... *Yes, I am coming soon...*

In other words, Jesus' personal interjections coming right out of the movie screen are few, but are centered on two crucial points that Revelation teaches. The first is that Jesus is coming back soon, *unexpectedly*. The second is that you need to be ready! Those who are ready will be blessed. Those who aren't ready will find themselves outside, cursed.

So what's the big deal about Revelation? What's the big deal about life? It's this! Jesus is coming back! Everything else taught in Revelation shows that it looks like evil is winning. This life looks unjust. It also reveals what goes on behind the scenes, that there are unseen forces of evil, beasts, dragons and evil prostitutes, but over it all there is Jesus. He is winning, but more than that. It's all about Jesus' final return. He is the victory rider on the white horse. Jesus is coming back!

We should not be ashamed as Christians to say we look forward to the victory of our King. We should live in light of his return. Hold yourself up for ridicule if necessary. You are not as concerned about the things of this life as you are for that future destiny. Remember you are so heavenly minded that you are fired up for earthly use. Nothing can touch you. Jesus is coming back!

This is life. This is its meaning. This is the answer to all the questions we have examined in this book. All those classic arguments 'I cannot accept God because of horrible things going on, abuse of the vulnerable, death.' Unbelievers find an answer for suffering and evil by getting rid of God. 'Well then there *is* no God.' But that makes it worse. It doesn't explain anything because even thinking atheists admit if you don't have God telling you what is right and wrong, you leave yourself with the dilemma that each one is entitled to their own opinion, so what is there to get upset about? You shall not murder. Who says? There are plenty who seem to think otherwise. Isn't each one entitled to their own opinion? And we are back to 'survival of the fittest,' indifferent to abuse of the vulnerable because everything is working out like Darwin said. There is no answer or solution to suffering and evil in this world …

Unless Jesus is coming back! And when he does, he brings both judgment for evil and his reward for the righteous. This is coupled with that *eternal* perspective we looked at towards the end of Revelation with a new heaven and new earth, which gives full compensation forever for those who suffered righteously, the healing of the nations, and eternal justice for the wicked. Those people who have suffered can look back in 50 million years and say all things have been put right and this reward makes it worth it. The only way that can happen is if Jesus is coming back to bring all that he promises.

And Jesus *is* coming back! Revelation has revealed to us far more about this than we knew before. Jesus will return for *final* judgment and that is what he means when he says, **Look, I am coming soon.**

But what Revelation has also shown us is that Jesus has been coming in partial judgments throughout the last 2000 years of history. 'Behold I am coming soon' is bigger than we ever thought before we opened Revelation. Yes, here in 22:7 it's talking about his final coming in person. But we have also seen through Revelation that it has such a richer meaning which leads up to that time. Look, I am coming *soon* is something we are meant to take seriously and literally. We are not meant to water it down, so that 'soon' doesn't really mean 'soon', since it's 2000 years from when John heard this, and it meant nothing to him or the churches or anyone through the last 2000 years when they read ...

> The angel said to me, 'These words are <u>trustworthy and true</u>. The Lord, the God who inspires the prophets, sent his angel to show his servants the things that <u>must soon take place</u>' (22:6).

Was the bit about *must soon take place* not really trustworthy and true? Can we conclude that it doesn't really mean *must soon take place* because it's not for at least 2000 years or more?

Revelation has *revealed* things. These things *have* taken place *soon* from John's time. We saw the one who opened the seals that brought partial judgments on this earth. It was Jesus. He came in judgment. Then came the trumpets and finally the bowls, all coming at the hands of the Lamb at the center of the throne. There is a sense in which it *did* take place from John's time *soon*. The coming of judgment warnings have been coming on this earth and will finally culminate in his personal coming here when he says, *'Look, I am coming soon! Blessed is the one who keeps the words of the prophecy written in this scroll.'*

There's more. There have been wedding preparations to be made for the great wedding banquet of the Lamb. They had to take place or the wedding could not take place. When you plan a wedding, you have all this stuff to do and you think you have all this time and before you know it, it's come upon you. It is coming soon — quicker than you would want. Why? Because all the preparations have to be made. This is the meaning of history! All the things we have seen in Revelation. We have also learned that these things refine God's people. The tribulation and suffering prepares the richness of the reward for those invited to the wedding banquet. Remember, it could be no other way. For the ecstasy of that wedding banquet to be what it is, the preparation had to take place. So the wedding is coming soon. And there are those you need to invite who have not yet come to faith. There are guests' seats at the wedding banquet that need to be filled. It won't happen until all the invitations to the guests are completed. In the sense of history, he has been coming soon all along, depending on where we are up to in the preparations.

We have learned in this book of Revelation there are Beasts, False Prophets, and Christians who have had their heads cut off (20:4). When could such a thing happen? We have learned there will be a uniting of one purpose of powers throughout the world that will oppose Jesus, and we saw how these could include powers such as governments, media, entertainment, and even education. These things also must happen, and they unfold the coming of our Lord Jesus. The preparation is occurring. Jesus is coming soon.

It's like watching a building site from the beginning of works. You drive past it each day. You see the foundations laid and when that frame goes up, you say it's all coming on so quickly. Well, actually there is quite a bit to go, but in the sense of progress, it is indeed coming quickly.

Revelation has taught us that progress has been made throughout history and Jesus has indeed been coming. The specific way in which Jesus has literally been coming soon is in partial judgment throughout the last 2000 years. Warning. Warning. Warning. That is Revelation. There is a very real sense in which through the last 2000 years, with Jesus releasing the seals, trumpets and bowls, that his *coming soon* has been real and alive for every reader of Revelation over those 2000 years. And it's all building up as we see the final preparations made before Jesus comes in person! *Look, I am coming soon!*

Now, what do your unbelieving friends think of all this? Jesus is coming back. They actually think you are nuts. You have lost your grip on reality. Who is that nutty preacher you listen to? How do you know the preacher is not nuts? How do you know you are not nuts?

Because of this: It's in red letters! It's Jesus himself who says, *Look, I am coming soon.* It's not the preacher's idea. It's not the church's idea. It's not your idea. It's Jesus endorsing the words which came before it in 22:6, which says these words are *faithful and true*.

How do you know Jesus is coming back? Because he said so!

It's the simplicity of these words of Jesus which imply we didn't have to make this book of Revelation so complicated. Everyone is debating Revelation, looking for ways to add up the 666, or looking for surgical implants in your wrists, or 200 million Chinese troops coming over the horizon. But its message is clear. Jesus is coming back. Revelation started out that way ... *Look! He is coming on the clouds!* Now it finishes that way. Jesus has proven it by coming through history with partial judgments. All those are down-payment evidence before your eyes, which assures you that he will really come in person when Jesus says, *Look, I am coming soon.*

The only question you need to answer is—are you ready? *Blessed is the one who keeps the words of the prophecy written in this scroll.* Jesus finishes Revelation where he began. *Blessed is the one who reads the words of this prophecy and takes it to heart* (1:3). Have you taken it to heart? Jesus left witnesses to write these things down ...

> I, John, am the one who heard and saw these things. And when I had heard and seen them, I fell down to worship at the feet of the angel who had been showing them to me (22:8).

John is the disciple whom Jesus loved. Jesus' best friend saw these things that were far greater than anything John had seen before, when he walked with Jesus on earth. John, the guy who saw Jesus raised from the dead. John, who saw Jesus still the storm, feed the 5000, and walk on water. But when he sees the cosmic sweep of history and action replay of the judgments upon the earth throughout history, the pictures of heaven, the return of the King in judgment, and finally the new heaven and new earth, John is so overwhelmed he makes the same mistake as he did back in 19:10, by falling at the feet and worshiping the first angel who had been showing him these visions through Revelation. What are you doing John?

> But he said to me, 'Don't do that! I am a fellow servant with you and with your fellow prophets and with all who keep the words of this scroll. Worship God!' (22:9).

Revelation is not from the angel. It's from God! Christians can fall for it if John can. It's not just the obvious history of so-called Christians worshiping saints and statues, but even holding undue reverence to a preacher. It's God's word that ministers to us, not a speaker. So what do you tell your skeptical friends when they say, 'You only believe whatever your church tells you'? You say 'No, we don't believe anything unless we see it coming from Jesus in the word he left us through his witnesses. We believe only in Jesus. And *he* said he is coming back.'

> Then he told me, 'Do not seal up the words of the prophecy of this scroll, <u>because the time is near</u>' (22:10).

It's not for sealing up. It's upon us now—**the time is near.** Everything that is happening in this book is unfolding before us. Don't seal it John! Tell it! Write it down and send it out to the churches! And that is what he did.

In contrast, Daniel was told about 600 years earlier (before Jesus gave this Revelation) to *seal up the prophecy* because the time had not come. Daniel 12:4, 8-9 had predicted a tribulation that God's people would go through, but didn't say when that end time would come. So the sealing up of Daniel's prophecies meant that they would not be fulfilled until the end, and Daniel was not in the end times (Dan. 12:13).

But John gets the sequel to Daniel and has to keep this prophecy open because this *is* the end times. Now in the last days comes the fulfillment in Jesus' life, death, resurrection and ascension. Jesus' coming is in partial judgments upon the earth, all the way up to his second coming in person.

> 'Let the one who does wrong continue to do wrong; let the vile person continue to be vile; let the one who does right continue to do right; and let the holy person continue to be holy' (22:11).

Now this is about as scary as it gets. What is God's message to you if you have heard Jesus is coming back and you are doing wrong? What do you think he says to you? Another call to repent? He actually says 'Let 'em be!' What? Let 'em be? What happened to 'heed the warning'? No, it's, **Let the one who does wrong continue to do wrong; let the vile person continue to be vile**. Just let him or her alone. Everything that has been warned about in this book will come upon you. This is like Romans 1:28. God *gave them over to themselves* to do what ought not to be done and they will receive the consequences of the judgment they bring upon themselves.

This isn't what we thought. We thought it would be 'Tell them to stop before it's too late!' Or 'this is your last warning!' But no, instead it's, 'Let 'em be.' Why? Why not warning? Because you have already been warned. Now we near the end of Revelation and it's, 'Let 'em be.' That is perhaps the scariest word of all, because it means that if you have been warned and kind of expect somehow that later you will be moved to change before it's too late, that you'll listen to the warning *later*, don't bet on it. *Let the one who does wrong <u>continue</u> to do wrong; let the vile person <u>continue</u> to be vile.* You will be comfortable with doing wrong right up to the day that it's too late.

It's like the warnings of the OT prophets, such as Isaiah 6:9-10. The message only hardens you. All God has to do to harden your heart is just leave you alone. And you will continue to do wrong all the time until it's too late.

This concluding message of Revelation is the final warning before it's too late. It goes out even when warnings will fall on deaf ears. It's meant to shock those who are truly his who have become 'lukewarm' or have 'forgotten their first love'. All the warnings to the seven churches—you are meant to read this and ask, 'What if I am the one who continues in doing wrong deliberately and it becomes too late for me?' Israel of old became hardened and only a remnant survived. The Israel of God that Paul talks about in Galatians 6:16 (the church of Jews and Gentiles), has become just as ancient Israel. Complacent. Whoever has ears let them hear! That was the constant refrain in the letters to the churches. It was meant to awaken those who had fallen asleep. Keep on going in slumber and he will come to you with the sword of his mouth. Keep on being lukewarm and he will spit you out of his mouth. Most will not hear. He who does wrong will just continue to do wrong. Later … Later … Later. But there is no 'later'.

That is the lot of most people. That is life. Most just keep on the same path they always have. 'I am just not moved to change anything right now. Maybe later.'

But the faint hope in this message is that maybe there are some who have been doing wrong who will see this as something they *can't* put off until later. 'Whoever has ears let them hear.'

And finally, there is also a good news message to the faithful persevering, **let the one who does right continue to do right; and let the holy person continue to be holy.** If you are walking with him and it's tough, and you don't know if you can keep going, this is written to encourage you. Don't give up! Keep on fighting through the tribulation to keep on *doing right* until the Lord returns. If you are trusting in him, he will keep you. He will complete the good work he began in you. This is the state he will find you in and it will count for eternity.

Let the one who does right continue to do right; and let the holy person continue to be holy. What about when I sin and fail to do right? Go back quickly to the Lamb who was slain on the cross for you and repent and get the assurance that it was in him you were cleansed. The ultimate doing *right* is trusting in Jesus. Get back up and continue to do right. Keep coming back to the one who did right on your behalf.

This text has a prophetic tone that is giving the certainty of the future. It's the certainty that the book of Revelation has given. There are those who follow the Beast and those who follow the Lamb. Those who have the Beast's mark and those whose names are written in the Lamb's book of life. It's predetermined. And yet, if you are one of his but have been lukewarm, it's also predetermined that these final words would scare the pants off you and wake you up! Repent and turn back to the Lord and begin to do right and your eternal destiny is set that you will make it. Even now. If you have ears, listen!

'*Look, I am coming soon! Blessed is the one who keeps the words of the prophecy written in this scroll*' (22:7).

Study Questions

1. What similarities are there between this text and the opening of the book of Revelation?

2. Jesus rarely interjects personally in the book. What is distinct about the times he does?

3. How does Jesus' coming back answer the questions of the skeptic?

4. Are Jesus' 'coming soon' and what 'must take place soon' to be taken literally?

5. Are there examples of ways Jesus has been coming soon over the last 2000 years?

6. How could we fall for the same idolatry that John did in falling at the angel's feet?

7. Why would God allow those who do wrong to continue doing wrong?

8. How does 'the one who does right continue to do right' encourage the reader?

9. Is there still hope in this text for the backslidden?

31
Testimony for the Churches
(Revelation 22:12-17)

Jesus is coming soon. He has also been coming in partial judgments since the time John wrote to these seven churches. Each day means we are one day closer to him coming in person ...

> 'Look, I am coming soon! My reward is with me, and I will give to each person according to what they have done' (22:12).

Did we get all the way to the end of Revelation and he gives us a salvation by works? We read here that he gives to each one **according to what they have done**. Well, it *is* judgment by works for those who rejected the Savior (20:12). What about the works of a believer? Our text goes on to explain that what Jesus does is wash our robes. Their works of sin have been dealt with. So it is not a works salvation. It is faith in Jesus' work. But is that all he is saying with *I will give to each person according to what they have done*? Salvation is indeed by faith alone. But, as many have said, *living* faith is never alone. It is worked out in our lives and will show itself in what we do. Hypocrisy will be exposed on this day as to *what you have done*.

If you really believe Jesus had to do everything on that cross to save you, it will transform your heart. It will give you a new humility that acknowledges, 'I was so evil: he had to do it all!' So if he did it all, will you still want to bother doing good? Yes, and 1000 times more, but with no fear of judgment! Instead you will have a heart of gratitude and love, not self-serving, self-saving, or self-righteousness. It will also show up on the Day of Judgment in what you have done! If you have trusted in Jesus you will have sought to live in obedience and look forward to this time ... *'Look, I am coming soon!* **My reward is with me.'** Why should I gain from his reward? Jesus brings the reward of salvation that is his victory, and yet he brings it not for himself, but for those who are his. This verse is drawn from Isaiah.

> See, the Sovereign LORD <u>comes</u> with power, and he rules with a mighty arm. See, his <u>reward</u> is with him, and his recompense accompanies him (Isa. 40:10).

God's *reward* is with him. But did you notice in 22:12 in place of God it says *Jesus'* reward? Revelation reveals it is Jesus who is God. And again, in the next verse (which causes all those nightmares for our Jehovah's Witness friends), Jesus says...

> I am the Alpha and the Omega, the First and the Last, the Beginning and the End (22:13).

Back in 1:8 and 21:6 it was God who says he is the Alpha and Omega. Here *Jesus* says *he* is the Alpha and Omega, the First and Last. Of course, this can only be describing the eternal God. As God said of himself, <u>I am the first and I am the last</u>; *apart from me there is no God* (Isa. 44:6). The LORD Almighty is the First and Last and there is no other God. And yet in 22:13 Jesus says he is that same one who is the First and Last. He is God who brings his reward. The JWs get in all kinds of confusion with this saying, 'Well then Jesus is *a* god but not the *Almighty* God.' But God says there are no other gods ...

> ... Before me no god was formed, nor will there be one after me (Isa. 43:10).

Any god other than the true God must be a false god (there are many 'gods' and 'lords', but only one true Lord and God, 1 Cor. 8:5-6). The JWs won't say Jesus is a false god, so they end up having to admit they have at least two true Gods. One Almighty God and another smaller god. But God says he is the only First and Last. He is God the Father. Yet here in 22:13 Jesus says he is also this same God, the First and Last! Not two or three gods. One God, one essence, three persons, Father, Son and Holy Spirit existing eternally in relationship. The JWs and the Muslims say this is all too complex and confusing. God is not a God of confusion. But as C.S. Lewis pointed out, it would not be confusing if we were making up our own ideas. When people make up their own religions, they never have anything as complex and difficult as this.[28] But the living God is beyond our comprehension. The wonder is not that God is beyond our thinking, the wonder is that God would bother to bring himself down to our level and make himself relatable and identify with us in our weakness by becoming a man in the person of Jesus.

Jesus is God. The OT titles for God (the First and Last) are now applied to Jesus in Revelation. Jesus comes at the end of Revelation in person and all of history comes down to the One who is the beginning and end of history. Revelation has been giving us this great sweep of history, and now look who shows up at the finish! The One who is the creator of history. He was there in the beginning of history. In the beginning was the Word. He created history and time, and history itself will conclude when he comes back. In fact, history and the Bible are all about Jesus. If you have put your trust in him, then you are on a sure and certain thing. How can you lose when the One who is sovereign over all history is sovereign over *your* history? No matter how bad things look, it's no wonder he can say he works it all for good for those who love him. He doesn't just see the beginning and the end. He *is* the beginning and the end. And he is with his people. What we've seen in Revelation is that despite the evil opposition raging, all is not what it seems. The Lord is with his people. More than that, he has spilt his blood for you. You are truly blessed indeed.

> 'Blessed are those who wash their robes, that they may have the right to the tree of life and may go through the gates into the city' (22:14).

We were introduced to this back in 7:14, *washing those robes in the blood of the Lamb*. It's all about the cross. Not only believing in *who* Jesus is, but *what* he did to take away your sin. Just as each one is judged according to the things they have done, he was punished for the things *you've done* to set you free!

So if you have trusted in him, then you have this ahead of you. You have the tree of life and get to go through those gates into the city. The same tree that human beings were barred from when man fell is now freely available! Now things have come full circle. Jesus,

---

[28] C. S. Lewis, *Mere Christianity* (New York: Simon And Schuster, 1996; Orig. 1943), p.145

the beginning and the end, came in between into the middle of history and washed your robes—with his blood, so that we can be with him at the *end* of history. What a great and glorious thing to be at this finish line. Jesus is the beginning and is there at the end. We will all meet him at the end, and the only thing that will count—the only thing that counts now is—have you had your robe washed? That stained robe. What is it stained with? Some of the things are listed in the next verse, for people who end up outside. You see, Jesus is bringing another reward. It's a reward of punishment for those who kept their own lordship in defiance of Jesus' Lordship. 'I will rule my life.' ... and their reward is to be outside. They wanted to be outside—of Jesus. So that is their reward.

> <u>Outside</u> are the dogs, those who practice magic arts, the sexually immoral, the murderers, the idolaters and everyone who <u>loves and practices falsehood</u> (22:15).

Will we feel sorry for those **outside**? Well, actually we will know they *wanted* to be outside, because it's for the one who **loves** continuing doing what they were doing. *Let the one who does wrong continue to do wrong.* They *love and practice falsehood!* They didn't want to be in God's presence. They end up on the outside, thrown into the lake of fire. It's a scary thought, the way Jesus put it in the gospel of Luke ...

> Someone asked him, 'Lord, are only a few people going to be saved?' He said to them, 'Make every effort to enter through the narrow door, because many, I tell you, will try to enter and will not be able to. Once the owner of the house gets up and closes the door, you will stand <u>outside knocking and pleading</u>, 'Sir, open the door for us.' But he will answer, 'I don't know you or where you come from.' Then you will say, 'We ate and drank with you, and you taught in our streets.' But he will reply, 'I don't know you or where you come from. Away from me, all you evildoers!' There will be weeping there, and gnashing of teeth, when you see Abraham, Isaac and Jacob and all the prophets in the kingdom of God, but you yourselves thrown out' (Luke 13:23-28).

We notice in 22:15 those liars get another mention in the hall of shame. There was a similar list in 21:8, and that list also ends with the liars. They *loved falsehood.* In the original language it literally says, 'they loved and lived a lie.' The Greek word translated 'falsehood' is the same word used by John of *false brethren* in his other writings. Not just any liars, but hypocrites who call themselves Christian but live falsely. He will give to each according to what they have done. They are unfaithful. These are the kind of people from Jesus' parable who could say 'we ate and drank with you.' Maybe they took the Lord's Supper? But now they are on the outside.

> 'I, Jesus, have <u>sent my angel</u> to give you this <u>testimony</u> <u>for the churches</u>.
> I am the Root and the Offspring of David, and the bright Morning Star' (22:16).

Remember this is the epilogue of Revelation. This is the conclusion. Jesus says he **sent** his **angel** to give **this testimony for the churches**. What churches? The seven churches that this was written to of course! Isn't this who Revelation was addressed to, if we go back to the start?

> John, To the seven <u>churches</u> in the province of Asia (1:4).

We have seen that God uses the number seven as his number of completion. So, by extension this book is addressed to all churches. Hence, this finish is coming back to where the book started. It was addressed to the churches in the first place and it finishes with Jesus saying he sent this testimony *for the churches*. This is the guide by which I have interpreted the book of Revelation. Taking it as to what it says of itself, as to whom it was written. The churches. It's real and alive and must soon take place *for the churches*.

When I met that pastor in India who was preaching through Revelation, and asked him if he was taking the popular Futurist view of Revelation, he said, 'We do not do isegesis here we do exegesis'. He meant we don't bring ideas from outside the text, but interpret based on what the text says of itself about who it's written to, the persecuted church, from the first century all the way through. That is when he told me that Revelation was alive for his people. The Christians in that part of India who don't accept the mark of the Beast and who won't deny their Christian faith often miss the jobs and business opportunities, i.e., their ability to buy and sell.

That's why I haven't gone with the idea that Revelation is only for the future with no relevance for the churches in the church age, because that would mean this book is not a *testimony for the churches*, but relevant only to some people in some small pocket of time in the future.

Rather, the first readers to whom this book was addressed would have taken hold of this last statement, that this book is a testimony for them! Revelation is alive, speaking to the churches from the first century and throughout the last 2000 years. And it speaks right up to the end ...

> The Spirit and the bride say, 'Come!' And let the one who hears say, 'Come!' Let the one who is thirsty come; and let the one who wishes take the free gift of the water of life (22:17).

Does this mean the Spirit and the bride ask Jesus to return? The reader is told **come** and **take the free gift**. But this is a call to the people, not Jesus. So which is it? A call for Jesus to come back, or a call to people to come and take the water of life? Commentators on Revelation are divided, but I wonder if it is deliberately ambiguous. 'Come back Lord Jesus' is the first plea. Then 'come in, you who are not saved' is the second. Have you ever felt that tension? We think, if only the Lord would come back soon. 'Come back Lord Jesus ... *but not yet*, not until my loved ones come to you.' So we urge them to come 'take of the free gift of life'.

When the last one comes in, Jesus will return. Have you ever thought about that? What is holding Jesus back, with all the evil going on? 2 Peter 3:12 talks about *speeding* the return of our Lord Jesus. How can we 'speed' the return of Jesus? Well, he will come back when the last one of his has come in, and that won't happen until *we* take the gospel to them and say, 'Come and take of the water of life.' So, as we say 'Come back Lord Jesus', we also say to the lost 'come and take'!

The Spirit and the bride say, 'Come!' And let the one who hears say, 'Come!' Let the one who is thirsty come; and let the one who wishes take the free gift of the water of life. It's a call to **whoever wishes**, like those seven churches who were lukewarm, compromising, indulging sexual immorality, idolatry and forgetting their first love. It's a message for *anyone* who is thirsty.

It's a message for *anyone* who finds something lacking in this life—thirsting for something. This is what this life will always bring ... something missing. But are you thirsty enough to consider all other attempts to quench your thirst as 'rubbish', like the apostle Paul did (Phil. 3:8)? How much does this water which gives eternal life cost you? Nothing! It's free to you. But it cost *him* everything, to wash your robe. He was the One who is the Alpha and Omega, the First and the Last. Only he could pay that eternal hell because he is the First and Last. He's eternal. It costs you nothing and yet it costs you everything. He doesn't want your outward efforts to make you right. He wants your whole heart! A humbled heart. A heart that is undone. A heart that thirsts. You've tried the world, the other gods. They leave you thirsty.

This is a wake-up call to the backslidden, but it's also a call to the weak and struggling. 'I don't know if I can make it. I have not lived as I should. Will I be able to stand on that day? I have tried and failed. Where do I really stand?' Well, this call says, 'Forget where you've been standing. If you are thirsty, come and take of the free gift of life!' And if you haven't lived as you should, then repent now and take hold of it! It's there now, still to be taken. 'But look at my weak past.' This is not about you and what you have done. It's a free gift of what *he* has done. Come. Whoever wishes! Let him take of the free gift!

Ask yourself what is so precious in this world that you would cling to, which would make it worthwhile to end up *outside* and reject this free gift? Write down those things (like those on this list in 22:15), whether it be idols, sexual immorality, etc. Write down what is holding you back from coming and embracing this free gift. Those things which you are clinging to that you will lose anyway if you are hurled into that lake of fire. Take that list and throw those things out! Look away from them and look to the Savior. *Believe* in the Alpha and Omega who gave himself up for you, even you.

This invitation goes out like no other, to **whoever is thirsty!** I think it was Martyn Lloyd-Jones who once said philosophers only invite other philosophers. They are above the rest of us. Who are they inviting to listen? Those who live in ivory towers? The ethicists invite those who have the moral capacity to follow their 'good ways'. But they have nothing to offer the hopeless sinner that can't lift himself out of the pit. Religious people invite you to follow religion. They invite the devotees. The disciplined. The devout. But that doesn't speak to the depressed and wandering soul. But this invitation goes out to the lowly, the vile — come, wash your robes. It's an invitation to the helpless that will say 'I surrender'. This is an invitation to *whoever is thirsty!*

And if the Spirit and the bride (the church) say, 'Come and take the water of life,' this means it's a call the church is to make. And if you are a believer, you are part of the church! Revelation is leaving us with the great commission—with *urgency*. 'Come!' Jesus, the true Alpha and Omega is returning, and we have been given this mission to proclaim the gospel. To call people to 'come, take of the water of life'. It's a call, in earnest.

So how much of your life is centered on this call? That is what we have been left with at the end of Revelation. What are you going to take away from Revelation? If you have forgotten everything else, then at least take this away. We are supposed to be witnesses following the faithful and true witness, calling people to '*Come, take the water of life!*' If you call yourself part of the bride, are you playing your part in that?

Study Questions

1. Is rewarding each one a works-based salvation?

2. How can Jesus' deity be defended from this text?

3. How does the 'Alpha and Omega' speak of God through history?

4. Why wouldn't we feel sorry for those 'outside'?

5. How does the mention of 'testimony for the churches' relate to the overall book of Revelation?

6. Is 22:17 a call to Jesus to come back or to unbelievers to come to receive life?

7. How can we speed the coming of Jesus?

8. What does Jesus mean by inviting whoever is thirsty?

9. Do you have things that still need to be left 'outside'?

32
Overview of Revelation 1-22
(Revelation 22:18-21)

Revelation finally ends with, 'Don't add and don't take away from Revelation.' So I hope I've been giving you the right interpretation, because if I've got it wrong, then look out for the plagues! Is that what these last words of Revelation refer to? You must have the right interpretation? Some have thought that. Others have said it's referring to the copyists. Before the invention of printing, manuscripts were all written by hand, so if those copying Revelation slipped up, would *they* receive the plagues? If this was the case, no one would have ever wanted to be a copyist for Revelation. 'I don't mind copying the rest of the Bible, but there ain't enough drachmas in the whole of Palestine to get me to write out Revelation. If I get one jot or tittle wrong, it's plagues upon me.' Is that what this text means when it says we are not to add or take away?

It's time to think of the overall message of Revelation. If anyone takes away or adds to the prophecy of this book, that is, the call to be faithful to Jesus who is coming back, to not give in to the world, the Beast, and Babylon with her false teaching, then they have not heeded the warning and will receive the plagues. The reason we know this is what it means is by looking at it through the eyes of John, the aging apostle. What did John think when he saw these last words of Revelation? He would have immediately thought of the OT ...

> Do not add to what I command you and do not subtract from it, but keep the commands of the LORD your God that I give you (Deut. 4:2).

It's the same thing repeated in Deuteronomy 12:32. Don't add or subtract from God's commands. Or as Deuteronomy 29:19-20 says, every curse written in this book will rest on him and his name will be blotted out. In Deuteronomy, the *context* is a warning to Israel against idolatry and immorality before they crossed over to the Promised Land. That's Revelation! From the warnings to the churches about idolatry and immorality, and all the way throughout, there are warnings before *we* cross over to *the* Promised Land—the new heaven and earth. Take the warning seriously.

> I warn everyone who hears the words of the prophecy of this scroll: If anyone adds anything to them, God will add to him the plagues described in this scroll. And if anyone takes words away from this scroll of prophecy, God will take away from that person any share in the tree of life and in the Holy City, which are described in this scroll (22:18-19).

There are plenty of **plagues** described throughout this book, culminating in the lake of fire. This is a warning against hypocrisy. Take God's word seriously. Don't take away or add to it. It's hard to believe that after this warning, people actually tried to write additional 'Revelation' books. These are the kind of guys who play chicken lying down on the busy freeway. 'I think I'll get away with this.' Gnostic works in the centuries that followed John included the Apocalypse (or Revelation) *of Peter, Revelation of Paul* and *Revelation of Thomas*. These are not taken seriously because they were written long after the apostles. Far more serious is the blight on the history of the church to add or take away from God's word in general. But even if people think they are getting away with it for a time, they won't, because the warning of Revelation closes with the same warning that has come up all through the book. Jesus is coming back.

> He who testifies to these things says, 'Yes, I am coming soon.' Amen. Come, Lord Jesus. The grace of the Lord Jesus be with God's people. Amen (22:20-21).

What an amazing way to finish this book! After a book of warnings and terrible sights and sounds, condemning backsliders and lukewarmers, it ends with a farewell of what? Grace. That final invitation we looked at previously, to *whoever*, no matter where you are at: 'Come and take the free gift.' It's grace that is needed for God's people and grace will bring us home. **The grace of the Lord Jesus be with God's people. Amen.**

When it says 'don't add to or take away, otherwise you will receive the plagues,' it can't be referring to the whole Bible because at the time of writing, the authoritative books of the Bible circulated separately and weren't put into one single volume until much later. So if we use the end of Revelation to tell our Mormon or Muslim friends that their scriptures **add** to God's word, they can rightly say this text does not refer to the whole Bible, just to the book of Revelation. And that's true. But think about the deeper implications.

There are other grievous warnings in Scripture about not adding to God's word. Proverbs 30:6 says don't add to God's word or he will prove you a liar. Or Galatians 1:8, if anyone adds to or changes the gospel, a curse upon him. So yes, this Revelation warning is referring specifically to the book of Revelation, but is it only coincidence that this warning comes at the close of the canon of Scripture? A warning that conforms with other parts of the Bible that you must not add to God's word, just happens to be at the very end of the Bible. In God's providence, he chooses for these words to close the canon of Scripture. The last words Christians are left with before Jesus comes back, written by the last living apostle, writing *his* last book, in the last book of the Bible, and the last words of the whole Bible just happen to say, 'Don't add anything to them or you'll get these plagues ... Jesus is coming back!'

It could be coincidence, but I wouldn't want to mess with it. And Mormons and Muslims don't just add more words, they add a different gospel. That is more in line with what is being warned against at the end of Revelation.

So it's not just a matter of our interpretation of the difficult parts of Revelation. There are devout Christians with different views throughout the last 2000 years, but whatever your interpretation, do you take the warnings seriously to follow the Lamb and reject the sin of Babylon? Do you take that away or add to it?

So as we come to the close of the book, let's finally try and picture John and how alive these warnings were for him in his old age as he sat there in that cave on that prison island. Let's look back over the book and picture it all from John's point of view when he first received this *Revelation* ...

'I was on the island of Patmos for standing for the Lord and his word. It was the Lord's Day and I was in the Spirit. Many times, sitting there in that cave I thought of those seven churches I ministered to back in Ephesus, Smyrna, Pergamum—all of them. I had been their Pastor and I was concerned for them. And it seems someone else was as well. Because there in that cave I heard a loud voice like a trumpet (Rev. 1). I turned around and the first thing I saw were these seven golden lampstands, and right in their midst was one in glory and splendor. His eyes were like fire. I fell at his feet as though dead, but he told me not to be afraid. He said *I am the First and the Last. I was dead but now I'm alive again forever.* He told me to write down a message to my congregations in those seven churches. The seven lampstands were the seven churches. So I sat down to write to them ...'

'*I, John am your brother and companion in the tribulation* ... what you are experiencing I feel it with you (1:9). And so, I was given this message to tell them how to cope in this tribulation—the patient endurance and suffering that are ours in Jesus. There were seven letters to seven churches. I knew seven is God's number of completion. Could this be a message to all of God's church? Yes, because he told me to write what I see, what is now in my time and what will follow in the future (1:19). I felt like weeping as I wrote those letters (Rev. 2-3). Of the churches where I had been their Pastor, only two of them had a report of being faithful witnesses. The rest were a sorry state indeed. Some had lost their first love. Others caught up in sexual immorality, false teachers, idols—lots of idols, some lukewarm and some experiencing Satan's attacks. And even worse, many of those who were *faithful* brothers and sisters were suffering persecution. They were in tribulation all right. Is this the church that Jesus had left here on earth?'

'But then he lifted me up in the Spirit (Rev. 4) and he showed me a different perspective. I got a peek into heaven itself! There he was on the throne! And there were 24 elders surrounding him. Of course, 12 apostles, 12 tribes of Israel, all of God's people represented. And there were these creatures representing creatures of all the earth, covered with eyes all over and they had wings. Then I realized I was looking into the very control room of the universe. All those eyes and wings, every action, in every direction, all seeing—nothing out of his control. He was reigning! From every possible angle. Then I understood it! What looked disastrous in the church below with all its struggles was *fully* in control from above. He *is* on the throne. Heaven's verdict: All under his power!'

'But then something stopped me in my tracks (Rev. 5). There in heaven was this scroll with seven seals, but no one could open it. I started weeping and weeping. Could it be that the history and salvation and judgment of the world would not, could not, go ahead because no one was worthy to open the scroll?'

'But then I saw him. The Lion and the Lamb who had been slain. He purchased men and women from every nation with his own blood. He paid for the sins of all those who would trust in him. That's why *he* was worthy to open those seals (Rev. 6). But what a shock when those seals were opened. Then I saw the sweep of history. Horsemen being released through history, and what were they bringing? Judgment. The first four seals. There was a white horse conquering, but then a red horse—blood, war and violence. A black horse—famine, starvation and disease. And finally, a pale horse—death. It was everywhere. People dying. So much so that people actually thought of it as normal! Here they were being warned through these partial judgments. This is exactly what the apostle Paul had said, *the wrath of God is being revealed from heaven against all the ungodliness and wickedness of men* (Rom. 1:18). It is happening now and through history.'

'And the message? This world is cursed, doomed and is under judgment! It's a world headed for a full judgment. But how long would this terrible world remain?'

'Then he opened the fifth seal and I saw under an altar (signifying the blood of the Lamb who saved them) those who had given their lives for the Lord. They asked the same question! How long, O Lord? How long will this world of evil remain? And he answered. As long as it takes, until the last one of mine comes to faith and gives his life up for me.'

'And the vision of history all led up to just that. Judgment. And there it was. The end! People running, calling for rocks and mountains to fall on them to hide from the wrath of God. And who could stand? Who *could* stand?'

'Then I saw who could stand (Rev. 7). Those sealed. Sealed with the Holy Spirit as the apostle Paul had said (Eph. 1:13, 4:30). And there were 144,000, that is 12 apostles multiplied by 12 tribes of Israel, together, but in the 1000s. I knew the number 1000 in the Scriptures is God's figure of a great, indefinite number. Jewish believers, the natural branches and those Gentiles grafted into Israel. The two joined as one in Christ together (Eph. 2:11-19). Sealed with the Holy Spirit. *They* were able to stand.'

'Then I saw it *all* again. It was like I was getting a great replay of history. There was a pattern, a repetition to these scenes of history. But this time more close-up angles. This time trumpets blasted. Why trumpets (Rev. 8)? Trumpets warn. How? More partial judgments. But this time more intense. Sun burning up the land, hail destroying, even killing, drawing blood, death and disease everywhere, creatures dying and waterways contaminated. Great parts of the world without clean drinking water. When? When would this happen? Wait! That is the world we live in now! What is the message? Warning! This world is under judgment! Find the Savior while you still can!'

'But as the fifth trumpet blasted (Rev. 9), something supernatural arose, and it wasn't good. It came out of the Abyss. That's Satan's realm. Evil creatures causing great grief, but there were two hundred million of them. That explains it! I knew there was an invisible warfare, but I had no idea how vast. We are under attack. A demonic army is against us! 200 million! There's a war going on. We can't see it, but we are in it—now!'

'The trumpets were warning, but the shock is that people aren't listening! They see death, disease and war before their eyes and they still think this is normal! They live in this dying world and they know they're going to die too, but they still *refused to repent of their sexual immorality and their idols.*'

'I felt like giving up. No one is listening and what can I do from this lonely cave on this forsaken prison island of Patmos? All I can do is write all this down and send it to the churches. Maybe someone, somewhere might read it someday.'

'It all seems out of control. But then I saw it's not out of control (Rev. 10). A mighty one so colossal, so in control of the world, that he had one foot on earth and one foot on the sea. And he gave me a scroll. He told me to eat it. He said it will be sweet to taste but bitter in my stomach. So I ate it. Then it made sense when he told me ... *Go! Prophesy about many nations.* Of course, the sweet gospel, so sweet, but so bitter when its rejected. And how could I keep proclaiming it with such rejection?'

'Who will keep the people of God through that? Then I got my answer (Rev. 11). I was to measure not only the temple but also the worshipers of God! Yes, measure! Measuring, God's way of saying he secures his people. The apostle Paul had taught that God's people were the temple with Jesus in their midst (Eph. 2:20 and 1 Cor. 3:17). I was told to brace myself.'

'There would be those trampling on God's people (the holy people of the city), and there would be only two witnesses, lampstands he called them (11:4). Now it made sense. The Lord told me at the start, lampstands were the churches, seven of them. So the witnesses were the churches, but why only two? Of course. The letters to the seven churches! There were only *two* faithful churches as a witness. The two lampstands. So there would only be a smaller faithful witness in the whole wider church of Jesus. Much of the church will be lukewarm or immoral or caught up in its wealth.'

'But the faithful witnesses breathed out a message of fire. Heaven or hell! The gospel of life ... or death. But those faithful witnesses were attacked and then decimated. Their persecutors rejoiced at the demise of the witnesses, the true church. *We beat the church* they said. But right then they were shocked. Jesus' people were caught up to be with him. It was the Day of Judgment. There was a great earthquake. Lightning, rumblings, peals of thunder, a great hailstorm. It was all over.'

'How could this broken-down people, the church, have ever made it to stand at the judgment of sinners? They were sinners themselves. Then I saw how (Rev. 12). He gave me another vision. Another perspective. I saw that same broken-down church, this time from the heavenly viewpoint. On earth she was in despair, shabby and beaten, but the heavenly verdict, the heavenly view? She was a beautiful woman, dressed in splendor! Clothed in the righteousness of the Lamb who cleansed her by his blood.'

'Again, it was the sweep of history, a replay from the perspective of this beautiful woman (the people of the Messiah). She gave birth to a male child (Jesus). But the Dragon, the devil tried to devour him. But Jesus was snatched up to heaven in full triumph. And because he paid for her sin at the cross, rose victorious from death, and ascended into heaven as King, he could throw the devil *and* his accusations out of heaven. The devil was defeated! His accusations could not stand.'

'But when that Dragon was thrown down, that just made him even more angry. Angry at the woman, the church (the people of Christ). He pursued her. But she was taken care of through this wilderness tribulation. She was nourished not on bread alone, but by the word of God. She would be all right. At least I thought so …'

'Until next (Rev. 13), I saw this beast coming up out of the sea at the beckon of the Dragon. The Beast was behind godless government powers throughout history. Unbelievers looked to those powers to keep them, to provide for them … they went along with the godless ways of the Beast. But those whose names were written in the Lamb's book of life would not bow down to those powers. So the Beast oppressed them. This calls for patient endurance and faithfulness on the part of the saints. And just when I thought it was safe to go back in the water, another beast came up, this time out of the earth!'

'A False Prophet Beast that would manifest in all kinds of false religions. The first Beast made it hard for those who stood for the Lamb even to the point of their income. The Beast (governments) introduced laws that went against God's law. So those who were faithful and who wouldn't compromise could miss out on opportunities for work or business. And because they wouldn't compromise for their income, it limited their ability to buy and sell. Those who followed the Beast didn't have that trouble. They took his mark.'

'Those who had the mark of God, the invisible seal of the Holy Spirit, showed God's mark in their actions and beliefs, standing firm. It was also clear who followed the Beast. *They* showed *their* mark in what they put *their* hands to and what they believed in *their* minds. The mark of the wrist and the forehead showed out in their lives. The mark of man. Rebellion. Man who falls *short* of the glory of God and of God's number of perfection 7. Man—created on the 6th day. God is Holy, Holy, Holy, 7, 7, 7. Man falls short, falls short, falls short. His number? 6, 6, 6.'

'There were those who were faithful who wouldn't give in to the Beast (Rev. 14). They kept themselves pure. This calls for patient endurance on the part of the faithful. Those who followed the Beast thought they were getting away with it. They carried on as usual. But if only they could've seen their end. I saw it. They were tormented day and night forever and ever. It wasn't worth it. Judgment was coming! And come it did. Once again, I was cast down with despair. How could *anyone* stand in light of a holy God?'

'And again, I saw how (Rev. 15). I got another view from heaven's perspective. No one could stand in themselves, but a new victory scene reminded me again of the finish line for the saints. They sang the song of Moses and *the Lamb!* The Lamb who was slain. Jesus. He died on the cross for the sins of all who put their trust in him. That's how they could stand!'

'But then, as if my old bones couldn't go around again, another replay. It was the sweep of history again. Yes, partial judgments again leading up to the end (Rev. 16), but this time intensifying—the bowls of God's wrath. I had never seen history in that light. This really is a world under judgment. It's right before our eyes. Death, disease and a dry uncompromising world. Everything around us through history has been warning us this world is dying. It's under judgment. But the inhabitants of the earth ignored it, as if this was normal. They still refused to heed the warning and repent and give glory to God.'

'All the powers of the world, godless political powers, media, education and religions all joined together. But how could they join as one? What do Muslims and Buddhists have in common? What do communist governments have in common with capitalist governments? Wouldn't they normally be enemies? What do the powers of godless media, entertainment, and social powers have in common? Yet they were all gathering together, *joined!* How? In one *purpose* (17:13)—to oppose the Christ as the only true Lord. They all had that one purpose. They all want to eliminate Jesus as Lord from society. And they said, *where is your Jesus now?*'

'Where is he? Behold he comes like a thief! And he did! Earthquakes and peals of thunder. The Day of Judgment. Armageddon! Now they gathered together for this battle, but it was a losing battle. Every nation gathered before him. Every knee bowed.'

'But then he showed me again behind the scenes of history from yet another angle. He had already showed me the holy woman in her splendor, the church. But now I saw her opposite number—*another* woman. An *unholy* woman (Rev. 17). A prostitute called Babylon. She is a great city. What city? The city where *you* live. The city you experience now! Just as the Dragon, the Beast, and False prophet were a counterfeit, an unholy trinity, so this woman was the counterfeit to the *holy* woman of splendor, the church. This was the seductive woman. The city with all the fun, lights, lusts, and luxuries.'

'But this seductive woman didn't last (Rev. 18). I saw this great evil woman fall. Fallen, fallen, is Babylon the great. And the call to the saints was ... don't fall with her! Look how she ends! *Come out of her my people!* She was boasting and enticing you with her lusts and pleasures, but if only you could see her end! She lay in ruins! Don't fall for her. You might think life seems to go on as always, forever, but suddenly it was all over. You thought you had more time, but it was all over in one hour. She fell.'

'But what happened to the saints (Rev. 19)? Then I saw them at the *end* of history. A great multitude I couldn't count, shouting with joy! All the people from the church were there! I could see them *all* at the end of time. I could see *you* too in their midst! ... If you were one of the faithful ones!'

'Then it all made sense. Now I was given the vision of the conclusion. I finally discovered what the meaning of life was. It was all a plan from before the creation of the world. *The* plan. The meaning of life ... was, a wedding!'

'Finally, all of the pain and struggles of life made sense. Why did the Christians have to go through it all? Why did good people have to suffer? And here was the answer. There had to be a preparation for that wedding banquet. The fine linen they wore represented their righteous deeds and suffering that were all building their individual rewards. Those deeds were also the refining which prepared them for the fullness of their rewards in this banquet. History had to unfold this way or the wedding banquet *could not* have taken place in all its richness, with the full rewards.'

'And there it was. The wedding. The bridegroom was not only a Lamb, but also the King. He came victorious on a white horse. The true King of kings and Lord of lords.'

'But in great contrast to the wedding supper of the Lamb, there was another supper. An ugly supper. The great supper of God's judgment. There were those eaten up in God's *judgment* supper. How did it come to this point?'

'Then I saw how (Rev. 20). A final sweep of history. But this time

Jesus' gospel message through history. 1000 years is like a day, and a day is like 1000 years. I'd seen how God used the number 1000 through the Scriptures as God's great, indefinite number. And this '1000-years' was also a great, indefinite number of the years sweeping the history of the gospel going forth. I could tell it was the gospel age because all through those years I saw this ugly threshing dragon that had been bound up, so he could no longer deceive the nations. But hasn't he always deceived the nations throughout church history? Isn't that what he does? Deceive? Then I realized—not in one crucial way. For century after century through all OT history, there was no salvation for *any* nation in *all* of history except for one tiny nation, Israel. Because the Dragon had deceived all the nations throughout those centuries! Ah, but when Jesus came, the Dragon was bound, and the good news *spread* to the *nations*. Jesus bound the strongman and plundered his goods. He took the nations. The gospel went forth to the ends of the earth. The Dragon was tied up.'

'So while it looked like the devil was winning on earth, in fact from this scene above he was tied up, bound from stopping the march of the King with his gospel to the *nations* during the long stretch of the church age. Jesus reigns. Jesus wins.'

'But just before the end, the dragon was *let loose* for a short, more intense time. There would be even more opposition. The dragon had always attacked. Oh yes, evil had always been around, but in this last short time, strange things were happening like never before. Even in so-called Christian countries they were seeking to stop religious education and prayers in schools! Jesus' name became a *publicly* accepted swear word. Unheard of laws allowing the killing of unborn human babies and euthanasia where people denied their life was given by God, and marriage was redefined—for people of same sex. Nothing like this had ever been seen before in all of history. All to defy Jesus. And this was happening in so-called Christian countries! But this intensity only lasted a short time ...'

'Then ... it was all over. Jesus came back. The Dragon was cast into the lake of burning sulfur.'

'And I saw a great white throne. He who gave his life was alive seated on it. Books were opened. Another book was opened—the book of life. If your name was not written in the book of life, if you had not repented and believed in Jesus, you were judged according to what you had done as recorded in books, and thrown into the lake of fire with the devil.'

'But for those who had trusted in Christ it was only the beginning of something getting better and greater (Rev. 21). Not only new resurrected bodies, but there was a complete renovation of a new heaven and earth. And this—even bigger. Heaven came down to earth! The New Jerusalem, the bride, God's people and God himself came down and dwelt with them. He wiped every tear from their eyes. It was the great reversal. It was a return to the Garden of Eden. God walking with his people on earth again!'

'So the people of God were together and they made up this beautiful building. Just as the apostle Paul had said, you are God's building. Joining Jew and Gentile in the gospel—the foundation of 12 apostles (the church), and 12 tribes of Israel (the Jews), all who believed in Jesus, 12 x 12 = 144. That number again. All God's people together made up this building.'

'Did Israel get their land? Yes, and a whole lot more than they could have ever asked or imagined. They inherited the whole earth! And did the Gentiles get heaven? More. Heaven *and* earth! All of the promises of God to Israel were 'Yes' and 'Amen' in Jesus ...'

'That's why there was no need for a bricks and mortar temple. Jesus and the Father *were* the temple! Together with his people—all the promises of God, 'Yes' and 'Amen' in Jesus, the true temple.'

'Finally, there was this picture of the return to Eden (Rev. 22). The river flowing down the middle of the street with the tree of life. It had all been a plan. It was a full restoration and celebration. What a wedding. What a honeymoon. What a bridegroom.'

'Then, when I thought I had seen it all in this vision of history ... out of the vision came the leading man. The King. The Lion and the Lamb, actually stepped out and spoke to me in person and said, *Look, I am coming soon.* All of what you have seen will really happen. Amen. Come Lord Jesus.'

He who testifies to these things says, 'Yes, I am coming soon.' Amen. Come, Lord Jesus. The grace of the Lord Jesus be with God's people. Amen (22:20-21).

Study Question

In one or two sentences explain each chapter of Revelation.

ABOUT THE AUTHOR

Bill Medley spent 15 years in the entertainment industry working as a comedian and actor. He was not brought up in a religious home and had no desire to ever become part of any 'organized religion'. In fact, he actually believed "Religion is for fools" and occasionally used religion as the butt of his jokes in his stand-up comedy.

No-one shared the gospel with Bill but he always thought one day he would investigate the religions of the world as an academic exercise. However, by age 32 and some life experience, he was ready to investigate in a deeper way. He set about reading the Scriptures of the five major world religions including the Bible, the Buddhist Scriptures, the Hindu Scriptures and the Koran. The uniqueness of Christ and his claims brought him to faith.

He has been the Pastor of Frankston Presbyterian Church in outer Melbourne Australia since 2006. He is married to Diana and they have three sons, Rick, Luke and Joshua.

OTHER BOOKS BY BILL MEDLEY

www.ingramcontent.com/pod-product-compliance
Lightning Source LLC
Chambersburg PA
CBHW070728020526
44107CB00077B/2102